MAKE THAT LEAP!
Starting Out as a Young Professional

To my children, Marieke and Jacob,
both now graduated and on the verge of a whole new life

MAKE THAT LEAP!

Starting Out as a Young Professional

Jan De Sutter

Make that Leap! Starting Out as a Young Professional

John Harper Publishing, London
www.johnharperpublishing.co.uk
ISBN 978-0-9934549-8-1

Text font, Palatino
Cartoons by Ted Goff Cartoons, Kansas City, USA
Printed and bound by Gutenberg Press Ltd, Malta
Distributed by Turpin Distribution Services Ltd, Biggleswade, UK

Table of Contents

Please make sure to use the self-assessment app that comes free with this book. You will get even more out of the book if you also use the app!

https://www.johnharperpublishing.co.uk/competency-passport

"A very impressive resume.
I really like your career goal
of ruling the world."

Foreword and acknowledgements

When my publisher, John Harper, first talked to me about writing a book for young professionals I was immediately sold on the idea, and already during that same meeting we started brainstorming how we would tackle this new adventure.

This is not my first book. Many years ago I wrote a 'survival guide for IT managers'. Being an IT manager myself at that time, I felt the urge to share my experience with younger colleagues. Even then I stressed the importance of 'soft skills' – skills in working with others as well as characteristics such as resilience and leadership – for technically proficient would-be managers. In 2015 – after experience as an EU official and president/member of a couple of European Union personnel selection boards – I co-authored a book with András Baneth on the EPSO (European Personnel Selection Office) Assessment Centre. This was – and still is – a bestseller in this small niche market. Having acquired a taste for writing on EU staff matters I then published another book on EU career development in 2016 and soon realised that a lot of its content could be readily exported beyond the limiting boundaries of EU administration. But I didn't know exactly how…

So when John came up with the idea of addressing fresh graduates – or young professionals – it was like an epiphany. Yes! Over recent years I had had the pleasure of meeting hundreds of young professionals, eager to join the EU administration. Many – if not most – had multiple university degrees in a variety of disciplines (law, economics, medicine, nuclear physics, engineering, business administration; the list went on) but they almost universally had one thing in common: they were unaware of the vital importance their soft skills, or lack of them, would come to play in their future careers. At the same time, as myself the father of two recent graduates – a medical doctor and a civil engineer – I could see them struggling too with the notion that 'being smart isn't enough'. John's idea was just perfect.

Why does anyone write books? It's certainly not in the expectation of becoming rich or famous. When considering the amount of time it takes to research, think, write, edit, and review a book the hourly pay is – to say the least – rarely worth the effort. And unless you write popular fiction – and are very, very good at it – or are a celebrity you haven't much chance of making it into the bestseller lists. But in my case at least, and I doubt I am an exception, the motivation for writing a book comes from within. As I explain in Chapter 10, intrinsic motivation comes from mastery, autonomy and purpose. Mastery is the feeling that you are good at something, and that you are getting better at it as you go along. Autonomy means that you can do things your way. And purpose, well you feel part of a bigger picture; you contribute to a better world. These three elements are – in my case – abundantly available, and that's what motivating me. And that's what I would like to thank John for.

I would also like to address a special word of thanks to Maria Grazia Goiettina, coordinator of post-graduate studies at the University Institute of European Studies, Turin, Italy. Her enthusiasm when I talked her about this project has inspired me a lot.

When I finished the first draft of this book I had the idea of creating a wiki, where people could download and review my texts. The idea was to obtain as much feedback as possible from people on the ground, young graduates, who could possibly recognise themselves in the situations I depicted. This gave us (the publisher and myself) the opportunity to look at the content of the book in a different – and hopefully better – manner. It is only appropriate to mention, as among the most helpful contributors to this wiki, Vivien Rigler (Hungary), Laure Baillargeon (France), Szimon Pozimsky (Poland), Andrea Baracco (Italy), Edith Van den Eede (Belgium), Sandra Cassotta (Denmark) and Françoise Cornette (Belgium). All these people are either young or starting professionals themselves, or related to the field of professional education.

Finally, I would like to thank my spouse, Lut, who has patiently indulged my nightly stretches behind the computer. After 26 years of marriage she knows how I work, and forgives me for that.

Jan De Sutter
February 2017

1. Why being smart isn't enough

"I'm seeking a job with low stress, interesting coworkers, a pleasant office and a fun boss. What do you have?"

So, you are finished. You have completed all your study credits and have your diploma in hand – but are you ready yet for the 'real world'?

While graduating is a great achievement, the change from student to working professional is a challenging one. You will find that the expectations and social norms on the work floor are very different than in the academic world. Your ability to work with people from different backgrounds and different levels of education, to cooperate with diverse personalities, to be a team player, and to work on projects with strict deadlines will all be put to the test. You are on your own now.

Many graduate students and young professionals are so absorbed in developing expertise in their field, their 'hard skills', that they neglect the importance of so-called 'soft skills' like communication, time management, or working in teams. These soft skills are very important at work, and being able to demonstrate them can really help you stand out in today's competitive job market. Employers look for the 'best of both worlds' in their new hires. They look for employees that have more than just the standard inventory of technical skills. They also want their staff to have the necessary soft skills, regardless of the field or academic background.

This opening chapter is about the difference between intelligence, hard skills and soft skills. Soft skills are what this book is about. In the chapters that follow we look at all the essential soft skills, one by one – how they are demonstrated and how you can improve them.

So what exactly is then the difference between hard skills and soft skills? In essence, *hard skills* are teachable abilities or skills that are easy to quantify. Examples of hard skills include a degree or certificate, speaking a foreign language, machine operation, computer programming, and so on.

Soft skills, on the other hand, are open to opinion and judgement, skills that are much harder to quantify. Also known as 'people skills' or 'interpersonal skills,' soft skills concern the way you relate to and interact with other people, to the way you behave.

Hard skills are skills where the rules stay the same regardless of

"People skills? What's wrong with
my #@&!*#! people skills?"

which organisation, circumstance or people you work with. In contrast, soft skills are skills where the rules change depending on the circumstances and the people around you. For example, computer programming is a hard skill. The rules for how you can be good at creating a computer program are the same regardless of where you work, and results of your work can be measured and put into numbers. Communicating, on the other hand, is a soft skill. The rules for how to be effective at communicating change and depend on the circumstances and the audience with whom you are communicating.

To illustrate this, just imagine the following two situations:

- situation 1: you catch a child 'red handed' in the candy box
- situation 2: a co-worker spends hours at work on Facebook

Of course you would deal with the two situations quite differently. Not only because those involved differ in age and maturity but also because of the different contexts (private or professional). Most probably the way you would explain to the child that they are not allowed to take sweets without permission would depend on whether it was your own child or somebody else's. Likewise you would adopt a different approach when challenging your fellow worker directly as opposed to 'snitching' to your manager (which I would not advise in a case like this by the way).

Hard skills are learned at school and university, from study and practice. There are usually specified levels of proficiency and a direct path to how to excel with each hard skill. For example, accounting is a hard skill. You can take basic accounting and advanced accounting courses. You can then work to get experience and take an exam and be certified as a professional accountant, and so on.

In contrast, there is no simple path to develop soft skills. Most soft skills have to be improved by real world experience, often by trial and error. There are many books and guides on soft skills (including this one), but they only take you so far, because there aren't any easy step-by-step instructions on how to master a soft skill. Soft skills are not easily measured; it takes a difficult assessment process, managed and done by professional evaluators and even then the results only serve to compare people, they are not absolute.

Soft skills help us do our jobs. They allow us to effectively and efficiently use our technical skills and knowledge. They improve

The IQ score bell curve

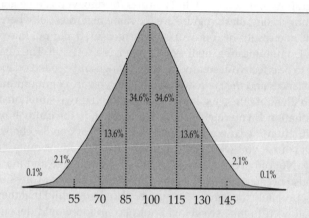

Figure 1.1: The IQ score bell curve

Standardised IQ tests are designed so that their scores have a 'bell curve' distribution in the general population with an average of 100, and a 'standard deviation' of 15. This curve has a peak in the middle where most people score and elongated ends where only a few people score. In statistics this is called a 'normal distribution.'

An IQ of 115 or more can be considered to be a high IQ score or level; it is one standard deviation above the average. Only about 15% of the population has an IQ level of 115 or above. Around 2% of the population has an IQ greater than 130, which is 'gifted' intelligence. This is an IQ of 2 standard deviations from the average IQ.

At the age of 21, renowned Serbian-American inventor Nikola Tesla earned his first PhD. He ultimately held four PhD degrees (Philosophy, Physics, Electrical Engineering, and Mechanical engineering). His exact IQ score is not known, because there were no tests at the time he lived, but it is estimated to have been around 200, which is exceptionally high.

the way we interact with other people. They enable us to get our work done on time, and to meet the expectations of our fellow workers, managers, and customers. They influence how we feel about our jobs, our motivation, and how others perceive us. While your technical skills can land you a job, soft skills will help you grow and enjoy life. Hard skills are the foundation of a successful career, soft skills are the cement.

Finally, bear in mind that soft skills are transferable between occupations. While you may have to go back to college to learn new hard skills if you change careers, you can always take your soft skills with you because they are valued in every field.

Intelligence

So what is the difference between *intelligence* and hard or soft skills? Intelligence by itself will not take you very far. It has to be constructively channelled into acquiring useful hard skills, and balanced by the social qualities of soft skills.

The definition of intelligence is somewhat controversial amongst psychologists, but by far the most widely used in practical settings is the psychometric approach, trying to capture the complex idea of intelligence into a single score known as the *intelligence quotient*, or IQ. Your IQ is said to be shaped by environmental and genetic factors, the relative importance of which has been subject of much research and debate. A person's 'general' IQ is taken from the results of standardised tests, but for recruitment and job selection purposes more specific ability tests on verbal, numerical and abstract reasoning are preferred.

An interesting idea first put forward by psychologist and psychometric research pioneer Raymond Catell is that there are actually two components to a person's intelligence. One is called *fluid intelligence*, the other *crystallised intelligence*.

Fluid intelligence is the ability to solve novel, abstract problems, requiring mental operations that make little or no use of the real world information that you acquired over your lifetime. Crystallised intelligence, on the other hand, represents the body of information that you have about the nature of the world and the

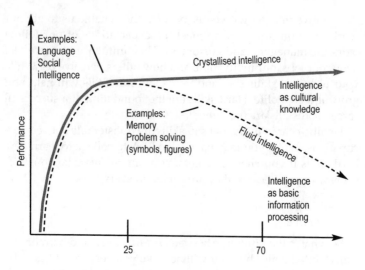

Figure 1.2: Crystallised and fluid intelligence

learned procedures and mental shortcuts that help you to make guesses about it; in other words life experience.

Interestingly enough, these two types of intelligence have quite different trajectories over a person's lifetime (see Fig. 1.2). Fluid intelligence develops quickly over the first years of life, but begins to deteriorate by the early twenties. People who work a lot with abstract materials, such as mathematicians, may find their powers diminishing somewhat by the age of thirty and older people find it harder to solve puzzles and mazes. Crystallised intelligence, on the other hand, may continue to increase, at least until very old age. In short, (life) experience does matter!

There is, however, not much we can do about the processing power between our ears. Our intelligence quotient – our IQ – is mostly fixed by our genes and the way we were brought up. At a given point in time, we are stuck with whatever IQ we have. The good news, however, is that our IQ is much less important to happiness and success in life than our *emotional intelligence* (EI), and that our emotional intelligence can be developed and improved considerably over time.

The New York Times science writer Daniel Goleman argued in his 1995 book *Emotional Intelligence: Why It Can Matter More Than IQ* that our feelings of love, hate, fear, and so on play a much greater role in thought, decision making and individual success than is commonly recognised. He defines emotional intelligence as a set of skills that include control of one's sudden desires, self-motivation, empathy and social competence in interpersonal relationships. Emotional intelligence can be described as interpersonal intelligence or, even more simply, as social skills.

In 1998 Goleman took these ideas into the workplace with a new book *Working with Emotional Intelligence*. He shows that outstanding performers are not defined by their IQ or even their job skills, but by their emotional intelligence. Analyses done in many corporations, government agencies, and non-profit organisations worldwide conclude that emotional intelligence is the indicator of excellence in virtually any job.

Emotional intelligence differs from IQ in that it can not be measured objectively. We may know when someone has it, but it can not be precisely quantified.

When we describe a person we often start by saying how smart (we think) they are and what they do for a living (doctor, architect, engineer...). But then we often give our opinion on how we per-

"Well, you certainly have a lot of
experience in tech support."

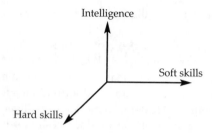

Figure 1.3: Intelligence and skills

ceive their behaviour. Are they friendly or a bully, a good listener or single minded, efficient or someone who wastes time? In fact, we often describe people in three 'dimensions': intelligence, hard skills, and soft skills (Fig. 1.3).

These three dimensions give a more or less complete image of a person, but – in our minds – they are distinctive traits, which can be good or bad, independent of each other. Allow me to illustrate this with two examples.

First, consider a 'typical' IT person – a software engineer, system manager, or tech support. We probably all know at least one person that qualifies. IT people are usually very smart (being an IT engineer myself, I am entitled to make this statement!), and most IT people are very good and passionate professionals. This means that in Figure 1.3 they would score high on both the 'Intelligence' and 'hard skills' axes. However, it is also true that many IT people are known to be 'nerds' and, as Wikipedia puts it, nerd is a 'descriptive term, often used pejoratively, indicating that a person is overly intellectual, obsessive, or lacking social skills'. In other words, they score low on the 'soft skills' axis.

The second example is about a 'typical' car salesman. Car salespeople will know everything there is to know about cars, mechanics, the models, and the brand of cars they are selling; they will have a good score on 'hard skills'. Good car salespeople also will score very well on the 'soft skills' axis, because – after all – they make a living by convincing other people to buy cars from them (not so many cars are sold online; it takes another human to convince us).

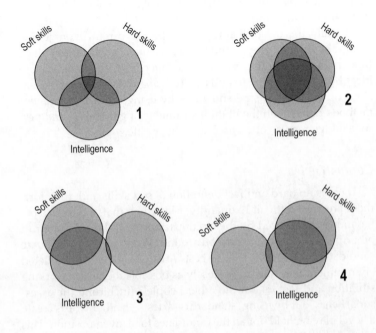

Figure 1.4: Different overlaps of intelligence and skills

However, there's nothing that requires a car salesperson to be smart. By this I'm not saying that all car salespeople are dummies, but it's not essential for their job. It's not in their job requirements.

In reality, these three dimensions cannot be seen independently as they do influence each other and overlap to varying degrees in different people (Figure 1.4).

Many of us will have a bit of an overlap between all three dimensions (example 1 in Figure 1.4). But being too smart and overly focused on doing one thing very well may interfere with a person's development of soft skills (the 'nerds' – example 4 in Figure 1.4). Also, some people may lack formal education and hard skills but are in fact very smart and have well developed soft skills ('street smart' – example 3 in Figure 1.4). The ideal is to have a big overlap of all three as in example 2.

Basically, this means that we have to be very careful in our judgements about other people, and try to get a nuanced, balanced view. Modern human resource management effectively implements these ideas by actively trying to find the truth about the different dimensions of a candidate's personality – by using refined assessment methods rather than the blunt instruments of gut feeling and personal judgement so often used in ordinary life.

Competencies

There is no hard and fast definition of soft skills and, therefore, these are very difficult to quantify. More than that, a person's behaviour is influenced by the circumstances and the behaviour of other people who happen to be around. When trying to evaluate candidates for a specific job, the best we can do is create a simulated environment that reflects as closely as possible the future working situation and factors out the other people's (including the assessor's) behaviour by using 'standardised' tests. In other words create a 'level playing field' for all the candidates for a given position. This set up is known as an Assessment Centre.

According to a definition by the talent solutions company Hudson 'An Assessment Centre is a set of concrete simulation exercises programmed to verify if the skills and competencies required for a specific job are present. Based on previously defined competencies, the Assessment Centre provides a clear understanding of your strengths or developmental needs and evaluates your potential.'

It is important to understand that the outcome of an Assessment Centre is a comparative list of the candidates as they were observed at that specific moment in time, doing those specific exercises, and being observed by a given group of assessors. The assumption is that the people on top of the list are the best *available* candidates. In no way is it assumed that they are the best *possible* candidates in absolute terms.

For a skill to be 'measurable' it has to be 'observable'. In an Assessment Centre this is done by putting the candidates in predefined situations (exercises) and watching their behaviour while they are executing the assignment. Moreover, the exercises are designed so that the focus is on a limited set of 'relevant' behaviour. Of course, a full scale Assessment Centre is a complex and expensive exercise, so it is only used by some employers for some jobs. In many cases a form of assessment takes place, but at a more informal and subjective level.

All forms of assessment are in various ways trying to measure a person's *competencies*. A competency can be defined as follows:

> 'A competency is a set of observable behaviours that provide a structured guide enabling the identification, evaluation and development of the behaviours in individual candidates.'

Competencies are job-related; for every type of job a different mix of competencies is needed. Because of this, during the selection process an employer will try to assess if a candidate has the necessary

Assessment Centres

It was the psychologist Max Simoneit who introduced the idea of assessment in the 1930s for selecting officers for the German Army (although it was ended in 1941 after too many politically favoured candidates did not pass the tests!) During World War II Assessment Centres were created by the British Royal Navy and the British Army. Today, all sorts of organisations use this method to select workers who have just graduated from university and have little or no work history and it is said that 68% of employers in the UK and USA now use some form of assessment as part of their recruitment/promotion process.

Assessment Centres are one of the most fair, objective and effective ways of identifying high-potential candidates who will fit in with a role and an organisation's culture. Research shows them to be far more predictive of future job performance than individual tasks, such as a job interview. This is because a number of different assessors get to see the candidates perform over a relatively long period of time and have the chance to see how they actually behave in a variety of situations (rather than what they might say in a typical job interview).

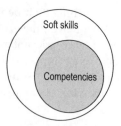

Figure 1.5: Competencies in relation to soft skills

competencies for that particular position. In other words, in an Assessment Centre (or other type of less structured assessment) not all
the soft skills are measured, only those that are relevant to the position, as in Figure 1.5. The same holds true for the hard skills. The two
sets of competencies (hard and soft) combined are also known as the
'core competencies' required for that job.

Competencies can be further broken down into a series of *behavioural anchors*. These are specific, easy to apply examples of
behaviours that show the competency.

With every anchor, there are some – positive and negative – indicators, or specific connected behaviours. Indicators can be associated with multiple anchors, as is shown in Figure 1.6. A
behavioural anchor is something that can be used, for example, to
define the level someone has reached on a particular competency
from 1 to 10. In this sense it is very similar to an indicator, but indicators tend to be simple 'positive' and 'negative' poles, whereas the
anchors define all points in between.

By way of example let us consider some anchors for the Communicating competency, which is discussed more fully in Chapter 5:

Behavioural anchors for Communicating

1. Demonstrating effective written communication skills.
2. Adapting written communication to the audience.
3. Writing clearly, in a visually appealing manner.
4. Explaining ideas clearly, simplifying the complex.
5. Being methodical, structured and precise in speech.
6. Adapting verbal communication to the audience.

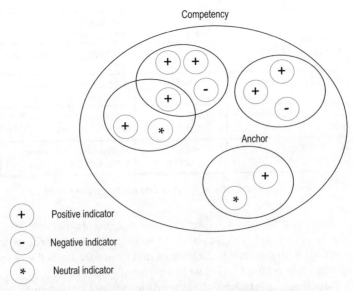

+ Positive indicator

- Negative indicator

* Neutral indicator

Figure 1.6: Competencies, anchors and indicators

7. Communicating clearly and knowledgeably.
8. Sharing information with others.
9. Seeking input from others.
10. Protecting private and confidential information.

Anchor 6 in this list can then be further expanded to the indicators as laid out in Table 1.1 on page 14.

For the purposes of this book I will use a general *competency framework* that is relevant to most graduate-level positions (putting to one side the very diverse hard skills required for these positions). This framework is in fact loosely based on the competency framework used by the EU administration for the selection, recruitment, and appraisal of their staff, but similar frameworks are used in other organisations and it is fairly representative of what is expected of an employee in the service industries or public sector. I call these 'essential competencies' and each of the chapters that follow is devoted to one of these competencies.

UNSATISFACTORY	1 - Extremely Weak 2 - Very Weak	Has difficulty tailoring communication to the needs of others.
IMPROVEMENT NEEDED	3 - Weak 4 - Fair	Does not always keep the audience in mind.
MEETS EXPECTATIONS	5 - Satisfactory 6 - Good	Tailors information to audience and individual needs.
EXCEEDS EXPECTATIONS	7 - Strong 8 - Very Strong	Effectively adapts verbal communication to audience.
EXCEPTIONAL	9 - Excellent 10 - Outstanding	Effectively distinguishes between 'need to know' and 'nice to know'.

Table 1.1: Indicators for one communicating anchor

Solving problems (Chapter 2) is at the centre of what most people do in their job. The capability to solve problems, to deduce, to come up with new, interesting ideas, and creativity are at the heart of what is expected from most professional employees.

Meeting expectations (Chapter 3) means not only coming up with results or producing output, but also – and more importantly – meeting the expectations of your customers, co-workers, or superiors.

Managing time (Chapter 4). Time is a scarce commodity and we all must meet deadlines (or targets) at some point. That is why it is important to be able to prioritise and organise our work effectively and avoid procrastination.

Communicating (Chapter 5). Meeting expectations means being able – in the first place – to listen to what the problem really is, then to analyse and solve it, and communicate the results in a convincing way.

Working in teams (Chapter 6). We all work in teams, we all depend on the results of other people's work, and other people depend on the results of our work. At work, one plus one can be more than two.

Being resilient (Chapter 7) is our capability to remain effective under difficult circumstances, and to bounce back from adversity.

Managing and leading others (Chapter 8) covers our ability to manage and steer other people to achieve results and our ability to motivate and inspire our fellow workers to achieve the goals of the organisation.

Learning and developing (Chapter 9), finally, is keeping our knowledge and know-how up-to-date, expanding it, and developing our soft skills on a continuous basis.

When you think of it, these competencies (and by extension our soft skills) are what make us, as humans, different from other living beings – and computers or robots. Organisations look for these competencies in their professional staff, whereas simple, routine, or repetitive activities can increasingly be automated (or outsourced to low-wage countries). This explains, of course, why employers are so interested in the competencies of their employees.

In this context I would like to refer you to the mind-challenging book *Rise of the Robots* by Martin Ford. It is essential reading for anyone who wants to understand what technological change means for their own job prospects as well as for society as a whole. After reading it, you will understand why soft skills will be the most important skills you possess in the years to come.

Once your competencies have been assessed it is possible to make a *competency passport*. This is an overview – in a graphical format – of how you were perceived by the assessors (Fig. 1.7).

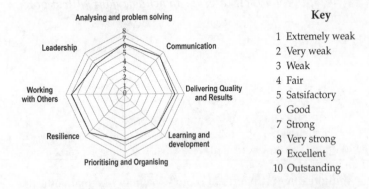

Figure 1.7: A competency passport 'spider's web'

To go with this book, I have created a simple app that will help you understand your own behaviour. The app asks you to fill in a self-assessment score card for each competency. Once you have done this, it will generate your Priorities – the issues you need to focus on – and the competency passport showing your strengths and weaknesses in a spider's web. I would encourage you to try the app before you read any further. You are sure to get more out of the rest of this book if you do so.

Try the app at:

https://www.johnharperpublishing.co.uk/competency-passport

Key points to remember

- *Having a degree is not enough to become a high-achiever.*

- *Soft skills are becoming ever more important at work.*

- *Competencies are about expected behaviour at work.*

- *Personal development is the process of understanding and developing yourself in order to achieve your fullest potential.*

2. Solving problems

"All we need to do is rename 'the problem' to 'the solution' and I think we're done here."

'Most people spend more time and energy going around problems than in trying to solve them' – Henry Ford

Solving problems is at the centre of what most people do at work. Any job at any level will bring problems to be solved, every single day. This chapter is about how to improve your ability to solve problems, without being overwhelmed by them.

Problem solving skills are among the top skills sought after in graduates. Employers want people who take *personal responsibility* to make sure targets are met, who can see that there might be a better way of doing things, and who are prepared to explore and implement change. They want people who don't give up when things go wrong but who will seek a way around problems. These may be comparable to academic problems or they may be more 'hands-on' such as those related to managing people or projects.

Many job ads simply ask for candidates who 'have the ability to solve problems'; but sometimes you will have to read between the lines:

- 'Someone interested in taking responsibility and with the confidence to challenge established practices and come up with new ways of working…'
- 'An analytical mind and the ability to understand and solve complex challenges are necessary…'
- 'We are looking for innovative minds demonstrating the ability to create interesting new things...'
- 'We need high-reaching graduates who will respond with enthusiasm to every issue they face…'

These requirements are all asking for the ability to solve problems, to make your own decisions and form your own opinions – without depending on other people, and to use your imagination to overcome difficulties.

In your work, you will be expected to:

- Solve daily problems independently where appropriate.
- Refer all questions you cannot answer to the appropriate person.
- Recognise problems that need to be addressed.
- Act promptly to solve or report problems.
- Recommend possible solutions when raising a problem.
- Work in teams to solve problems and exchange information.
- Make decisions only after getting all facts from all stakeholders.
- Think out-of-the-box.
- Use good judgement in making decisions.
- Consult your supervisor for matters outside your authority.

Knowing when to try to solve a problem by yourself and when to involve others is a key aspect of this competency. Every situation is different, but if you stop and think before you act, you will improve your chances of making the right call. If you are not sure, be prepared to ask a more experienced colleague.

Going back to the concept of 'behavioural anchors' which we

looked at in Chapter 1, let us now take a look at what the anchors are for the 'solving problems' competency.

Anchors for 'solving problems'

- Increasing efficiency and improving quality.
- Involving others in solving problems and making decisions.
- Factoring organisational goals into decisions.
- Making clear, transparent, and timely decisions.
- Dealing with complexity.
- Identifying the relevant aspects from a mass of information.
- Proposing useful and practical solutions.
- Gathering information from various sources.
- Using judgement and analysis to find solutions to problems.

Now that you've seen the anchors, take a look at Table 2.1 on pages 20-21. This asks a simple question: which of these behaviours sound like a description of what you do and how you react to situations? Be honest with yourself – it will help you identify the areas where you need to work on your performance.

You will find a similar table for each of the competencies in the following chapters and don't forget you can also use the app!

General problem solving approach

A *problem* is a deviation from the standard. A problem happens when there is a difference between what 'should be' and what 'is' – a difference between the ideal and the actual situation. It is something that wasn't expected: too late, too expensive, poor quality, or not working as anticipated. Problems are always connected with solutions, even though there may not always be a perfect solution, just a 'best possible' solution.

Solving problems is the process of working through the details of a problem to reach a solution. Problem solving may include mathematical or step-by-step operations and can be a measure of a person's critical thinking skills.

Table 2.1: Which of these sound like you?

UNSATISFACTORY	IMPROVEMENT NEEDED	MEETS EXPECTATIONS	EXCEEDS EXPECTATIONS	EXCEPTIONAL
Has difficulty distinguishing between critical and noncritical issues.	Tends to focus on simple operational issues.	Finds solutions that effectively address issues and are easily sustainable.	Stays focused on critical problems until they are successfully resolved.	Analyses and prioritises critical problems accurately and quickly.
Loses focus when resolving larger issues.	Proposes solutions that are usually short-term.	Collaborates effectively with others to solve problems and make decisions.	Finds solutions that change the workplace both in terms of increasing efficiency and enhancing the quality of products and services.	Maintains a sense of urgency in solving even complex problems.
Misunderstands or misinterprets key elements of information.	Collaborates with others only when asked to.	Keeps organisational and departmental goals in mind when solving problems and making decisions.	Makes processes more efficient.	Consistently and effectively seeks input from all fellow workers and stakeholders.
Rarely proposes innovative solutions.	Makes decisions that are sometimes not clear.	Makes sound decisions based on facts and experience.	Is highly collaborative in terms of seeking input to solve problems and make decisions.	Is agile and decisive.
Rarely collaborates with fellow workers and stakeholders.	Tends to put off decisions on more complex issues.	Understands and summarises the main issues involved.	Makes decisions that consistently support and facilitate desired results.	Always has 'big picture' in mind and helps others see it.
Makes decisions that have minimal or no impact.	Misses logical links between items of information.	Tackles main problems and is not distracted by secondary issues.	Takes on board all the available information and fits everything together.	Makes decisions that consistently align with organisational and departmental goals.
				Analyses and interprets the available data correctly and completely.

Table 2.1 – continued

UNSATISFACTORY	IMPROVEMENT NEEDED	MEETS EXPECTATIONS	EXCEEDS EXPECTATIONS	EXCEPTIONAL
Has difficulty articulating rationale for decisions.	Is distracted by side issues.	Proposes reasonable but not particularly visionary solutions.	Stays focused on critical problems until they are successfully resolved.	Consistently proposes solutions that reflect a balanced analysis and sound judgment.
Often defers decision-making to others.	Proposes solutions that are impractical because of their implications.	Proposes workable solutions.	Proposes solutions that deal effectively with all aspects of the problem.	Refers to the available sources and assesses the relative significance of each one.
Omits important facts and details from his/her analysis.	Proposes solutions that do not take all the factors into account.	Takes into account different sources of information available.	Makes processes more efficient. Analyses problems by comparing and contrasting options drawn from all available sources.	Identifies and resolves inconsistencies or contradictions in available information.
Is overwhelmed by high volumes of information and gets lost.	Is more descriptive than analytical in his/her approach	Explores different options in search for solutions.	Tests different options to determine which provides the optimum solution.	Considers all the options before deciding on the best way forward.
Does not identify inconsistencies or contradictions in available information.	Makes proposals without thinking through their implications.	Considers the implications for his/her proposals.	Weights up options and anticipates possible objections to preferred choices.	Reacts to developments as the implementation unfolds.
Bases analysis based on information from only a few of the available sources.	Does not make a convincing case for his/her recommendations.			
Relies more on intuition than on analysis.				

How doctors, scientists, and engineers approach problems differently

Doctors, scientists and engineers are trained to have different approaches to solving problems. These three types of problem solvers can be seen as examples representing the training methods each field is known for. Of course, any individual would use a mix of these problem-solving methods based on their knowledge and experience, but they may never have received formal training in methods other than the ones they are familiar in.

The doctor. Medical doctors are trained to think about differences and categories. A patient's symptoms are processed, and then historical information is used to find the most common diagnosis associated with the gathered evidence. This is an approach to problem solving based on probabilities. This method is very efficient when a patient has a problem that has been encountered before. However, when the patient has something not seen before, it is a very inefficient way of treating the problem, and the doctor will move to less and less common solutions.

The scientist. In contrast to the doctor, the scientist is trained to look at a problem in the abstract and use testable assumptions (models) to isolate all the component parts of a problem and solve them (individually, if possible) in a logical way. Breaking down the problem into its individual parts can determine the independent root causes. Then, using those root causes, the scientist can arrive at a solution to the overall problem. Solving problems in this way is more resource- and time-intensive than the doctor's method, but if the right hypotheses are made, this system can handle a broader range of problems and generate new data that are applicable to other problems.

The engineer. One way to think of the engineer's method is as a combination of the scientist and doctor's methods. The scientist starts with a new set of hypotheses for each problem, and the doctor starts with a set of solutions that can be applied. The engineer is trained to take a known solution and then use that as a starting point to find a solution that applies to the problem. A very simple example can illustrate this. The most common way to find the area of a triangle is to multiply the base and height and to divide the result by two. This rule has been proven by mathematicians, and applies to all types of triangles (right, equilateral, isosceles, obtuse, and acute). So, if an engineer has to calculate the surface of a triangle, he will simply apply this rule, and not try to reinvent the theory behind it.

Some problems are clearly harder or more complex than others, and in many cases the path towards a solution is not clear. There is a general approach though, the steps of which are listed below:

- Problem identification
- Problem analysis
- Generating possible solutions
- Making a decision
- Implementation
- Seeking feedback

At any stage of this process, it may be necessary to return to an earlier stage – for example, if further problems arise or if a solution does not appear to be working as desired.

A somewhat simplified mnemonic for this approach is IDEAL:

- **I**dentify the problem
- **D**efine the problem
- **E**xamine the options
- **A**ct on a plan
- **L**ook at the consequences

I will add to this in the following pages.

Problem identification

'*A problem well put is half solved*' – John Dewey, US educationalist and psychologist

Problem identification involves detecting and recognising that there is a problem, and identifying the nature of the problem – in other words, defining the problem. Being able to state the problem clearly is the first important step to effectively solving it.

When faced with a problem, our natural tendency is to come up with possible solutions. Therefore, thinking and discussion concentrate on the merits of the proposed solution(s), rather than an in-depth discussion of the possible causes of the problem itself. Inexperienced problem solvers will soon find out that a great solution isn't worth much, if the problem it tries to solve was misidentified.

Sometimes, finding or identifying a problem is more of a break-through than the actual solution. For example, Galileo recognised the problem of needing to know the speed of light, but did not come up with a solution. It took ages of advances in mathematics and science to solve this problem. But Galileo still received credit for identifying the problem.

Sometimes problem identification may be nothing more than the art of asking the right questions at the right time (this is actually the best kept secret of coaching).

Problem analysis

'If I had an hour to solve a problem I'd spend 55 minutes thinking about the problem and 5 minutes thinking about solutions' – Albert Einstein

After the problem identification, *problem analysis* involves col-lecting more information about the problem and increasing under-standing. This phase is all about fact finding and analysis, building a more complete picture of both the goal(s) and the barrier(s). This stage may not be necessary for simple problems – or issues – but it is for more complex problems. The following things need to be done in problem analysis:

- Identifying the stakeholders
- Understanding the root causes
- Identifying the constraints

Identifying the stakeholders

A *stakeholder* is anyone who is affected by the problem and the solution. The following questions can be helpful in identifying the stakeholders:

- Who are the main users?
- Are there any other users whose needs must be addressed?
- Who are the beneficiaries or customers?
- Who else is affected?
- Is there anyone else who cares?
- Who will evaluate and approve the solution?

- Who will monitor and provide feedback?

Stakeholder analysis is a process of systematically gathering and analysing qualitative information to determine whose interests have to be taken into account when solving a problem. An interesting read about this topic can be found on the website of the World Health Organisation (http://www.who.int/workforcealliance/knowledge/toolkit/33.pdf).

Understanding the root causes

A *root cause analysis* is an organised way of uncovering the 'roots' – or underlying causes – of an identified problem, or the symptoms of a problem. The fishbone diagram (or Ishikawa diagram, after its creator, the Japanese organisational theorist Kaoru Ishikawa) identifies the possible causes for an effect or problem. It can be used to structure a brainstorming session. It immediately sorts ideas into useful categories (see Figure 2.1).

Not all the root causes are equally important. That is why an-

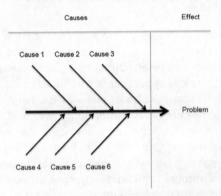

Figure 2.1: A fishbone diagram

other way of looking at the root causes is the Pareto diagram, named after the Italian polymath Vilfredo Pareto (Figure 2.2).

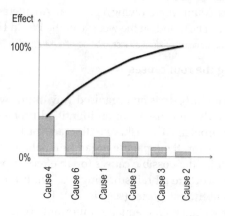

Figure 2.2: A Pareto diagram

The Pareto principle (also known as the 80/20 rule, although it is really just an observation – see Chapter 4) states that, often, around 80% of problems can be attributed to 20% of causes. Mathematically, the 80/20 rule is approximately followed by a power law distribution, and many natural phenomena have been shown empirically to reveal such a distribution. Therefore, in many situations, you have an easy access to dramatic improvements by focusing on the most important causes and ignoring the rest. Basically, the problem-solver guesses the benefit delivered by each action, and then selects a number of the most effective actions that deliver a total benefit close to the maximum possible one.

Identifying the constraints

Constraints are limitations on the degree of freedom you have in providing a solution. Constraints can limit your ability to deliver a solution as you imagine it. Therefore, each constraint must be carefully studied as part of the problem solving process, and some

Correlation and causation

'There are lies, damn lies, and statistics' – Mark Twain

In root cause analysis we often rely on statistical data based on past observations. In this way we try to understand the underlying (hidden) patterns in data sets. Over the last decade or so we have seen a lot of hype around what is now known as 'data mining'. According to the American IT research and advice firm Gartner, data mining is the process of discovering meaningful correlations, patterns and trends by sifting through large amounts of data stored in repositories. Data mining, used by companies in many sectors, employs pattern recognition technologies, as well as statistical and mathematical techniques.

However, reducing a complex situation (many variables, many rows of data) to a simple set of numerical values, such as median, variance, correlation, and linear regression can be tricky. It is therefore important to understand the difference between correlation and causality. For example, on a beach in summer there is a relationship between the sales of ice cream and the number of cases of sunburn. The existence of such a relationship makes it possible to estimate one variable (in this case, the number of cases of sunburn) from observation of another variable (sales of ice cream). However, there is no direct causality between the two. This means that you cannot influence one fact by controlling the other. For example, if you ban selling ice cream, you will not influence the number of cases of sunburn. The correlation is still valid because the two facts share the same cause (sunshine). So, correlations can be divided in at least three classes:

- Causality (A causes B)
- Correlation with a common reason (C causes both A and B)
- Accidental correlation (there is no C causing A and B)

While the first two are a reliable way for detecting patterns in data sets, the accidental correlations might lead to wrong conclusions. You can find a lot of strange and even funny accidental correlations, for example on http://twentytwowords.com/funny-graphs-show-correlation-between-completely-unrelated-stats-9-pictures/

constraints may even cause you to reconsider the entire approach you initially imagined. Below is a non-exhaustive list of some possible constraints:

- What is the available budget?
- Do internal or external political issues affect possible solutions?
- Are there environmental or regulatory constraints?
- Are there legal restrictions?
- Is the schedule defined, are there deadlines?
- What (human) resources are available?

For someone at the start of their career, the biggest constraint is going to be what they are actually *allowed* to do.

How much freedom you will personally have to tackle problems will also depend on the set up you are working for. In the public sector you are likely to be very restricted by rules and procedures. In big private sector companies, too, even the chief executive officer (CEO) or managing director cannot just decide to do their own thing. They have their own constraints. Indeed the scope for personal initiative tends to shrink the larger the organisation – which is why there is a constant process of innovation originating in small start-up enterprises. A talented but unpredictable innovator can be the proverbial square peg in a round hole in a large organisation.

"Remember that great idea you had
that we ridiculed and ignored? It
appears that we need it after all.
What was it?"

Generating possible solutions

'Be passionate about solving the problem, not proving your solution' –
Nathan Furr, teacher of innovation strategy

During this stage you create a range of possible solutions, but with
little or no attempt to evaluate them at this point. In a group situation
this stage is often carried out as a brainstorming session, letting each
person in the group express their views on possible courses of action.
Different people will have different expertise in different areas and
it is useful, therefore, to hear the views of everyone.

During brainstorming, postpone judgement on whether solutions are achievable, practical, or reasonable. This is the time for creative thinking, not critical thinking. Creative thinking is like putting
your foot on the accelerator of a car. Critical thinking is putting
your foot on the brake. There is a time for each but not at the same
time, otherwise the engine will stall.

I recommend that you take a look at the TED talk by business
guru Tom Wujec: 'Got a wicked problem? First tell me how you
make toast.' His books are well worth reading too.

Making a decision

It is now time to look at the possible solutions and analyse them
for their pros and cons. Some solutions may have to be eliminated
due to the constraints that were previously identified.

Work out the criteria you are going to use to evaluate the pros
and cons. Agree upon both the criteria and their relative importance. Decide whether you will evaluate ideas mostly on the basis
of cost, timeframe, interference with existing operations, or anything else you need to think about.

Assess the importance of each criterion relative to the other criteria. If the criteria are all equal in importance, your evaluation will be
based on how each potential solution measures up to all the criteria.
If the criteria have different importance, assign a unique weighting
to each.

Finally, you make a decision on which course of action to take. Decisions can be made through either an intuitive or a reasoned process.

Intuition is a combination of your past experience and your personal values. It is worth taking your gut feeling into account, especially for simple problems, but complicated decisions require reasoning.

There are a number of factors that can prevent effective decision-making. These can include (among others):

- Not enough information.
- Too much information.
- Too many stakeholders.
- Emotional attachments, or the lack thereof.
- Incomplete problem definition, analysis or invalid solutions.
- Too many, or contradictory constraints.
- Lack of experience or knowledge of the problem.
- (Political) taboos or inability to think outside the box (see p. 35).

For those at the start of their careers, the scope for decision-making can be limited by lack of personal authority and having to do what superiors say. Judging when you have scope to make decisions, and how much scope you may have, can be a challenge.

Implementation

'An idea that is developed and put into action is more important than an idea that exists only as an idea' – Edward de Bono, psychologist, author and inventor

Implementation means acting on the chosen solution. During implementation new problems may arise, especially if identification or analysis of the original problem was not carried out properly. If this happens you have to go back to the previous stages.

This involves monitoring the implementation to make sure it goes to plan. Project management is a whole subject in its own right on which there are many useful books.

Seeking feedback

The final stage of problem solving is verifying that the implemented solution has been successful. Feedback from the stakeholders can provide this. It is good practice to keep a record of results and any additional problems that occurred. This is a very important stage, because in this you verify if the stakeholders' expectations were met, and to what extent.

Working in teams

'Coming together is a beginning, staying together is progress, and working together is success' – Henry Ford

In organisations, the individual competency of solving problems is closely related to the competency of working in teams.

Depending on the situation, teams can have a different name: task force, work group, study group, commission, committee, or such like. Teamwork frequently cuts across lines of hierarchy.

You need three types of people in any team effort:

- Deciders - they hold the authority and are the 'bosses'.
- Doers - the implementers who get the job done.
- Experts - they bring the knowledge, expertise and/or charisma to the table.

In order to have really productive problem solving meetings, the best behaviour of all participants is in Table 2.2:

Maximise	Minimise
Listening	Criticising
Appreciating	Impatience
Seeking usefulness	Being judgmental
Clarifying	Boredom
Accepting	Rejecting

Table 2.2

Why do we need teams to solve problems?

First, when you are working in a team there is a higher chance that most of the things you are uncertain about will come to the surface and the answers will arise naturally.

Second, it is often quite hard to understand every detail of a problem when you are alone.

Third, through their cooperative but also competitive nature, teams promote both critical thinking and creativity in the form of new questions and explanations within discussions and debates.

Finally, when you are alone, the temptation to procrastinate is greater than when in an interactive environment. Although taking breaks is important, dipping in and out of your work mode can waste time, and add to frustration and inefficiency.

'Too many cooks spoil the broth' is an expression meaning that a team becomes inefficient if too many people are involved, as it becomes harder to coordinate, communicate and maintain discipline. In workplace situations the ideal size of a team tends to be around three to four people, but sometimes more are needed, for example if a variety of specific technical expertise is needed. I will go into more detail on this in the chapter on working in teams.

The dangers of groupthink

The term 'groupthink' was first described in 1972 by American social psychologist Irving Janis. It is a phenomenon that occurs when a group makes incorrect decisions because group pressures lead to a deterioration of 'mental efficiency, reality testing, and moral judgment' (*Victims of Groupthink: A psychological Study of foreign-policy decisions and fiascos*, by Irving Janis.) Groups affected by groupthink ignore alternatives and tend to take irrational actions that dehumanise other groups. A group is especially vulnerable to groupthink when its members are similar in background, when the group is insulated from outside opinions, and when there are no clear rules for decision-making.

Janis documented eight symptoms of groupthink:

- *Illusion of invulnerability* – Creates excessive optimism that encourages taking extreme risks.
- *Collective rationalisation* – Members discount warnings and do not reconsider their assumptions.
- *Belief in inherent morality* – Members believes in the rightness of their cause and therefore ignore the ethical or moral consequences of their decisions.

- *Stereotyped views of out-groups* – Negative attitudes to those seen as the 'enemy' make effective responses to different opinions seem unnecessary.
- *Direct pressure on dissenters* – Members are under pressure not to express arguments against any of the group's views.
- *Self-censorship* – Doubts and deviations from the perceived group consensus are not expressed.
- *Illusion of unanimity* – The majority view and judgements are assumed to be unanimous.
- *Self-appointed 'mind guards'* – Members protect the group and the leader from information that is problematic or contradictory to the group's cohesiveness, view, and/or decisions.

Only strong individuals can stand up against groupthink, but adopting some of the following measures may reduce the risk:

- The leader assigns the role of critical evaluator to each member.
- The leader avoids stating preferences and expectations at the outset.
- Each member of the group routinely discusses the group's deliberations with a trusted associate and reports back to the group on the associate's reactions.
- Outsiders are brought in with a brief to challenge the views of the group.
- At least one articulate and knowledgeable member is given the role of devil's advocate (to question assumptions and plans).
- The leader makes sure that a sizeable block of time is set aside to survey warning signals from rivals; leader and group construct alternative scenarios of rivals' intentions.

Of course, if you are new in your job, you may find yourself unable to do much about it when groupthink takes over.

Ways of thinking

A problem can be addressed by different ways of thinking and we are now going to look at five of these: critical, creative, lateral, strategic, and black box.

Critical thinking

'It is the mark of an educated mind to be able to entertain a thought without accepting it' – Aristotle

Critical thinking is the process we use to reflect on, evaluate, and judge the assumptions underlying our own and others' ideas and efforts. The Socratic method, named after the classical Greek philosopher Socrates, is at the heart of critical thinking. It is a method of controlled questioning in order to explore complex issues, get to the truth of things, open up problems, challenge ideas, analyse views, distinguish what we know from what we don't know, and follow a line of thought to its logical conclusion. The key to distinguishing Socratic questioning from questioning in general is that Socratic questioning is methodical, orderly, and profound and it usually focuses on fundamental ideas, principles, theories, issues or problems.

According to authors Richard Paul and Linda Elder in their book *The Thinker's Guide to the Art of Socratic Questioning* (2007) there are nine types of Socratic questions:

- Questions of clarification
- Questions that probe purpose
- Questions that probe assumptions
- Questions that probe information
- Questions about viewpoints or perspectives
- Questions that probe implications and consequences
- Questions about the question
- Questions that probe concepts
- Questions that probe inferences and interpretations

Socratic questioning teaches us to dig beneath the surface of our ideas.

Creative thinking

'The significant problems we face cannot be solved at the same level of thinking we were at when we created them' – Albert Einstein

Creative thinking uses very different approaches from critical thinking; it involves a much more relaxed, open, and playful ap-

"Come on, people. We need a
creative epiphany right now.
Who has one?"

proach. 'Thinking outside the box' is a metaphor that means to
think differently, unconventionally, or from a new perspective; it
refers to creative thinking.

When thinking creatively you are looking for many possible solutions, rather than just one. You allow yourself to make wild and
crazy suggestions, make mistakes, and you do not judge ideas early
in the process. You allow yourself to doodle, daydream or play with
a theory or a suggestion.

Creative thinking is more about attitude and self-confidence than
it is about talent. Creativity is often disorderly, unstructured, and unpredictable. Strong emotional self-control is needed to allow creative
thinking states to arise, as it is important to be able to cope with risk,
confusion, disorder and the feeling that you are not going forward.

Looking back, every great idea seems obvious. But how can you
be the person who comes up with those ideas? In his book *Thinkertoys – A Handbook of Creative Thinking Techniques* (2006) Michael
Michalko unveils the secrets of creative genius and brings creative
techniques within everyone's reach. This book presents dozens of
field-tested, immediately usable tools for generating ideas and stimulating creativity, and provides an understanding of many creativity techniques that can be applied to problems, opportunities, or

situations. The principles and methodologies include a variety of options developed by Michalko, and the strategies are easily changed to fit specific needs or industries.

Be aware however that thinking outside the box and being creative may have its risks if you are new to a job. New ideas are not always going to be welcomed by colleagues or sometimes even by managers. Your colleagues may resist your ideas and even operate against you. You will have to judge the situation carefully.

Lateral thinking

'Everyone has the right to doubt everything as often as he pleases and the duty to do it at least once. No way of looking at things is too sacred to be reconsidered. No way of doing things is beyond improvement' – Edward de Bono

Dr Edward de Bono created the term 'lateral thinking' in his influential book *The Use of Lateral Thinking* (1967). De Bono became known as a pioneer in the fields of creativity and lateral thinking, advancing the idea that the human brain is a self-organising system. It was from this insight that he developed thinking tools and creativity methods designed to help people and organisations transform their thinking by avoiding the normal thought-blocks that inhibit their everyday thinking.

According to De Bono, lateral thinking deliberately distances itself from standard perceptions of creativity as either 'vertical' logic (the classic method for problem solving: working out the solution step-by-step from the given data) or 'horizontal' imagination (having many ideas but being unconcerned with the detailed implementation of them).

De Bono defines four types of thinking tools:

- *Idea-generating tools* intended to break current thinking patterns – routine patterns, the status quo.
- *Focus tools* intended to broaden where to search for new ideas.
- *Harvest tools* intended to ensure more value is received from idea generating output.
- *Treatment tools* that promote consideration of real-world constraints, resources and support.

One famous technique that is promoted by de Bono is his 'Six Thinking Hats'; you can read more about this on pages 147-148.

Strategic thinking

The work of management theorist Henry Mintzberg, and other authors, points towards the conclusion that the critical strategic question is not the conventional 'What?' but 'Why?' or 'How?' Strategic thinking is closely related to the managing and leading competency.

Strategic thinking helps managers and leaders review policy issues, perform long term planning, set goals and determine priorities, and identify possible risks and opportunities. But strategic thinking is not just relevant to managers and leaders. From the very start of your career the ability to demonstrate strategic skills will be an asset and will get you noticed. Organisations are always looking for people who can make the next step, and the ability to think strategically is a sign of someone who is capable of going far.

Strategic thinking involves developing an entire set of critical skills:

- Strategic thinkers have the ability to use both the logical and the creative capabilities of their brain.
- They have the ability to balance a tremendous amount of creativity with a sense of realism and honesty about what is achievable in the longer term.
- They have the ability to develop a clearly defined and focused vision for the organisation, and a personal vision.
- They have the ability to clearly define their objectives and develop a strategic action plan with each objective broken down into tasks and each task having a list of needed resources and a specific timeline.
- They have the ability to design flexibility into their plans by creating some benchmarks in their thinking to review progress.
- They are remarkably aware and perceptive. They will listen, hear and understand what is said and will read and observe whatever they can so that they have very helpful and strategic information to guide them.

- They are committed lifelong learners and learn from each of their experiences. They use their experiences to enable them to think clearly on strategic issues.
- They are committed to and seek advice from others. They may use a coach, a mentor, a fellow worker, an advisory group or some other group that they can confide in and offer up ideas for feedback.
- They have the ability to be non-judgmental and they do not allow themselves to be held back or restricted by judging their own thinking or the thinking of others when ideas are initially being developed and shared.
- They have the ability to be patient and not rush to conclusions and judgements. Great ideas and thoughts require time to develop into great successes in the future to reach their vision.

Black box thinking

'Failure is not the opposite of success, It's part of success' – Ariana Huffington, co-founder and editor-in-chief of The Huffington Post

In his book *Black Box Thinking: The Surprising Truth about Success* former England table tennis champion Matthew Syed explores the surprising truth about success, and why some people never learn from their mistakes.

'Black box thinking', as you may have guessed, refers to the flight data recorders all airplanes have to carry for recording dozens of flight parameters and the conversations in the cockpit. They have been compulsory in commercial airplanes in the US since 1967. Syed's point is that flying has become safer than any other form of travel because of the lessons learned from past failures. In 2014, even accounting for Malaysia Airlines Flight 370's 239 deaths, the rate per million flights fell to a historic low of 0.23. Compare that to the US healthcare system. In 2013, a US study in the Journal of Patient Safety put the number of premature deaths associated with preventable harm (misdiagnosis, wrong drugs, injury during surgery, post-operative complications etc.) at more than 400,000 a year – the equivalent of two jumbo jets falling out of the sky every 24 hours. Why? In aviation, failure is regarded as a 'precious learning opportunity for all pilots' but in the healthcare business there is great reluctance to acknowledge and investigate failures.

Each success is the child of many failures. Sir James Dyson for example made 5,127 prototypes of his Dual Cyclone vacuum cleaner before he got it right.

Black box thinking is basically about how you learn from failure and in his book Syed shows how in various contexts success results from a particular way of thinking that embraces failures and methodically integrates the lessons learnt from them. Whether developing a new product, perfecting a skill or just trying to get a critical decision right, black box thinkers aren't afraid to face up to mistakes, indeed they see failure as the very best way to learn. Rather than denying their mistakes, blaming others or attempting to talk their way out of trouble, these individuals capitalise on errors to build their future success.

Key points to remember

- *Your ability to solve problems is an important skill sought after by recruiters.*

- *The first step towards a solution is a clear understanding of the problem.*

- *For most real-world problems there is no straightforward path to the solution.*

- *Solving problems requires teamwork, involving different points of view and expertise.*

- *Critical thinking, creative thinking, lateral thinking, and strategic thinking are all important tools in the problem solving process.*

- *Failure is not the opposite of success; it's part of it.*

And finally... some things to avoid

- *Constantly bothering your fellow workers for help in solving daily problems.*

- *Referring all questions to others.*

- *Trying to solve everything by yourself, not asking for help.*

- *Always raising problems, never offering solutions.*

- *Ignoring facts before resolving a problem.*

- *Making decisions on your own, without consulting fellow workers or your supervisor.*

- *Ignoring problems that need to be addressed.*

- *Procrastinating.*

- *Keeping information to yourself.*

- *Always going for the 'low hanging fruit' or easy solutions.*

- *Passing the buck to others.*

- *Relying too much on your 'gut feeling'.*

- *Making proposals without thinking through the consequences.*

- *Turning a deaf ear to other people's solutions.*

3. Meeting expectations

"Are we supposed to eliminate quality or improve waste?"

Meeting people's expectations at work means not only being able to do your work, solve problems, come up with solutions or produce output, but also deliver on your promises – to everyone, including yourself. Meeting expectations is about taking personal responsibility and initiative, within a set environment and following the given rules and procedures. Meeting expectations is also about working to your full potential, beyond your strict job description, going the 'extra mile', and surprising with better than anticipated results.

Meeting expectations is relevant at all stages of a career, but it is absolutely vital at the start. To put it simply, if you don't meet expectations – if you don't deliver what is expected of you – you could soon find yourself out of a job.

In your work, you will be expected to:

- Do your work in an enthusiastic and effective manner.

- Work in a professional manner and complete tasks on time.
- Perform job tasks in a satisfactory manner.
- Demonstrate a willingness to accept extra work.
- Propose new services or improved ways of working.
- Familiarise yourself with procedures, rules and regulations.
- Observe company policies.
- Keep organised, neat and accurate records.
- Keep all documentation updated as needed.
- Keep up with the knowledge and know-how for your position.
- Attend job related professional development activities.
- Attend job related social activities.
- Meet production standards for your position.
- Prepare for the meetings you attend.
- Refrain from conducting personal business on company time.
- Be courteous to the public at all times.
- Listen to clients carefully in order to determine their needs.
- Follow the company's dress code.
- Go the 'extra mile'.

Anchors for 'meeting expectations'

- Taking responsibility.
- Taking initiative.
- Overcoming obstacles.
- Delivering quality work on time.
- Working to a high standard of quality.
- Managing workload efficiently and effectively.
- Understanding the value of innovation and continuous improvement.
- Linking up various elements of the work.
- Demonstrating efficiency and effectiveness in your work.
- Managing and sustaining change initiatives.

Now, just as we did in Chapter 2, take a look at Table 3.1 on pages 44-45 asking which of these behaviours sound like a description of what you do and how you react to situations.

And don't forget, you can also use our free app to compile a scoresheet for yourself competency-by-competency.

What is work?

'Work consists of whatever a body is obliged to do, and play consists of whatever a body is not obliged to do' – Mark Twain in 'Tom Sawyer'

A formal definition of work could be: 'Any activity involving mental or physical effort done in order to achieve a result.'

- A *task* is a unit of work, that is, a set of activities needed to produce some result.
- A *result* is the final consequence of a task that can be expressed qualitatively or quantitatively.
- A *job* is a collection of tasks and responsibilities that a worker is responsible to conduct; jobs have titles.
- A *role* is a set of responsibilities or expected results associated with a job. A job usually includes several roles.
- A *career* is something that someone wants to pursue for the rest of their (working) life.

Usually, work is related to being paid; most people work to get a salary or revenue. Intuitively, one might think that higher pay should produce better results, but scientific evidence indicates that the link between compensation, motivation and performance is much more complex. Why else do people have hobbies, do sports, or volunteer – and be highly motivated and well-performing – without any financial compensation? In his TED talk on 'The way we think about work is broken', Barry Schwartz argues that, apart from a pay check, there are intangible values that our current way of thinking about work simply ignores. When Schwartz interviewed hospital janitors about the challenges of their jobs, all the motivators they listed dealt with the expectations of other people. Good janitors knew not to vacuum the floor when patients were napping, or not to mop the floor when a patient was walking the hallways and restoring his strength. Being a hospital janitor involves interactions that require kindness, care and empathy. In this way, even for a simple, low wage, job it is indeed possible to exceed expectations and go beyond the job description.

Behavioural scientists usually divide work into two categories: 'algorithmic' and 'heuristic'. An algorithmic task is one in which

Table 3.1: Which of these sound like you?

UNSATISFACTORY	IMPROVEMENT NEEDED	MEETS EXPECTATIONS	EXCEEDS EXPECTATIONS	EXCEPTIONAL
Finds excuses for not dealing promptly with problems and requests.	Does not always take responsibility for dealing promptly with problems that arise at work.	Takes his work seriously and applies himself to tasks.	Tackles assignments and accepts full responsibility for the results.	Has a highly developed sense of responsibility and accountability.
Refers problems to third parties instead of tackling them directly.	Is slow to react to developments that affect achievability of results.	Is quality-conscious and does the necessary to achieve high standards.	Reacts to developments that affect achievability of objectives.	Anticipates problems and has solutions already worked out in advance.
Blames external factors for failure to deliver quality work.	Is reluctant to go beyond the call of duty.	Understands procedures and workflow within his/her department.	Keeps up with events and takes initiatives that have a positive impact on quality of work.	Goes the extra mile to ensure best possible results.
Does no more than the minimum required to complete tasks.	Does not deal adequately with complex tasks.	Follows established guidelines where appropriate.	Acts without waiting to be told: takes initiative.	Takes initiatives to make procedures and workflows more efficient or effective.
Sticks strictly to own job description.	Takes the first solution that comes along without standing back to weigh other options.	Works beyond the confines of job description if necessary.	Takes remedial actions when quality is in danger or compromised by deadlines.	Finds ways of delivering the best possible results under difficult circumstances and tight deadlines.
Is deflected or stopped by obstacles and does not find ways around them.		Deals with matters in appropriate and timely manner.	Sets himself demanding standards and does not settle for second best.	Puts a large amount of personal effort and creative thought into work.
Settles for quick and easy solutions.	Is overly perfectionist, indecisive, or impatient with others.	Strikes acceptable balance between quality and deadlines.	Combines good work-life balance with efficient and effective behaviour at work.	Thrives in challenging situations.

Table 3.1: Which of these sound like you? – continued

UNSATISFACTORY	IMPROVEMENT NEEDED	MEETS EXPECTATIONS	EXCEEDS EXPECTATIONS	EXCEPTIONAL
Works inefficiently or becomes overwhelmed with workload.	Has a limited perspective and understanding of the importance of quality improvement.	Performs to expected standards and in accordance with procedures in place.	Understands and communicates the importance of quality improvement.	Manages own workload as well as the workload of others effectively and efficiently.
Procrastinates.		Manages to get all his/her work done in time and to a good quality standard.	Manages several projects effectively and efficiently.	Consistently offers original, inventive ideas for improving products and services.
Resists change: prefers to continue to do things as they always have been done.	Makes few if any links between separate items of information.	Understands the value of quality improvement.	Results enhance productivity and quality of the department.	Focuses on both the general elements and the details of the situation.
Does not grasp the bigger picture.	Has difficulty handling more than one task or project at a time.	Identifies weaknesses that impede processes and recommends changes	Ensures that operational changes are successfully implemented and sustained over time.	Has a clear understanding of the bigger picture.
Cannot handle more than one project at a time.	Rarely monitors change initiatives after implementation.	Sustains change through clear documentation and regular monitoring.		Demonstrates efficiency by getting more done in less time while maintaining quality of results.
Moves to next project before ensuring successful, sustainable implementation of previous projects.				

you follow a set of pre-established instructions, down a single pathway to one conclusion. That is, there is an algorithm for solving it. A heuristic task is the opposite; because there is no algorithm you have to experiment with possibilities and find a new solution. During the twentieth century, most work was algorithmic, but today, in much of the Western world algorithmic work is disappearing, as it is offshored to wherever it can be done cheaper, or automated.

Most graduate-level workers are so-called 'white collar' workers whose job involves mostly heuristic work. The term white collar used to simply characterise non-manual workers, but now it refers to workers or professionals whose work is knowledge-intensive, non-routine, and mostly unstructured. Previously, in the West, clerical workers wore white shirt collars and manual workers wore blue, hence the expression.

According to American organisational theorist Russell Ackoff, the content of the human mind can be classified into five categories:

- *Data – symbols*. Data is raw; it simply exists and has no significance beyond its existence. It can exist in any form, usable or not. It does not have meaning of itself.
- *Information* – data that is processed to be usable. Answers to 'who', 'what', 'where', and 'when' questions. Information is data that has been given meaning by way of relational connection. This meaning can be useful, but does not have to be.
- *Knowledge* – application of data and information. Answers the 'how' question; knowledge is information organised in a way that makes it useful.
- *Understanding* – appreciation of 'why'. For example, elementary school children memorise knowledge of the times table. They can tell you that 2 x 2 = 4 because they have amassed that knowledge (as it is in the times table). But when asked what 123 x 456 is, they cannot respond correctly because that calculation is not in their times table. To correctly answer such a question requires understanding.
- *Wisdom* – evaluated understanding. Unlike the previous categories, wisdom deals with the future because it incorporates vision and design.

White-collar work is about the exchange of data, information, knowledge, understanding and wisdom.

The inner game of work

In his book *The Inner Game of Work: Overcoming Mental Obstacles for Maximum Performance* (2000), Tim Gallwey defines work in terms of a triangle with the words performance, learning and enjoyment at the points. He stresses that all three of these are important and that, therefore, if enjoyment is decreased, performance is also decreased. This has obvious effects for many traditional work cultures; he says:

> 'When either the learning or the enjoyment side is ignored, performance will suffer in the long run. When it does, management feels threatened and pushes even harder for performance. Learning and enjoyment diminish even further. A cycle ensues that prevents performance from ever reaching its potential.'

What is quality?

'Quality in a service or product is not what you put into it. It is what the client or customer gets out of It' – Peter Drucker

Romanian-born American engineer and management consultant Joseph Juran defined quality as 'fitness for use' but this is – to say the least – not the whole story. Allow me to use a very practical example to illustrate this. Say that we are talking about smartphones. We all know that there are hundreds of different models and brands out there, and that there is a constant evolution going on, almost forcing people to buy a new smartphone every two years or so. Unless you were really ripped off, or your smartphone recently broke, you can definitely say that the model you are using today is 'fit for use'; you can use it for what it's meant to do, that is to communicate with others. But does that mean that it is of 'good' or 'excellent' quality? Or, inversely, that the 'fitness for use' of an older model has dropped over time? Of course not, because we all have different

**"Go tell the workers that I'm
serious about this quality crap."**

needs – or call it expectations, and these needs evolve over time. Technology freaks will 'need' the most recent, fancy model to show off to their friends, while elderly people will probably be satisfied with the simplest, cheapest, and even out-dated model. In fact, our 'needs' and 'expectations' are to a large extent driven by the market and the outrageous competition between the manufacturers of smartphones. In order to survive, they have to produce, and sell, new models at an ever-increasing pace. Manufacturing costs are dropping constantly, and so are the profit margins. This can only be made up for by selling higher volumes. The bottom line is that 'fitness for use' is not 'fit for use' as a comprehensive definition of quality; we have to take the expectations of our clients into account.

The ISO (International Organisation for Standardisation) definition of quality goes as follows: 'The totality of features and characteristics of a product or service that bear on its ability to satisfy stated or implied needs.' More directly, one can say that a product or service has good quality when it complies with the requirements specified by the client. A *requirement* is a singular, documented physical and functional need that a particular design, product or process must be able to perform. In the business world, requirements are also called *specifications*.

In the context of office work, quality can be seen as a measure of the degree to which the expectations of your client (your boss, your company, your customers, or the general public) are met. However, 'expectations' are deeper and wider than 'requirements' or 'specifications'. Expectations are your client's vision of a future state or action, usually unspoken but nevertheless very important to your success. These expectations are not always clear and obvious. Your supervisor may want a piece of work to be 'quick and dirty,' or to be personally 'involved in all the details' or 'not involved at all,' or expect that your work is of 'high quality' without giving any further details as to what that means in practice.

In the end, the quality of your work is decided by the person who asked for it, not by people in general. It is not related to cost, and adjectives or descriptors such as 'high' and 'poor' are not applicable as such.

Understanding what is expected

Imagine your boss asks you to produce a plan to improve the workflow for a routine activity. You come up with something that tweaks the existing arrangements – it is 10% more efficient. You have met your boss's expectations.

Maybe that was what your boss was looking for – or maybe they were actually looking for something more, something that was 'thinking outside the box', that would transform the activity and be 35% more efficient. You did what was asked but did you really meet your boss's expectations? Sometimes it can be a challenge to figure out what your boss is expecting of you. It is not always only what they ask. Do not be afraid to probe and engage in a conversation with your boss.

Bureaucracy

In the description of meeting expectations it is also said that the results have to be delivered 'within set procedures'; clearly, what is meant here are the procedures as imposed by the organisation you work for.

Many organisations are *bureaucracies* – and there is nothing wrong with that, as such. Bureaucracies allow for specialisation –

employing people to do what they are best at. Professor Mintzberg labelled a highly bureaucratic organisation as being like a 'machine.' The machine organisation is defined by its standardisation. Work is very formalised, there are many routines and procedures, decision-making is centralised, and tasks are grouped by functional departments. Jobs are clearly defined; there is a formal planning process with budgets and audits; and procedures are regularly analysed for efficiency.

The term bureaucracy is French in origin, and combines the French word *bureau* – desk or office – with the Greek word *kratos*, meaning rule or political power. It was coined sometime in the mid-18th century and was a satirical pejorative from the outset.

Bureaucracies have a tight vertical structure. Functional lines go all the way to the top, allowing top managers to maintain centralised control. These organisations can be very efficient, and they rely heavily on economies of scale for their success. However, formalisation leads to specialisation and, quite often, functional units may have conflicting goals that can even be inconsistent with overall objectives.

Bureaucracies have been criticised as being too complex, inefficient, or too inflexible. The dehumanising effects of excessive bureaucracy became a major theme in the work of Franz Kafka. Others have defended the necessity of bureaucracies. The German sociologist Max Weber argued that bureaucracy constitutes the most efficient and rational way in which one can organise human activity, and that systematic processes and organised management levels are necessary to maintain order, maximise efficiency and eliminate favouritism. But Weber also saw unrestricted bureaucracy as a threat to individual freedom.

To end on a lighter note on bureaucracies, I'd recommend you to read *The Peter Principle*. The first edition of this book by Laurence J. Peter and Raymond Hull was published in 1969, but the main ideas still hold true today. It is a very funny book that will for sure deepen your understanding of how life in an organisation really works.

Time management

Meeting expectations is closely related to your ability to manage time. The modern concept of time management really began with the scientific management techniques pioneered by American mechanical engineer Frederick Taylor (1856-1915). His goal was to increase worker productivity (see Table 3.2). To do this, he conducted time and motion studies and began to focus on the best ways for jobs to be performed to maximise the work completed in a given amount of time.

Time management has also been used as a tool for increasing the productivity of white-collar workers, for whom work output may be hard to measure. In this respect, modern managers in these areas look for ways to monitor worker productivity in terms of time use.

Time management is a tool for improving employee efficiency. But it is also very relevant as a personal tool. If you manage your time well, you will get your work done faster and better.

Effectiveness	Efficiency	Productivity
Effectiveness is about doing the right task, completing activities and achieving goals.	Efficiency is about doing things in an optimal way, for example doing it the fastest or in the least expensive way.	Productivity is an average measure of efficiency. It can be expressed as the ratio of output to inputs used, i.e. output per unit of input.

Table 3.2

Performance management

Performance management is a process by which managers and workers act together to plan, monitor and review work objectives and overall contribution to the organisation. More than just an annual performance review, performance management is a continuous process of setting objectives, evaluating progress and providing on-going feedback to ensure that workers are meeting their objectives and career goals.

One of the cornerstones of performance management is the *job description*. Through their job description a worker will know in general terms what is expected without having to refer to more complete instructions for a task at hand. Complex positions in the organisation can include many tasks, which are sometimes called functions.

Job descriptions are lists of the general tasks, or functions, and responsibilities of a position. Usually, they also include whom the position reports to, and specifications such as the qualifications needed by the person in the job, salary range for the position, etc. It is important to make a job description practical by keeping it dynamic, functional and current. A well-written job description will help the manager avoid hearing a refusal to carry out a relevant task because 'it isn't in my job description.' A poor job description will keep workers from trying anything new and from learning how to perform their job more productively. Good job descriptions will help them to grow within their position and make a bigger contribution to the organisation.

Bear in mind that job descriptions often have a certain amount of padding or vague requirements. You need to understand what the really important elements are. Your new colleagues might be able to help with that.

Expectation management

'*Always give people more than what they expect to get*' – Nelson Boswell, US author of self-help books

Expectation management is very valuable. Managing expectations proactively will increase your chances of success, a great performance review, and ultimately have a positive effect on your career progression.

The first thing to do is to make sure you understand exactly what is expected of you. Understanding your job description and learning about the procedures that are to be followed for your particular role or job is clearly a first step in understanding what is expected. Managers sometimes fall into the trap of assuming that everyone else has the same understanding of a situation, project, deadline, or task. If you supervise a team, make sure to share your expectations with them. Giving others a picture of what you think a success would be for the team and each individual, will give them a way to move forward. The SMART model (Specific, Measurable, Achiev-

"Meeting my expectations will be
easy. Just be better than you are,
and smarter than you are,
and work harder than you can."

able, Realistic and Time-framed – see pages 255-256) can be a useful
tool in this respect.

One of the best ways to manage expectations is to make sure you
communicate with everyone on a frequent basis. To keep in control
of your performance, constant conversation provides opportunities
to measure progress, assess risks, and adjust actions. By keeping
your boss in the loop, you also ensure that they are aware of your
progress and successes along the way. If you are a manager yourself, share with the people you manage how you expect them to
tackle possible problems, so that these can be dealt with in a timely
manner and don't become obstacles to your own success.

Finally, plan for contingencies. When objectives are set, 'what
if?' questions are rarely part of the conversation. Some tasks will be
easier than others and some are more dependent on circumstances
beyond your control. The landscape can change quickly if a critical
assumption does not end up holding true. Assess the risks and
identify potential options for addressing the most likely scenarios.
That way you will be less likely to be caught by surprise. If you find
yourself leading others, speak to your team about the risks they perceive and how you can help them reduce these risks to achieve their
objectives. Also, being honest about a delay is a thousand times better than promising to deliver and then missing your deadline.

Anticipating expectations

The traditional definition of quality is the ability to meet customer expectations. This is not always the whole story.

I as a customer have no clue about the new features that will come as part of the new Apple iPhone or the Samsung Galaxy for that matter. But time and again, the new features cause me to say 'This is exactly what I was looking for!' People often expect to have their needs not just met, but also *anticipated*. As Henry Ford famously said, 'If I'd asked people what they wanted, they would have said a faster horse'. He came up with his Model T, a horseless car.

So our definition of quality has to be tweaked to something like this: ability to meet your customer's – in this case your boss's – unknown expectations. But how can you do that?

The answer is rather simple: understand your boss. It is easier to surprise someone you know than a stranger on the street. When you know someone, you know what he or she wants. When you really know someone, you know what they want before they know it.

Anticipating needs starts with paying attention. Who is your boss? What do they care about? What makes them tick? Conversely, what annoys them and makes them feel their time is being wasted? What are their biggest frustrations? So, for example, instead of just asking at the end of an interaction if your supervisor is satisfied, ask them what you could have done to better meet their expectations. People think in terms of finding an answer to their question or a solution to their problem. That is what meeting expectations is all about.

Dealing with a 'bad boss'

In an ideal world, we would all have fantastic bosses – people who help us succeed, who make us feel valued, and who are just great people. Unfortunately, that's not always the case. Maybe your boss is a micromanager or a bully – or an insensitive, abusive, or incompetent person. In my own career I have had quite a few 'bad bosses', and I definitely recall situations where I was the bad guy myself. The thing is that you still have to make the best of the situation and get your job done, but how?

**"This is where you all went wrong,
causing my plan to fail."**

Here is a general approach for 'managing up' a difficult boss:

- Manage your own negative emotions regarding their behaviour. Control your impulses to react emotionally or defensively. Don't take it personally. Look at negative feedback as an opportunity for improving your own behaviour.
- Try to understand the reasons for your boss's difficult behaviour. Is it because of their personality – who they are – or because of external circumstances? Find out what makes them tick.
- If your boss has a personality problem accept the fact that you will not be able to solve it. Don't let their problem affect your work, and stay on good terms with other leaders in the company (and keep your job).
- If it's a matter of external circumstances that cause your boss's behaviour, communicate your concerns and try to find a solution *with* them, not *against* them. Let them feel you understand their situation, and work together.

How to recognise a bad boss

As a new arrival in the workplace you may feel uncomfortable with your boss but be unsure whether the problem lies with you, or with them. Having not so much experience you may be inclined to believe that the boss is always right, and that you are to blame. Here are some signs that indicate that your boss is not as good as they believe themselves to be:

- Everybody is afraid of your boss, not just you
- He is always right
- He blames others when things go wrong, including his own boss
- Your boss is a micromanager
- Your boss does not provide guidance
- He does not communicate, is a bad listener
- Your boss is quick to blame you for mistakes, but rarely gives positive feedback
- He has zero-tolerance for other people's mistakes
- Your boss has favourites
- Your boss constantly changes their mind
- You are not given a chance to grow
- Your boss is self-centred
- He takes credit for other people's work
- He is manipulative

A recent poll from job-search site Monster found that 32% of employees say they have a 'horrible' boss; while only 15% say they have an 'excellent' one; so before blaming yourself, think twice. It will be good for your self-esteem.

Personal responsibility

'The power behind taking responsibility for your actions lies in putting an end to negative thought patterns. You no longer dwell on what went wrong or focus on whom you are going to blame. You don't waste time building roadblocks to your success. Instead, you are set free and can now focus on succeeding' – Lorii Myers, in *Targeting Success* (2011)

Personal responsibility is the willingness to accept the importance of standards for individual behaviour, and to make active personal efforts to live by those standards. But personal responsibility also means that when you don't meet expected standards, you don't look around for some factor outside yourself to blame.

Our brain is inclined to flatter and shield our self-image from blame when we make mistakes. Despite how hard it may be to fight against the mechanisms of your ego defence system you must make the effort. In doing so, you will find that trying to take responsibility for your actions and ownership of your mistakes is valuable for many reasons:

- It allows you to make better decisions. Self-justifications distort reality. The more you use them, the more you create an alternative universe for yourself. This leads to a decreased ability to make good choices, as the information you're using to do so is distorted. Most dangerously, one self-justification leads to another, setting off a domino effect that sends you more and more off track. Once you justify one bad decision, you're deeper into it, and you'll make a decision that digs you even further into it ... and so the cycle continues.
- It keeps little problems from turning into big ones. If you can own up to a mistake as soon as you make it and do your best to correct it or make it right, you can prevent it from turning into a huge problem that is going to be very hard to solve.
- It allows you to learn from your mistakes. You can't learn from your mistakes if you can't acknowledge you've made them! And if you don't learn from your mistakes, you're certain to repeat them. That is a formula for quickly going nowhere.
- It causes the respect of others. We hide our mistakes from other people when we worry they will think less of us once they've seen that we've messed up. Honestly admitting your mistakes, apologising for them, and then working to make things right almost always has the opposite effect: people will respect you for it.

There are two ways to explain things we get wrong: someone did something because of the situation, or, because of who they are. We usually use the first explanation for what we do ourselves – 'I forgot we had agreed to discuss this beforehand because I just have so much on my mind right now.' We tend to use the second explanation about others' behaviour: 'He totally forgot we had agreed to discuss this beforehand because he is self-centred and couldn't care less about others.' In the second case we don't evaluate their behaviour, but their personality – they don't just *do* bad stuff, they *are* bad. The person is stupid, useless, selfish, immature, evil, lazy, etc. We judge them to be failed human beings. This kind of criticism is called a 'global label'. Global labels are rarely correct, but your brain finds them very satisfying to develop. They allow you to see the other as deliberately hurting you. It is their fault, and you are the victim, so you feel entitled to punish and attack them.

Initiative

> *'Initiative is doing the right thing without being told'* – Victor Hugo

Not everything will be in your job description. You will have to take the initiative at times. Initiative is all about *taking charge*. A person with initiative is motivated to do things. If you take the initiative, you are willing to get things done on your own. However, taking the initiative can be risky; if you do something on your own initiative, then there is nobody else you can blame if it goes wrong.

When you show initiative, you do things without being told; you find out what you need to know; you get going when the going gets tough; and you identify and take advantage of opportunities that others pass by. You act, instead of react.

Initiative has become increasingly important in today's work. Organisations want workers who can make quick decisions and take action without waiting for someone to tell them what to do.

The good news is that initiative is a skill that you can develop. The first step is to make your own career plan. Research has shown that people who have a long-term career plan are more likely to take the initiative. The next step is to build your self-confidence. It takes courage to show initiative, especially if you fear that people may disagree with your actions or suggestions. Set yourself small goals so you can achieve some quick wins. Then push yourself to do bigger things. Have a good look at the GROW model as described in Chapter 11; you will find it to be a good tool to develop your self-confidence.

Unforeseen obstacles

'The greater the obstacle, the more glory in overcoming it' – Molière

Sometimes, things are not working out as expected, or you have to overcome an unforeseen obstacle. For sure, these are situations of high stress, but you have to deal with them.

Anticipating the various possible results and/or reactions that others may have in a situation is extremely helpful in many ways. Thinking about all the possible actions and reactions of others to a situation makes your planning process more complete. What you ultimately piece together will likely not only have a solid plan 'A', but it may have a plan 'B', 'C', etc. as well.

When you take the time to anticipate, you are less likely to be surprised when and if what you thought might happen actually does happen. When you are less surprised you are less likely to be destabilised and you will be in better control of your emotions. When you are in control of your emotions you have the upper hand. You never know precisely what's around the corner, but you don't allow that to throw you off your game. Train yourself to anticipate possible challenges, to be prepared.

Of course, not everything can be anticipated, and really unforeseen – or unforeseeable – obstacles can block your way. You will have to find a workaround. You may be forced to 'think outside the box'. This means approaching problems in new, innovative ways; abstracting problems differently, and understanding your position in relation to any particular situation in a way you had never imagined before. Thinking outside the box, like any skill, is one that can be developed through practice; you may find some ideas on WikiHow (http://www.wiki-how.com/Think-%27Outside-of-the-Box%27).

Finally, you have to see these unexpected situations as learning opportunities. Being pushed out of your comfort zone creates a learning opportunity, as long as you are not drawn into your *panic zone* (see pages 159-161).

Quality management

'It is not necessary to change. Survival is not mandatory' – W. Edwards Deming

'Kaizen' is a Japanese word that has given its name to a management technique referred to as *continuous improvement* (see *Kaizen: The Key to Japan's Competitive Success* by Masaaki Imai). When applied to the workplace, it refers to activities that continuously improve all functions and involve all workers, from the top executives to those at entry-level. Many companies use variations on kaizen/continuous improvement so it is worth being aware of the concepts and vocabulary.

Kaizen was first implemented in Japan after the Second World War, influenced by the ideas of the American quality guru W. Edwards Deming. It has since spread around the world and been adopted in a wide range of environments, including government and business.

Deming provided a simple, yet highly effective technique that serves as a practical tool to carry out continuous improvement in the workplace. This technique is called the PDCA Cycle or simply Deming Cycle. PDCA is an acronym of Plan, Do, Check and Action. The Deming Cycle provides a conceptual as well as practical framework while carrying out Kaizen activities by the workers – see Figure 3.1. Notice the similarities to the GROW model (pages 253-255).

Kaizen is continuous improvement that is based on certain guiding principles:

- Good processes bring good results
- Go see for yourself to grasp the current situation
- Speak with data, manage by facts
- Take action to contain and correct root causes of problems
- Work as a team
- Kaizen is everybody's business

One of the most notable features of kaizen is that big results come from many small changes accumulated over time. However, this has been misunderstood to mean that kaizen equals small changes. In fact, kaizen means everyone being involved in making improvements.

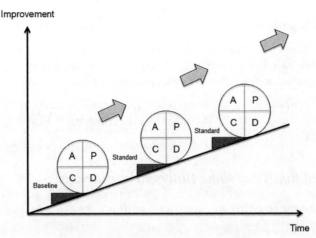

Figure 3.1: The Deming cycle – Plan (P),
Do (D), Check (C) and Action (A)

Key points to remember

- *Quality is the degree to which a product or service meets the expectations of the customer.*

- *Expectation management, personal responsibility and taking initiative are key for meeting and exceeding expectations.*

- *Whether it's verbal or written, communicating ideas, deadlines and other messages to your boss and fellow workers is a must.*

- *Taking the initiative, and the capability to overcome unforeseen obstacles, are important qualities.*

- *Bureaucratic rules are there for good reasons but they have to be applied with insight and common sense.*

- *Quality management by continuous improvement is a responsibility for all.*

- *Align your own goals to the team's goals.*

- *Staying abreast of the latest developments in your industry can show continuous improvement and help you become a more efficient and effective worker.*

- *Identify what differentiates you professionally from the rest and make it a characteristic that your boss can depend on.*

And finally... some things to avoid

- *Being impolite or impatient with others.*

- *Ignoring basic office procedures.*

- *Ignoring the established departmental dress code.*

- *Gossiping or ignoring the rules for confidentiality.*

- *'Office politics'.*

- *Using office equipment for personal purposes.*

- *Not properly using and maintaining office equipment.*

- *Not using equipment and materials for their intended purpose.*

- *Ignoring safety rules and procedures.*

- *Surfing, chatting, or otherwise abusing the internet for non-professional purposes.*

- *Coming late for scheduled meetings, or not showing up.*

- *Extending coffee breaks, lunch breaks without a reason.*

- *Coming in late in the morning, and/or leaving early in the evening.*

4. Managing time

'The bad news is time flies. The good news is you're the pilot' – Michael Altshuler

As a student, you probably discovered the need to manage your time when you arrived at college. In high school, classes filled your day, teachers structured your assignments, and you had little freedom. In college, you had less in-class time, more homework and group assignments, and a great deal of freedom and flexibility.

As a working professional, you will find that even better time management skills are needed. With the exception of planned meetings there may well be no fixed schedule for your working day. Your supervisor will only tell you when they expect you to deliver your work – if that. In college you only had to worry about when to complete your study points, and these were all of equal importance. In the workplace, some activities are more important than others, and some are more urgent than others. This is quite a different situation, and you will have to deal with it. You will have to change your old habits.

But what is time management? Time itself can't be managed. It is constant and it always goes forward, never backwards. Everyone has the same amount of time in an hour, a day, and a week. Therefore, time management does not mean that you are trying to manipulate time, but that you are trying to make the best possible use of the time available.

Time management is the act of taking conscious control over the amount of time you spend on specific activities. Time management is about setting goals, effective scheduling, prioritising and choosing what to do and what not to do, delegating tasks, analysing and reviewing your spent time, organising your workspace, keeping your concentration and focus on your work, and motivating yourself. You manage your time to increase your effectiveness, your efficiency, your productivity, and in the end to meet the expectations of people around you.

In your work, you will expected to:

- Set specific goals and priorities for completing tasks.
- Monitor progress and change plans if needed.
- Complete all work tasks by their deadlines.
- Keep organised, neat, and accurate records.
- Work at a rate that is similar to your fellow workers.
- Maintain a to-do list to help you stay on top of deadlines.
- Prioritise your tasks and properly plan your work.
- Delegate assignments to subordinates when appropriate.
- Avoid procrastination.
- Attend scheduled meetings and arrive on time.
- Observe time reporting rules and regulations.
- Plan and account for the use of overtime.
- Observe scheduled work and meal breaks.
- Call your supervisor if you must be late or absent.
- Avoid tardiness and report to work on time.

Anchors for 'managing time'

- Understanding goals and implementing plans to achieve them.
- Mobilising the appropriate resources to achieve goals.
- Developing and implementing metrics to measure results.
- Anticipating and solving problems.
- Setting realistic deadlines and milestones.
- Managing workload efficiently and effectively.
- Prioritising tasks appropriately.
- Linking up the various elements of the work.
- Being flexible in taking into account new aspects as they arise.
- Collaborating effectively with others.

Now, as in previous chapters, take a look at Table 4.1 on pages 66-67 asking which of these behaviours sound like a description of what you do and how you react to situations.

Tasks

Ever since Adam and Eve were expelled from the Garden of Eden most of us have had to work for a living. But even though we have to work in exchange for a financial reward, there is nothing wrong with actually enjoying our work. After all, we spend a big slice of our waking hours at work, and spending that time in an enjoyable and productive way is part of what makes life worth living. Agreed, your boss, your fellow workers, or the work you have to do are not always exciting, but 'feeling in control' of what you do – and how you do it – will at least give you some degree of job satisfaction and happiness.

The most elementary building block of work is a task. A *task* is an activity that needs to be accomplished within a defined period of time (or by a deadline) to reach work-related goals. One can see a task as an (abstract) three-dimensional object: input, output and time. The *input* is what you do; the efforts, knowledge, energy, focus or whatever other contribution you make to get the work done. The *output* is the result; it can be a message, a report, a presentation or any tangible or intangible deliverable of your work. The *time* is the difference between the moment you started working on

Table 4.1: Which of these sound like you?

UNSATISFACTORY	IMPROVEMENT NEEDED	MEETS EXPECTATIONS	EXCEEDS EXPECTATIONS	EXCEPTIONAL
Does not follow an orderly method of setting objectives, scoping out difficulties, detailing work, or planning for task completion.	Does not have a clear picture of organisation's goals; lacks perspective to pull elements into a strategic view; plans often lack substance and specificity.	Creates effective plans with defined purpose and results.	Plans with organisation's goals in mind.	Creates innovative, ambitious plans, which align with organisation's goals and serve as reliable roadmaps to desired results.
		Breaks complex tasks into process steps, prioritises activities, itemises resources and estimates costs.	Plans clearly identify roles, responsibilities and timeframes.	
Fails to prepare in advance.	Has difficulty marshaling and informing resources to work together to achieve desired results.		Informs and mobilises resources—staff, stakeholders, technical experts—to achieve shared vision, mission, and goals.	Effectively influences, informs, and mobilises resources—staff, stakeholders, technical experts—to achieve shared vision, mission, and goals.
Is not able to integrate multiple activities and resources into a cohesive, actionable plan.	Has difficulty defining and implementing appropriate metrics to measure success.	Organises, informs and supports resources to achieve goals.	Implements metrics that effectively and efficiently measure results.	Develops and implements reliable, effective metrics to measure results; identifies and recommends changes to improve efficiency and effectiveness.
Is unwilling/unable to create or track metrics.		Monitors progress and determines how processes may be changed to improve quality and/or efficiency.	Recommends improvements based on results.	
Allows work to continue without monitoring.	Becomes ineffective when plans need to change.	Adapts to changes in plans effectively.	Anticipates and adjusts for problems and roadblocks.	Proactively anticipates, analyses and solves problems and motivates others to do the same.
Ignores small problems until they become significant, jeopardising deadlines and effective utilisation of resources.	Identifies problems but does not effectively address them.	Addresses problems in process or resourcing quickly and effectively.	Resolves problems in early stages.	
	Neglects work-life balance. Uses overtime as only strategy to cope with heavy workload or tight deadlines.		Factors in 'what if' and plans for contingencies.	Consistently sets realistic deadlines and milestones, and always has a 'Plan B'.
			Sees how different elements fit together	

Table 4.1- continued

UNSATISFACTORY	IMPROVEMENT NEEDED	MEETS EXPECTATIONS	EXCEEDS EXPECTATIONS	EXCEPTIONAL
Sets unrealistic deadlines and milestones.	Is overly perfectionist, indecisive, or impatient with others.	Manages to get all his/her work done in time and to a good quality standard.	Sees how new input affects the state of play and re-assesses the situation if necessary.	Manages own workload as well as the workload of others effectively and efficiently.
Works inefficiently or becomes overwhelmed with workload.	Leaves the task of establishing priorities to others.		Encourages others to share ideas and integrates others' thoughts and opinions in own plans and priorities.	Prioritises tasks appropriately, both for himself and for the unit.
Procrastinates.	Does not play an active role in identifying the issues and prioritising accordingly.			Differentiates clearly between matters of primary and secondary importance.
				Fits things together and draws conclusions.

the task and when your work was complete. It is important to be aware that these three dimensions are connected; they influence each other.

I sometimes use the metaphor of a balloon, filled with air. This is a three-dimensional object too, right? When you squeeze the balloon (in this way changing one dimension) this will influence the other two dimensions. By analogy, when you change one 'dimension' of a task this will also have an impact on the other dimensions. Say your manager changes the (expected) output; you will then be forced to either change your input or the time it takes to complete the task. If you reduce your input then either the output will have to be less or it will take you more time to complete the task (or both).

Here is another nice use of this metaphor. What happens if you squeeze a balloon too hard? It will burst. Well, the same thing happens with tasks. Say the deadline (or the time allotted) is too tight: you will never manage to complete

Figure 4.1

the task. If the (expected) output is too high you will never make it in time and neither will you complete the task if your input is too low.

Processes

Tom Davenport, Professor in Management and Information Technology at Babson College (Massachusetts, USA), defines a process as:

'A specific ordering of work activities across time and place, with a beginning and an end, clearly defined inputs and outputs, a structure for action.'

The purpose of a process is to transform input into output. This transformation is done through the support of resources (people, money, infrastructure, information…) and according to – formal or informal – specifications (or expectations if you wish).

A process can be broken down into *steps* and organised in a *workflow*. Each step (task) is performed by an actor (a person or a group of people) with a given role in the workflow. Very often processes (also known as procedures, or operations) are automated and run on a computer network or 'in the cloud'.

The output of a process can be material (a *product*) or non-material (a *service*). In fact, often it is a combination of both (e.g. a paper file is the material component, while the content is the service component of a written report).

Most of the tasks you will have to do are in some way part of a process: you are an 'actor' with a given role, transforming input into output according to some specifications (meeting expectations).

The nice thing about this view on matters is that it makes your life easier in terms of managing your time. You know the input, what is expected and how much time you have to execute the task. You also have an idea of how important your tasks are.

Projects

'Crash programs fail because they are based on the theory that, with nine women pregnant, you can get a baby in one month' – Werner Von Braun

Projects have always been a part of life, ever since the first groups of humans worked together to gather, plant or hunt. Over the years, the idea of project management – planning and directing the activities executed by a group of people with a fixed objective and over a limited period of time – has been refined and formalised into a profession.

The Project Management Institute (PMI), a leading organisation in the development of project management principles and certification standards, defines a project as 'a temporary endeavour undertaken to create a unique product, service, or result.'

Projects and processes differ mostly in that processes are ongoing and repetitive, while projects are temporary and unique.

The objectives of projects and processes are fundamentally different. The purpose of a project is to reach its objective and then terminate. Conversely, the objective of an on-going operation (a process) is to sustain the organisation. Projects focus on change, while processes focus on status quo. Projects are undertaken at all levels of an organisation and they can involve a single person or many thousands. Projects can involve one or many organisational units, including joint ventures and partnerships.

If you are part of a project team it is very important that you are aware of the overall planning of the project, and where exactly you fit in in terms of timing, because a delay at your level can have devastating effects on the general project timing. Be aware of that!

Signs of poor time management

The following list covers some of the most common signs of poor time management, regardless of the quantity of work you actually bring to a conclusion. If you recognise some of these signs in your own behaviour, there is possible room for improvement.

- *Poorly defined goals* – Your goals help you to identify your priorities. They outline what you want to achieve, when you want to achieve it by, and why the task is important. If you do not have clearly defined goals, how are you supposed to know which tasks need to be done first?
- *Poor punctuality* – You are regularly late for your appointments or in completing your tasks. This may be due to you accepting too many tasks or your inability to assign the correct amount of time to your activities.
- *Rushing* – We all have to rush a little, from time to time, but if you find yourself constantly rushing from one appointment to another then you have an issue. You have to allow sufficient time between appointments to cope with unforeseen events such as a previous meeting overrunning, or simply traffic jams.
- *Impatience* – Impatience is usually a sign of poor time management. You may accuse other people, or technology, of delaying you but the truth is that you have failed yourself by failing to manage your time properly.
- *Perfectionism* – You spend so much time trying to prepare and make sure that you perform your tasks perfectly that you either fail to start or go incredibly slowly. In reality, most of the time, 'good enough is best'.
- *Indecisiveness* – You are unable to choose an option and run with it. You spend excessive time going over the options without coming to a conclusion.
- *Saying 'Yes' to everything* – Constantly saying 'Yes' will leave you with an excessive workload. One of the quickest ways to improve your time management is to be assertive and learn to say 'No'.
- *Doing everything yourself* – It doesn't matter at what level of the organisation you are, there are always tasks which can be delegated, automated or outsourced. These tasks need to be identified and removed from your workload.
- *Procrastination* – Sometimes you know what needs to be done but you keep putting it off. Eventually, when you decide to complete the task, the deadline is usually approaching and you are under pressure to complete the task in time.

- *Lack of energy* – When you constantly have to work extra hard to catch up, your energy levels begin to drop and you lose motivation. It becomes harder to catch up and so you fall further behind which drains you of even more energy.

**"I feel it's important to always
have a plan to ignore."**

Poor time management impacts every area of your life, from work to relationships. Don't confuse being busy with being an accomplished time manager. Getting more work done does not automatically mean that you are managing your time effectively; if the extra tasks are unimportant, you are just filling your schedule. Focusing on getting the *important* tasks done is the key to effective time management.

Estimating time

'Work expands to fill the time available for its completion' – Parkinson's Law

It is important to realise that a time estimate is not a fixed number, but a range of possibilities, a statistical entity. If somebody wants to talk to you 'for five minutes' it may take 15 minutes, and if it is important it may be more like 45 minutes.

In order to improve your own estimation of how long a given task will take it is a good idea to keep track of your own work (your own timesheet) and use the average time you spend on similar tasks as the basis of your estimate. You can still decide if you want your estimate to be 'safe' (a generous allocation of time that will cover 95% of cases) or 'aggressive' (a tight allocation of time that will cover 50% of cases), depending on the importance, the urgency and circumstances you are in at that moment.

STOP

The 'STOP' tool was introduced by Tim Gallwey in his book *The Inner Game of Work: Overcoming Mental Obstacles for Maximum Performance* (2000). Not everything we do at work is about ceaseless activity. The hard part is to remain conscious of what we are trying to achieve while busy working. The STOP tool is used to:

- **S**top
- **T**hink
- **O**rganise your thoughts, and
- **P**roceed

STOPs can be of any duration, maybe only for a few seconds. For example, to quote Gallwey:

- STOP before you speak
- STOP at the beginning of each work day
- STOP at the end of each work day
- STOP at the beginning and end of any work/project
- STOP to make a conscious change
- STOP to address mistakes
- STOP to correct miscommunication
- STOP to learn or coach
- STOP to rest

And a good signal that it is time for a STOP is when working just isn't fun anymore.

Multitasking

'The first law of success is concentration – to bend all the energies to one point, and to go directly to that point, looking neither to the right or to the left' – William Mathews, 19th century

Multitasking is doing multiple things – or performing multiple tasks – at the same time. Since the 1990s, psychologists have conducted experiments on the nature and limits of multitasking. The results of these experiments suggest that multitasking is not as efficient as work performed on a single task. Because the brain cannot fully focus when multitasking, people take longer to complete tasks and are more susceptible to error.

When people attempt to complete many tasks at one time, or alternate quickly between them, the error rate goes up and it takes far longer – often double the time or more – to get the jobs done than if they were done sequentially. This is largely because the brain is forced to restart and refocus. Ultimately you want to shift important facts from your short-term memory to your long-term memory. Research shows that this process takes about 8 seconds of focused attention on a specific item. A study by David Meyer and David Kieras at the University of Michigan found that in the interim between each exchange, the brain makes no progress whatsoever. Therefore, multitasking people not only perform each task less well, but also lose time in the process.

In terms of your time management this basically means that you'd be better off planning to execute your tasks in a sequential way, keeping your focus on one task at a time.

Our limited multitasking capabilities are also brutally challenged by modern technology. Office computers, Voice-over-IP telephones, smartphones and tablets are all designed to give us 24/7 accessibility. Besides the devastating effect on our work-life balance technology also hampers our time management skills.

In his 2011 book *The Shallows: What the Internet is doing to our Brains*, one of my favourite authors, Nicholas Carr states: 'Once I was a scuba diver in a sea of words. Now I zip along the surface like a guy on a Jet Ski'. Carr is finding it harder to concentrate and attend to long pieces of reading and writing. He also crystallises one of the

most important debates of our time: as we enjoy the internet's boun-
ties, are we sacrificing our ability to read and think deeply?

Even though I used to be an IT professional myself, it is my opinion that information and communication technology has not lived
up to its promise of improving our productivity, especially in the
white-collar arena. One of the reasons for this is the introduction of
too much multitasking amongst our workers, pushing them far too
often outside their comfort zone, into their panic zone and eventually towards a burnout.

One can conclude that having a good personal strategy for mastering technology is vital for your ability to manage time.

The art of delegation

No matter how efficient and masterful you are at your job, you
have the same number of hours in the day as your fellow workers.
There are only so many tasks you can achieve within a given amount
of time, so to free yourself up and lighten the load: delegate!

The key to successful delegation is to be totally clear about what
you are expecting for the result. How much direction you provide
to get from point A to B will depend on the level of expertise of the
person doing the task. You can read more about the art of delegation in Chapter 8.

Goal setting

*'The greater danger for most of us is not that our aim is too high and
we miss it, but that it is too low and we hit it'* – Michelangelo

Top-level athletes, successful business people and high achievers
of all kinds use *goal setting*. Setting goals gives you long-term vision and short-term motivation. By setting sharp, clearly defined
goals, you can measure and take pride in the achievement of those
goals, and you can see progress in what might previously have
seemed a long and pointless journey. You will also raise your self-
confidence, as you appreciate your own ability in achieving the
goals that you have set.

As mentioned in Chapter 3 'SMART' stands for goals that are
Specific, Measurable, Achievable, Realistic, and Time-bound. You

may have realised that it is important – both for your motivation and your development – to push the boundaries of your comfort zone by working in your *learning zone* (see pages 160-161). But how can you achieve all this in your daily work at the office?

Edwin Locke and Gary Latham in their book *A Theory of Goal Setting and Task Performance* (1990) identified five elements that need to be in place for us to achieve our goals: clarity, challenge, commitment, feedback, and task complexity.

- *Clarity* – When your goals are clear, you know what you are trying to achieve. You can also measure the results accurately. That is why SMART is such a useful mnemonic. However, when a goal is vague it is not easy to measure, and it is not motivating. You may not even know you have achieved it. Write your goal down and be as detailed as possible. Then think about how you will measure your progress towards this goal.
- *Challenge* – Is the goal outside your comfort zone? Consider how the goal makes you feel.
- *Commitment* – Try to visualise in your mind how you will feel when the goal is achieved. Does it motivate you?
- *Feedback* – Measure your own progress and ask for feedback from others. Schedule time to analyse your progress.
- *Task complexity* – Is the behaviour to achieve your goal inside your learning zone? Is the task not too complex, thus pushing you into your panic zone? If so, break it into smaller, less complex sub-goals.

Prioritising

I am sure you know the feeling of getting up for work in the morning with the sense of having so much to do that you don't know where to start. There are times when everything that you have to do seems like a priority, which makes it tough to figure out where to begin.

Don't worry; there are many techniques that can be used to prioritise the tasks you have to perform. Usually, these techniques are very simple and somewhat intuitive, but they work. Here I discuss a few – you can decide for yourself which of these works best for you.

To-do list

By far the simplest technique for day-to-day management is the *to-do list*. This is simply a list, in no particular order, of all the things you have to do, your tasks.

Don't keep your tasks on different post-it notes or in your head but at the beginning of each day or week, write on a sheet of paper what you want to get done and by when. Clearly, when making a new list you should not forget to transfer the tasks you have not finished from your previous list. You can refine this technique a bit by adding the amount of time you think it will take you (estimate) to perform every task and reorder the list in descending order (longest tasks first). You then work your way down the list assuming that the most important tasks are the ones that will take you the most time. Obviously, every time you complete a task you have to strike it from your list.

In many instances your to-do list related to the processes you participate in is generated by a workflow system; the tasks will be in your inbox and the deadline for execution will clearly be indicated. When you are part of a project team your project-related tasks will be given to you by the project manager, who is responsible for the overall timing and output of the project.

The 80/20 principle

Management thinker Joseph M. Juran first put the 80/20 principle into currency in the 1940s, calling it the Pareto principle (after the Italian economist Vilfredo Pareto, who in the 1890s observed that 80% of the land in Italy was owned by 20% of the population and that this distribution seemed to apply in many other cases too). The assumption is that most of the results in any situation are determined by a small number of causes.

This principle can also be applied to prioritising your tasks, based on the idea that most of the results (output) will be generated by a small proportion of your effort (input). When looking at your to-do list you simply pick those tasks that will produce

the most (relevant) output and you take these as your priorities.
The remaining tasks are executed when there is time left.

The ABC method

The ABC method is a powerful priority setting technique that
you can use every single day.

Once again, your to-do list is the starting point. Behind every
item you put a letter A, B or C depending on the following criteria:

- A – Very important. This is a task that you must do and for
  which there can be serious consequences if you fail to do it.
- B – A task that you should do, but it only has mild consequences.
  This means that someone may be unhappy or inconvenienced if
  you don't do it, but that's about it.
- C – A task that would be nice to do, but for which there are no
  consequences at all.

The Eisenhower matrix

Although it was Stephen Covey who made this method popular
in his book *First Things First*, the concept is originally credited to
US President Dwight D. Eisenhower. Whenever confronted with
something that needed to be done, he would ask himself two questions: First, is the task important? Second, is it urgent?

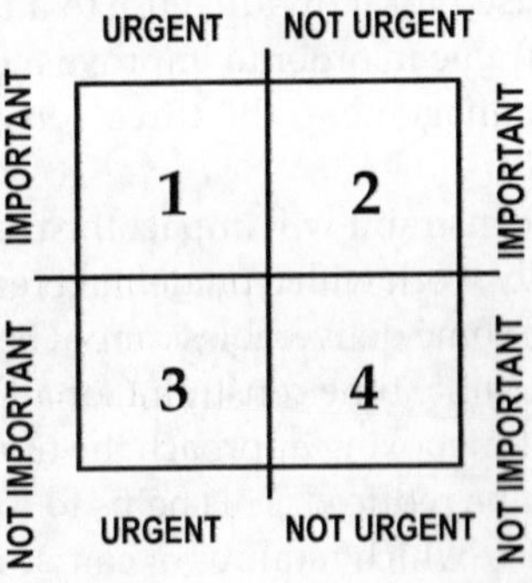

Figure 4.2: The Eisenhower matrix

Based on this, the task would end up in one of four categories: important and urgent, important but not urgent, not important but urgent, and neither important nor urgent.

Obviously the first priority has to go to the tasks that are both important and urgent (quadrant No. 1 in the matrix in Figure 4.2). However, what is not so obvious is that tasks labelled important but not urgent get the next priority (No. 2). This is what Eisenhower's point was all about: 'What is important is seldom urgent and what is urgent is seldom important'. Tasks that are in quadrant No. 3 are typical candidates for delegation, and the ones in No. 4 can even be dropped because they are neither urgent nor important, so why bother?

Tasks performed in the context of processes or projects are almost by definition important. Their urgency depends on the time constraints of the process or the timing of the project and whether the task is on the critical path or not. Doing your planning for the coming week is for sure important, but it probably is not urgent. Phone calls from outside are probably not important (unless you are waiting for one) and many text messages or emails are not important either.

Timeboxing

Timeboxing is a time management technique whereby the schedule is divided into a number of separate time periods – or timeboxes. Each timebox has its own deliverables, deadline and budget. It is also used for individual use to address personal tasks in a smaller time frame in order to improve the productivity of the user. In project management, the three constraints are time, resources, and result.

Changing one constraint will impact the rest. Without timeboxing, projects usually work with a predefined result. Under these circumstances, when some deliverables cannot be completed you will either have to adjust the time constraint, or add extra resources, or do both. With the timeboxing approach the time constraint is fixed, but the result may be reduced. This helps to focus on the most important deliverables, which requires of course a clear prioritisation (see also the section on expectation management in Chapter 3).

Individuals can use timeboxing for personal tasks. By using a reduced scale of time (e.g. one hour instead of a full week) and well-defined deliverables, personal timeboxing is said to help control perfectionist tendencies. Personal timeboxing also helps to overcome procrastination and many people find that the time pressure created boosts their creativity and focus.

Planning tools

'In preparing for battle I have always found that plans are useless, but planning is indispensable' – Dwight D. Eisenhower

Besides your to-do list it is a good idea to plan all your activities, whether they are process-related, project-related, related to your working conditions, or your personal life.

In the old days most people had a 'personal organiser' – a small, usually leather-bound book – and they had it with them all the time. With the advent of the internet and smartphones these have been gradually replaced by a version 'in the cloud'. The iCalendar protocol is supported by most – if not all – platforms, which means that you can have one organiser for all your activities or tasks (both private and professional) and that you have access (read/write) from wherever you are (provided of course you have access to the internet). You can also share (parts of) your calendar with other people and even invite people for activities you plan to do. Some companies even offer 'cloud scheduling software' which makes scheduling activities with other participants even more convenient (think of Doodle).

However, 'a fool with a tool is still a fool'.

If you use these tools you have to do it right. You have to put ALL your 'A' and 'B' (or '1' and '2') tasks or activities in there and respond accordingly when you receive the alert that the 'event' is about to start. You also have to schedule some time for the other activities and for the necessary breaks; in most situations it is sufficient to leave these time slots blank. Don't put every little activity in your calendar because otherwise you will have too much overhead or feel overwhelmed by all the things you are supposed to do (and be disturbed time and again by the alerts). It is also a good idea to work with larger blocks (with a minimum of say half an hour) so that you don't have to switch your focus too often.

Attention management

In their book *The Attention Economy*, Thomas H. Davenport and J. C. Beck define the concept of attention as follows: 'Attention is focused mental engagement on a particular item of information. Items come into our awareness, we attend to a particular item, and then we decide whether to act.'

There are different kinds of attention. *Proactive* attention is the kind of sustained focus you need to draft an important memo, lead a team meeting or come up with creative solutions to a business problem. *Active* attention is necessary when you are making smaller day-to-day decisions, writing to-do lists or attending meetings. *Inactive* attention is more suited for tasks like deleting unnecessary emails or filing paperwork.

When an item of information has our attention we store it in our short-term memory, and the more focused our attention is, the more items of information we store. Short-term (or working) memory acts as a kind of 'scratch-pad' for temporary recall of the information, which is being processed at any point in time. It holds a small amount of information for a short period of time. The short-term memory has a limited capacity. Experiments by George Miller in 1956 suggest that the number of objects an average human can hold in working memory (known as 'memory span') is between 5 and 9 (7 ± 2, which is sometimes referred to as Miller's Law). However, memory span varies widely from person to person, and modern estimates of the average are usually lower, in order of just 4 or 5 items. Moreover, our memory span is not constant during the day and it depends to a large extent on our physical state and the environment we're in.

Based on this information, here is a way to organise your workday by managing your attention span. This technique is based on the work of Graham Allcott, author of *How to Be a Productivity Ninja* The goal is to help you become more efficient at the office by figuring out when during the day you are the most or least focused.

Then you match those times with tasks that require the appropriate
level of attention:

- Make a list of all the tasks (big and small) that you complete in
  a typical day.
- Next, decide whether each task requires proactive, active or inactive attention.
- Think back over the last couple of weeks and ask yourself when
  you felt focused and productive. What time was that?
- With this information in mind, create a work schedule that
  matches the appropriate tasks to your attention level throughout
  the day.

Of course, you will have to make some exceptions. Even if you
don't have as much flexibility as you would like, it is still useful to
know what level of attention you need for a certain task. Just remember that attention management is about you dictating your
time rather than having your tasks dictate to you. After all, only
you know your brainpower best.

Procrastination

Procrastination is carrying out less urgent tasks in preference to
more urgent ones, or doing more pleasurable things in place of less
pleasurable ones, and thus putting off tasks to a later time, sometimes to the 'last minute' before the deadline. Procrastination is negative behaviour in the context of effective time management.
Procrastination is wasting time.

A form of procrastination is also known as the *student syndrome*, the phenomenon whereby people will only start to fully
apply themselves to a task just at the last possible moment before a
deadline. (This is true of many more people than just students!) The
student syndrome usually includes more of a plan and sincerely
good intentions. In project and task estimating, a time or resource
buffer is applied to the task to allow for overrun or other scheduling
problems. However, with student syndrome, because tasks are
started at the last moment possible, the buffer for any given task is
wasted beforehand, rather than kept in reserve. In this context it is

also worth citing Parkinson's Law (first advanced by C. Northcote Parkinson in his 1958 book *Parkinson's Law: or the Pursuit of Progress*): 'work expands so as to fill the time available for its completion'. I would even add: 'and then some'.

If you are honest with yourself, you probably know when you are procrastinating, but how do you fight this bad habit?

The first step is *awareness*. When you find yourself doing low-priority tasks from your to-do list while higher priority tasks are put aside, or when you are waiting for the right mood or the right time to tackle an important task, or when you say yes to unimportant tasks that others ask you to do knowing that you have other work on your plate, you are probably procrastinating.

The next thing is to ask yourself the question WHY you are procrastinating. Is it because you don't like the task, you find it unpleasant? Is it because you are simply disorganised and can't distinguish priorities? Or is it because you are afraid of doing the task, or in other words that the task will push you into your panic zone?

I suggest having a look at the TED talk 'Inside the mind of a master procrastinator'. Tim Urban explains the mechanisms of procrastination in a hilarious way and makes you think about your own behaviour. He also has a very good blog ('about almost everything'), which can be found at http://waitbutwhy.com/

Clear desk

Is your monitor framed with layers of post-it reminders? Is your workspace hidden under stacks of papers, or your guest chair buried under a pile of outerwear? A majority of people admit they judge co-workers by how messy they keep their work environment. Co-workers will associate a messy office with your organisational skills and assume their project or proposal will get lost in the landfill that is your desk.

Most people spend at least 30 minutes to an hour a day looking for things. In addition to saving time and money, a clear desk policy helps organisations reduce the risk of information theft, fraud, or security breaches caused by sensitive information being left unattended and exposed.

So, is a clear desk better for the workplace? As with many things in life, there is no clear-cut answer to this question. Proponents claim that people see measurable life improvements from becoming neat and tidy, and they can point to millions of euros in annual revenue as evidence of success. In contrast, many creative individuals with Nobel prizes and other prestigious awards prefer – and in fact cultivate – messy environments as an aid to their work.

Working at a clear desk seems to encourage people to do what is expected of them. But research also shows that a messy desk may confer its own benefits, promoting creative thinking and stimulating new ideas. Disorderly environments seem to inspire breaking free of tradition, which can produce fresh insights.

Once again the conclusion is that this is a matter of individual awareness and responsibility. If the clutter on your desk is too intimidating to tackle, you can set a regular reminder on your calendar to tidy up your workspace once a week. But if you feel comfortable in your mess and if you do not breach any official policy with that, then, by all means, stick to it.

Is doing overtime good or bad?

Allow me to give a consultant's answer: 'it depends'.

There is nothing wrong with overtime as long as you are personally motivated for it. By this I mean that it is your own decision – based on your personal assessment of the situation – and it is not your boss who randomly imposes it on you. If imposed, there have to be good and compelling reasons for this and it has to be known and scheduled beforehand.

There is nothing wrong with overtime if you do it for the right reasons. Some people 'burn hours' by just being at the office, spending their time in daydreaming, surfing the internet, socialising all day long, or drinking coffee in the cafeteria. Doing overtime while not being productive but merely to build up a compensation time later on is not good, because you are actually 'stealing' time from your employer.

There is nothing wrong with overtime if it doesn't affect your productivity. But human beings are not machines that can go on and on without resting. Our attention span is limited in time and we can only be truly productive for a certain period of time, after which our output – or the quality of our work – decreases.

cont....

There is nothing wrong with overtime if it is necessary to deliver something urgent and important to schedule. President Eisenhower once said: 'Usually, urgent things are not important, and most important things are not urgent.' These wise words have been converted by management consultants like Stephen Covey into personal productivity (or time-management) methods. The basic idea is to focus first on what is really important AND urgent, then on what is important but maybe not so urgent, and postpone – or even drop – the other tasks. Don't waste your time on things that are not important, and don't be inclined to opt for overtime to carry out work that may be 'urgent' but not important.

There is nothing wrong with overtime if you don't hurt yourself by doing it. By this I mean that you are taking serious risks of running into a burnout or a depression when doing overtime is your only strategy for coping with high workloads or tight deadlines. This will at a minimum affect your motivation and productivity.

There is nothing wrong with overtime if you don't hurt your fellow workers by doing it. Especially when you are in a managerial position and try to 'set a good example' by burning lots of time at the office, you may be putting pressure on your fellow workers to do overtime against their will (see first argument above). Those people – your typical workaholics – who are doing overtime just to please the boss are hurting their fellow workers by doing so.

Finally, there is nothing wrong with overtime if you keep control over your work-life balance. Work-life balance is a very individual thing and differs widely from person to person. It is even variable over time. Don't project your personal situation on that of your fellow workers. Bear in mind that a good work-life balance is essential for your resilience.

In conclusion, there is no clear-cut, black-and-white answer to this question. An important point is not to confuse overtime with the consequences of procrastination. I once had a fellow worker who turned weekend working into a virtue: 'I worked overtime to finish this'. In fact, she was forced into spending the weekend doing it because she did not do the job during the week when she should have (and could have). It is important for fellow workers and managers alike to distinguish true overtime from false.

Speed-reading

A word here about speed-reading, because it has a place among the 'best practices' of time management.

Speed-reading, also known as diagonal reading, is about skimming through reading material to gather its general meaning and purpose. You look through the documentation and read the titles, pull-out quotes and any diagrams or bullet lists. You then go back and read the table of contents and the summary, if applicable. This sets your mind up to better understand the purpose and terminology before you dig into the text. In fact, you already practise speed-reading – most likely without being aware of it – whenever you flick through a newspaper or magazine, or browse the internet, in search of stories that you're really interested in.

Most diagonal readers give the content a first pass by reading a text 'passively' – just like one would browse a magazine, look at photographs, or watch television, i.e. they are not really paying attention to the small details, rather they are waiting for something to really pop out at them. The average person reads about 240 words per minute, whereas a diagonal reader 'scans' closer to 15 words per second or about 900 words per minute. So, there are at least three, and up to five important sections of an article that a diagonal reader will see in the approximately 10 seconds they will initially allocate to a text:

- The title or headline.
- The subtitles or subheadings within the text.
- Any bold, underlined, quoted, or otherwise highlighted text.
- Pictures, graphs, charts, or images of any nature.
- A summary of the article.

Effective speed-reading takes a lot of practice to master – usually years – and it is not the purpose of this book to turn you into a proficient speed-reader. There are, however, some ideas you can usefully apply when reading an everyday text:

- Don't read everything
- Don't read in order
- Don't try to understand everything

Let us now expand a bit further on these ideas.

One mistake is to think that you have to read everything. You don't. You have to read with a purpose. Usually, this is the extraction of information from a piece of text. Once you have that information – you're done. There's no need to read any longer. In fact, I would say that most of the texts you will encounter are simply filler (or 'payload'); you don't need to read all of it, just the relevant parts. Also, well-written texts contain a lot of repetition. I have a rule: if I start reading a text and after a few sentences I still haven't found what I am looking for, I move on.

Another mistake is the idea that you have to read start-to-finish. There is no reason you can't start by reading the conclusion or summary, then go back to the introduction or jump around through different paragraphs or chapters. Sometimes it's worth picking what you're interested in from the table of contents or index and starting there. It's more than likely that you are reading this book in this way, so why not do it for all the documents you have to deal with?

The other common, but wrong, idea is 'perfect' understanding. There's no such thing. Of course, your understanding will go down a bit when you speed read, but that is not really a problem. When you read, you have to read for a purpose and for certain bits of information anyway – no one cares if you remember every single fact and figure from a text, or what the 7th word in the third sentence on page two was.

A consequence of this is that you don't need to understand absolutely everything in a piece of text. We mostly read to understand main concepts anyway. If you really must understand everything, you can take notes (or draw a mind map), and you can always re-read certain sections to note down facts and figures.

A few other ideas that will help you with speed-reading:

- *Summaries are often as good as the whole text itself.* If you are lucky, there will be a management summary or an introduction to the text you are reading. So, if there is, first have a look at this, as it may provide you with all the answers you need right away!
- *Eliminate distractions.* If you are surrounded by noise, even background noise like music, do everything you can to get rid

of it. Isolate yourself with nothing but the text and a comfortable reading position. By eliminating potential distractions, your mind can better focus on absorbing the words on the sheets of paper or your screen.

- *Focus the right senses on reading*. Although many people are used to reading out loud or imagining a voice attached to the words, your mind may soak up the material faster by 'cutting out the middle men' and connecting them straight from the eye to the brain. Read without moving your lips. In fact, by using your finger or a pen as a guide, you can actually read and comprehend the material faster. Your finger can act as a pacesetter for your brain, going as fast as you can retain the information.

- *Read faster by using your peripheral vision* to focus on seeing the text as a whole before understanding the words individually. By using an imaginary line down the middle of the page, your mind can start to sort the text into blocks. You will start to read the pages in a diagonal fashion, rather than a linear way. This also allows you to focus on key words, rather than spending time on decorative phrases.

- *Take frequent breaks* by pacing yourself accordingly. By taking breaks, you give your mind a chance to rest and recuperate since it is absorbing information much faster than it's used to. Read the text in portions, and take short breaks.

- *Don't speed read all the time*. The above speed-reading tips can only be used when going through material produced by others. When you are revising your own texts, trying to make the meaning clearer, building good arguments, or just weeding out spelling errors, you should NOT speed-read. In that case you have to pay close attention to every word and idea to tidy up your text and make it is as good as you can.

Note of caution: you need to differentiate between various reading tasks. For example, translators do speed read for scanning purposes or oral/written summarising, but they cannot translate a text they don't read in full detail. Translators do not have the freedom of deciding what parts of a text are important.

Key points to remember

- *Use 'safe' estimates of the time you will need to complete a task unless there are reasons to the contrary.*

- *Focus on one thing at the time.*

- *Use a to-do list to schedule your daily activities.*

- *Schedule breaks.*

- *Delegate whenever appropriate.*

- *Work smarter, not harder.*

- *Stay in control.*

And finally... some things to avoid

- *Failing to prepare, prioritise, or have a plan.*

- *Setting unrealistic deadlines and milestones.*

- *Not monitoring progress.*

- *Sticking to the original plan regardless.*

- *Not completing all work tasks by their deadlines.*

- *Being disorganised, sloppy, or inaccurate.*

- *Not keeping up with the pace of your fellow workers.*

- *Saying 'yes' to everything.*

- *Doing everything by yourself.*

- *Procrastination.*

- *Arriving late for meetings, or not attending at all.*

- *Sloppy time reporting.*

- *Abusing overtime.*

- *Reporting to work late, or leaving early.*

5. Communicating

"What do you mean the computer is
down and I'll have to communicate
the old way? What old way?"

Effective communication is vital to an organisation's success. Research has shown that effective communication leads to an improvement in overall company performance. Good communication also increases job satisfaction; employees feel empowered if bosses or managers are really listening to employees, and respond. Because of this, for you too, communication is key to personal success. Communicating is perhaps the most important of all the soft skills because so many of the others depend upon it.

In today's multimedia world, there are more ways than ever before to communicate: email, text messaging, voicemails, blogs, tweets, videoconferences, and social media. But one thing hasn't changed: there are effective and ineffective ways to express yourself. All professionals need to know how to communicate if they want their message to come across.

In her best-selling book *Shut Up and Say Something*, Karen Friedman shows her readers how to convincingly communicate in any business situation. This book shows how to explain complicated concepts, minimise communication mistakes, avoid misinterpretation, bring across vision, and influence decision makers.

There are literally thousands of books, websites, and training courses on effective (business) communication, so I will limit myself to the most important ideas and tools you can use to understand and develop this important skill.

In your work, you will be expected to:

- Communicate clearly when speaking or writing.
- Listen carefully and ask questions when needed.
- Use appropriate communication tools for the situation.
- Speak clearly and respectfully to others.
- Maintain confidentiality.
- Provide others with information in a clear and timely fashion.
- Write documents with no typos or formatting errors.
- Check spelling on all documents before sending them out.
- Report all accidents or incidents.
- Be open and honest in all your communication.
- Keep your supervisor informed of problems as they develop.
- Respect the company's style guides and standards

Anchors for 'communicating'

- Shows effective written communication skills.
- Adapts written communication to the level of the audience.
- Writes clearly, in a visually appealing manner.
- Explains ideas clearly, simplifies the complex.
- Is methodical, structured and precise in speech.
- Adapts verbal communication to the level of the audience.
- Communicates clearly and knowledgeably.
- Shares information with others.
- Seeks input from others.
- Protects private and confidential information.

Now, as in previous chapters, think about which of these behaviours sound like a description of what you do and how you react to situations. Our first table considers oral (spoken) communication – there are similar tables for written communication and social media later in the chapter.

Table 5.1: Which of these sound like you? (Oral communication)

UNSATISFACTORY	IMPROVEMENT NEEDED	MEETS EXPECTATIONS	EXCEEDS EXPECTATIONS	EXCEPTIONAL
Speaks in an unstructured fashion, jumps from one point to another, does not get to the point, or does not achieve flowing delivery of ideas.	Gets lost in complexity and does not succeed in making his/her points clearly.	Speaks clearly, persuasively, and concisely.	Uses verbal communication that is consistently clear, persuasive, and adapted to the audience.	Is methodical, precise and structured in speech, is articulate and makes good use of language and gesture.
Makes contributions that are often unclear or inaccurate.	Dwells too much on detail and does not get to the point.	Focuses on the needs of specific individuals and groups.	Goes straight to the point when answering questions.	Anticipates information needs and gives full and complete answers to questions.
Gives minimalist or no answers to questions.	Is rather vague or evasive when answering questions.	Keeps to a logical order when explaining things.	Illustrates answers to questions with appropriate and relevant examples.	Explains even complex issues and ideas clearly and succinctly, simplifies the complex.
Does not finish sentences or stops mid-sentence and expects the audience to second-guess and draw conclusions.	Does not always clearly structure his/her ideas; has difficulty in articulating his/her thoughts.	Copes well with questions and provides relevant information.	Explains issues and ideas clearly and succinctly.	
Gets blocked and has difficulty in finding the right words to express himself.	Is hesitant and transmits uncertainty with body language or tone of voice.	Speaks clearly, connects with his/her audience and gets messages across with relative ease.	Strikes a good balance between detail and the need for clarity.	Convinces sceptics and opponents of his/her points of view.
Speaks too fast and is difficult to follow. Has bad articulation or truncates his/her words.	Does not engage spontaneously with his/her audience.	Engages spontaneously with his/her audience.		

Oral communication

Oral communication can be either formal or informal: conversations and discussions happening at meetings are often informal while interviews and public speaking opportunities are more formal.

With advances in technology, new forms of oral communication continue to develop: video conferencing combines sound and video so that workers in distant locations can both see and speak with each other. Other modern forms of oral communication include Podcasts (sound clips that you can access on the internet) and Voice over IP (VoIP), which allows callers to communicate over the internet. Skype is an example of VoIP.

There are many situations in which it makes sense to choose oral over written communication. Oral communication is more personal and less formal than written communication. If time is limited and a matter demands quick resolution, it may be best to have a face-to-face or telephone conversation. Oral communication can be especially effective in addressing conflicts or problems. Talking things over is often the best way to settle misunderstandings or disagreements. Finally, oral communication is a great way to give individual feedback and inspire or motivate a team.

Conversations

Catherine Blyth wrote an interesting book called *The Art of Conversation*. Every day we use cell phones and computers to communicate, but it's easy to forget that we possess a communication technology that has been in research and development for thousands of years: face-to-face conversation. Catherine Blyth points out the bad shape that conversation has fallen into – and then, taking examples from history, literature, philosophy, anthropology and popular culture, she gives us the tools to rebuild.

Most people are not good listeners, they just wait their turn to speak, and once they have the floor they follow their own agenda. Try to remember how you felt the last time someone 'listened' to you in this way. Do you want to do this to others?

Research suggests that we only remember between 25 and 50 per cent of what we hear. That means that when you talk to your boss, your fellow workers, or partner for 10 minutes, they 'hear' less than half of what you say. Now turn this around and it reveals that when you are being presented with information, you aren't hearing the whole message either. You can hope that the important parts are caught in your 25-50 per cent, but what if they are not?

Interviews

An interview is a formal conversation where questions are asked and answers are given. Interviews can happen in a wide variety of contexts such as journalism, research, and psychology but as a young professional you will most likely be confronted with job interviews.

In a job interview, your communication starts with the first impression ('you only get one chance to make a first impression'). Until we get to know someone, our brain relies on snap judgements to try to categorise the person, predict what they will do, and anticipate how we will react. According to research done by Alex Todorov, Professor of Psychology at Princeton University, this is an evolutionary survival mechanism.

There is much more on this topic in Annex 2.

Public speaking

In his book *TED Talks* Chris Anderson, the head and curator of the TED (Technology, Entertainment, Design) platform asks his readers a very radical question: Why bother to give a talk? Why not instead simply email the text to every possible member of the audience?

'An 18-minute talk contains maybe 2,500 words. Many people can read 2,500 words in less than 9 minutes and retain good comprehension. So why not do that instead? Save the auditorium cost. Save everybody's travel. Save the chance that you might flub your lines and look foolish. And get your talk across in less than half the time it takes to speak it....

One of the reasons I was so captivated by TED was the discovery that talks really can offer something more than the printed word. But it's not a given, and it's not even true in every case. That something extra has to be thought about, invested in, developed. It has to be earned.

What is that something extra? It's the human overlay that turns information into inspiration'.

Public presentations tend to have one of three general purposes: to convince, to inform, or to entertain. The first step in preparing a public speech is to decide on the purpose of the communication. As Chris Anderson says it, the only thing that truly matters in public speaking is not confidence, stage presence, or smooth talking. It's having something worth saying. Out of the purpose will come the main ideas to be included in the presentation.

The ideas are then organised to include an introduction, a body, and a summary or conclusion. One of the most viewed TED speakers is Sir Ken Robinson. He says that most of his talks follow the same, simple structure:

- Introduction – settling in, what will be covered
- The Context – why this matters
- Main Concepts – high level, some examples or statistics
- Practical Implications – pros and cons, consequences
- Conclusion – summarising the main ideas

Pay particular of attention to the beginning (the introduction) and the end (conclusion) of your talk because these are the things that will be remembered most.

A good talk answers three questions: *What? So What? Now What?*

Visual aids

Visual aids can be a useful part of oral presentations, but do not think about them as unavoidable. Visual aids have to be meaningful, creative, and interesting in order to help the speaker get a message across. Visual aids are supposed to help to illustrate and strengthen your points, not be a distraction from what you are saying. The key to successful use of visual aids is that they effectively support the theme of the presentation; they support its message but

"This information is so exciting I feel
obliged to tone it down a little with
these boring slides."

do so without being confusing, complicated, or even too entertaining. Visual aids are not the presentation! Too many speakers just read out loud what's on the PowerPoint slides. Your audience could have done that themselves in the comfort of their office or at home.

The late Steve Jobs, co-founder of Apple, put it even more strongly: 'People who know what they are talking about don't need PowerPoint.'

As a trainer and coach I regularly speak in front of a classroom audience. When I do, I methodically refuse to give the (paper) handouts to the students before my talk, and I don't use a video or overhead projector. I want the students to look at me; I want them to listen to what I am saying and watch my body language. At the very most, I make some simple drawings on a white board or flip chart to reinforce my words, but I never use an already prepared drawing.

Speak with passion

The delivery of an effective speech needs the speaker to think about his or her vocal pitch, rate, and volume. It is important to incorporate changes in vocal pitch, to add emphasis, and to avoid boredom. It is also helpful to vary the pace at which you speak and incorporate pauses to allow the audience to reflect upon particular elements of the overall message.

Why bullet points are bad for presentations

You have probably heard this before: don't use bullet points in your presentations. The reason for this is that bullet points make information harder to remember when the lists are accompanied by spoken information.

In 2014, the International Journal of Business Communication published the results from 'The Use of Visualisation in the Communication of Business Strategies', a study designed to gather empirical evidence regarding whether the use of visualisation is superior to text in the communication of business information. The results of that experiment confirmed that lists of text are ineffective for presentations. Slides with visuals are definitely more effective than slides with text. In other words, when your slides contain lists of text, your audience will struggle to pay attention to your slides, they will find it very hard to agree with your message, and they will remember less information.

Your voice is multitalented; it can sound assertive, cautious, critical, funny, motivational, compassionate, or neutral, and it does all this through pitch, tone, volume and pronunciation. Taking passion out of your voice will bore your audience.

On the subject of tone of voice and body language you should have a look at Will Stephen's TEDx talk 'How to sound smart in your TEDx talk'. In this hilarious video he demonstrates just about every trick in the book of public speaking. A must see!

Body language

'The body is the unconscious mind.' – Candace Pert

Non-verbal elements such as posture, gestures, and facial expressions are important factors also. Some movement may be helpful to hold listeners' attention or to increase importance and focus, but constant shifting or pacing is to be avoided. Likewise, hand and arm gestures can be used to point, describe, or emphasise, but these too have to be varied, carefully timed, and adapted to the audience. Now, I am not saying that you always have to act and behave like Steve Ballmer in his famous 'Monkey Boy Dance', which you can view on You Tube, but using all your body is definitely a good thing if you want to seize your audience's attention. Finally, good speakers make frequent eye contact with their audience; they let their facial expressions show their own interest in the ideas they are presenting, and dress in a way that is appropriate for the occasion.

It is often claimed that only 7% of our oral communication is brought across by what we actually say, 38% is attributed to the tone and speed of our voice, while 55% of our message is passed through our non-verbal communication, our body language. These figures go back to the work of Professor Albert Mehrabian at UCLA, as explained in his book *Silent Messages*, originally published in 1971. However, many trainers and non-verbal communication gurus forget to mention that Mehrabian based his findings on studies that only dealt with the communication of positive and negative *emotions* via single spoken words. He was trying to understand the mechanisms of feelings of like and dislike. He did not intend this 'rule' to apply across the board to all communication; so, unless a communicator is talking about his or her feelings or attitudes, these numbers are not applicable.

A more applicable set of statements is used by trainer and consultant Pamela Thorne in her dissertation 'Debunking the Body Language Myth':

- Words are only part of a message, but they are a vital part. We also communicate through body language and tone of voice.
- Non-verbals support the words by conveying the speaker's feelings.
- When speaking about feelings and attitudes, and there is a mismatch between the words and the body language, we tend to put more trust in the non-verbals.
- If we have only words, as in emails, it is possible to misunderstand the emotion behind the words.

Body language has been watched and discussed for centuries, going back at least as far as ancient Greece and Rome. However, scientific studies first appeared only in the 1950s, and truly took off in the 1960s.

In the earliest days of the scientific study of body language, there was widespread agreement that it was nothing more than a series of individual, isolated actions, each with a different and specific meaning. However, over time we have come to understand that body language is far more complex and varied. Because of this, even defining the difference between non-verbal communication and verbal communication remains an area of disagreement among experts.

Non-verbal and verbal components of communications are inevitably interwoven and can't be completely drawn apart into separate components. This does not mean, however, that you can't learn to interpret the body language of others and – to some extent – control your own. I can only suggest you read as much as you can about body language and its applications, from the academic and scientific perspective as well as from the real world, practical, perspective. But keep in mind that understanding body language and applying this knowledge is an inexact science. Body language comes in clusters of signals and postures, depending on internal emotions and mental states. Recognising a whole cluster is far more reliable than trying to interpret individual elements, but even the most intuitive and attentive people can misinterpret or misunderstand body language messages.

A rather thorough summary of our body language signals, of use to French speakers, can be found in the 2011 book *Ces gestes qui vous trahissent* by Joseph Messinger. I further suggest you have a look at CreativityWorks (http://www.creativityworks.net/). They have a short animated video where these ideas are clearly expressed. Another must-see is Amy Cuddy's TED talk 'Your Body Language Shapes Who You Are'. I am sure you will be inspired!

Fear of public speaking

Public speaking fear and stress is one of the most common fears. A little bit of anxiety as you prepare for a presentation is normal. Even the best speakers get anxious before they get on stage or speak in front of a large group. If you are not a little bit anxious you are either exceptionally lucky or maybe not really putting enough of yourself into what you are doing. Never expect to be completely anxiety free. What you need is to turn that anxiety into energy for giving a great presentation, not holding you back from speaking.

Although the 'stress hormone' cortisol is linked to many health detriments it is also our 'get up and do things hormone.' Just like we have 'eustress' (good stress, see page 157) and 'distress' (bad stress), we need cortisol to stimulate our sympathetic nervous system and kick-start our bodies into action.

Public speaking fear and stress comes from our fear of being judged or the fear of forgetting what we need to say. Doubts over our own ability, combined with the knowledge that others are obliged to pay attention to what we are saying, create a feeling of fear that is difficult to overcome. On top of that, our mind tends to focus on the mistakes we make, and our fear is then confirmed. Instead, think of the idea that your audience is not there to judge you, but because they believe you have something interesting to say. So make it interesting!

The power of vulnerability

It takes courage to speak to a group. It takes courage to tell stories where you show your own weaknesses and mistakes. *It takes courage to be vulnerable.*

It will come as no surprise that I am a huge fan of TED. Brené Brown's TED Talk on 'The Power of Vulnerability' is a first-class example of why I am such a fan. I love when she talks about 'courage':

'Courage, the original definition of courage, when it first came into the English language – it's from the Latin word *cor*, meaning heart – and the original definition was to tell the story of who you are with your whole heart. And so these folks had, very simply, the courage to be imperfect. They had the compassion to be kind to themselves first and then to others, because, as it turns out, we can't practice compassion with other people if we can't treat ourselves kindly. And the last was they had connection, and – this was the hard part – as a result of authenticity, they were willing to let go of who they thought they should be in order to be who they were, which you have to absolutely do for that connection.'

If you really want to create a connection with your audience, you MUST be willing to be vulnerable.

Think about the alternative: showing no vulnerability. I suspect we all remember at least one professor at university who stood behind a lectern, reading from his notes in front of him or relying heavily on some PowerPoint presentation to make sure that he didn't miss a word of what he was saying. Chances are that he didn't allow his students to interact – or ask 'stupid' questions – because he wasn't 100% sure of how to handle these. Alone in his ivory tower, he was only talking to himself; there was no passion, and there was no connection with his audience.

How did you feel about this professor? Did you trust him? Did you want to go to his room and discuss the course with him? I am almost certain the answer is 'NO!' This is because he did not show real humanity. Because we get the feeling that he is not being kind with himself and therefore highly unlikely to be kind with others. Because he is not willing to be vulnerable. You could have simply studied from the syllabus instead of going to the class.

Just have a look at the TED talk of Malte Spitz, 'Your phone company is watching', and you will understand what I mean by showing your vulnerability.

More resources

There are literally hundreds of books and other resources about delivering presentations and speaking in public so I will limit myself to pointing out just a few.

First, I warmly advise you, if you understand French, to read the book *Prendre la Parole en public* by Bernard Blein as it contains a wealth of very practical ideas.

There is also an interesting slide deck called 'Death by Power-Point' available on SlideShare. It explains the dos and don'ts if you want to use PowerPoint anyway.

Another book worth mentioning is the *HBR Guide to Persuasive Presentations* by Nancy Duarte. There are, by the way, many other Harvard Business Review Press (HBR) books and publications covering the topics of the current book.

You can watch some of the masters at work and learn from them on the TED website (https://www.ted.com/playlists/77/11_must_see_ted_talks). If there's one you absolutely must see, it is Dan Pink's 'The Puzzle of Motivation' – but maybe wait until you have read the rest of this chapter and try to figure out which 'best practices' Dan is using. 'American Rhetoric Top 100 speeches' is another great resource.

Finally, I would like you to know about Toastmasters. Toastmasters International (https://www.toastmasters.org/) is a world leader in communication and leadership development. Their membership is 313,000 strong. Members improve their speaking and leadership skills by attending one of the 14,650 clubs in 126 countries that make up a global network of meeting locations.

Written communication

The first requirement of *written communication* is that it is easily understandable. Clarity of writing usually follows clarity of thought. So think what you want to say, then say it as simply as possible. Readers are primarily interested in what you have to say. By the way in which you say it you may encourage them either to read on or to give up.

One advantage of written communication as compared with oral communication is that written messages do not have to be delivered on the spot; instead, they can be edited and revised several times before they are sent so that the content can be moulded to maximum effect. Another advantage is that written communication provides a permanent record that can be saved for later. Since they are permanent, written messages also enable recipients to take more time in reviewing the message and providing more appropriate feedback. For these reasons, written forms of communication are often considered more suitable for complex messages and contexts where traceability is key. In the context of misunderstandings or faced with a fellow worker whose unclear expression or reception of ideas is a constant source of concern, having a written record of what was said/agreed or instructed is very important. Depending on oral communication in this situation can be detrimental to one or both parties involved (colleagues or manager).

However, there is also a potential downside associated with written communication. Unlike oral communication, the sender of a written communication does not generally receive immediate feedback to his or her message. In addition, written messages often take more time to compose, both because of their content-rich nature and the difficulty that many people have in composing such communications.

In all organisations, staff have to write many different types of documents. Whatever the type – a project outline, a technical report, minutes, a press release or speech – a clear document will be more effective, and more easily and quickly understood.

Writing style

Your writing style is one of the most important ways in which you present yourself and the organisation for which you work. For this reason, many organisations have what is called a style guide.

A style guide is a set of standards for the writing and design of documents; it establishes and enforces style to improve communication. Maintaining a writing style builds an organisation's brand. It is good for your productivity since you don't want to re-invent the wheel each time you compose a new text. Style also sets the tone for consistency and readers benefit from a consistent style because they have less work to do.

The bottom line is that it is important to develop your own writing style, if possible in line with the style guide of your organisation.

Structuring documents

Authors make decisions about how to present information to their readers. They choose from a variety of structures to organise their texts:

- *Chronological/Sequence*. Chronological texts reveal events in a sequence from beginning to end. Words that signal chronological structures include: first, then, next, finally, and specific dates and times.
- *Cause/Effect*. Informational texts often describe cause and effect relationships. The text describes events and identifies or implies causal factors.
- *Problem/Solution*. The text introduces and describes a problem and presents solutions.

Table 5.2: Which of these sound like you? (Written communication)

UNSATISFACTORY	IMPROVEMENT NEEDED	MEETS EXPECTATIONS	EXCEEDS EXPECTATIONS	EXCEPTIONAL
Creates documents that are poorly written, unstructured, grammatically incorrect, or contain too many spelling errors.	Creates documents that are disorganised or contain many grammar or spelling errors.	Keeps sentences and paragraphs short and concise.	Creates documents that are consistently clear and persuasive.	Writes documents that are always complete, concise, clear, concrete, correct, considerate and courteous.
Uses incomplete sentences or bad punctuation.	Uses too long sentences, too verbose, or overly complex.	Leaves out words that do not contribute to the main focus of the communication.	Creates documents that are concise and comprehensive and convey all the ideas that need to be addressed.	Writes documents that consistently address all the needs of specific individuals and groups within the audience.
Creates documents that are either overly simplistic or too complex and therefore not adapted to the audience.	Creates documents that are somewhat disorganised and/or not appropriate for the audience.	Writes documents that are syntactically and semantically correct.	Explains issues and ideas clearly and succinctly.	Writes visually engaging documents, illustrated with tables and graphs enhancing the messages to be conveyed.
		Focuses on the needs of the audience.	Strikes a good balance between detail and the need for clarity.	
Creates visually unappealing documents; large blocks of continuous text without punctuation or white space.	Uses slang, jargon, acronyms, or unexplained concepts or ideas.	Uses simple language, without over-using clichés, jargon, and expressions or trying to impress with difficult words.	Makes appropriate use of colour coding, text formatting, capitalisations enhancing the underlying structure and ideas.	
	Makes inappropriate use of colour coding, text formatting, capitalisations, ...	Creates visually appealing documents with appropriate use of whitespace, indentations and graphical elements.		
	Uses no illustrations or visual elements.			

- *Compare/Contrast*. The author use comparisons to describe ideas to readers. Images, metaphors, and analogies are used in compare/contrast   structures.
- *Description*. Descriptive details help readers visualise information.
- *Directions*. How-to texts frame the information in a series of directions (e.g. 'frequently asked questions' or FAQ).

If the essence of a text cannot be taken in at one glance, it is a good idea to add an introduction (abstract, management summary) and possibly a conclusion. Aristotle put it that: 'A whole is what has a beginning and middle and end': technically, the *protasis*, *epitasis*, and *catastrophe* (a word which survives in modern English but with a rather different meaning!). The introduction is intended to grab the reader's interest and establish the theme of the remainder of the text. The conclusion restates the key points and summarises the main message that is being conveyed. It is known that we remember both the beginning and ending of a story and mostly forget what was said in the middle.

Identifying the structure of a text helps readers to read efficiently. Readers can anticipate what information will be revealed in a selection when they understand the text structure. Understanding the pattern of the text also helps readers organise their ideas for synthesising and summarising, and remembering the key messages.

Grammar, spelling and punctuation

Correct grammar, spelling and punctuation are key in written communications. The reader will form an opinion about you, the author, based on both the content and the presentation, and errors are likely to lead them to get a negative impression.

Some employers state openly that any CV or résumé containing spelling or grammatical mistakes will be rejected immediately, while a BBC news article (http://www.bbc.co.uk/news/education-14130854) quotes research that calculates spelling mistakes cost online businesses 'millions' in lost sales.

Checking for poor writing and spelling mistakes is showing respect for your readers, since it will take them longer to understand what you are trying to say if they have to struggle to follow the text. You have to make their life easy.

It is good practice to review all written messages before sending to print, or hitting the 'Send' button in the case of emails, as it is likely that there will be errors. Do not assume that spelling and grammar checkers will identify all your mistakes for you: words can be spelled correctly but misused, and whole words may be missing, wrecking the sentence and the entire message. If at all possible, take a break before rereading and checking your writing, because you are more likely to notice problems when you read it again.

Even if you know spelling and grammar rules, you have to double-check your work or, even better, have it proofread by somebody else. Our brains work faster than our fingers can type and accidental typographical errors inevitably sneak in.

Using tables and pictures

A table is a way of arranging data in rows and columns. Any time you have lots of related facts and figures to present, a table is a useful approach to organising them so that the audience can quickly see and understand how they relate to each other.

Tables can be used to enhance your text to help bring across the information being presented. Tables are to be used for essential information only, adding to, and not just repeating identical material already in the text. A table cannot just appear out of nowhere: you need to introduce the reader to the table by referring to it in the text, preferably before the table is presented. Use the text to draw the reader's attention to the importance and key points of the table, but don't repeat details as this defeats the very purpose (efficiency and clarity) of having a table.

Let us take a look at an example: Table 5.3 on page 106. As you can see from the table, with the exception of Russia, all major countries in the world have seen an increase of their population between 2015 and 2016. The most rapid growth can be noted in Nigeria (2,70%) and Pakistan (2.12%).

Make sure that your tables are understandable. Some readers may be speed-reading: they turn their attention to the tables (and

Country	2015 (Million)	2016 (Million)	Change (%)
China	1375,96	1382,32	0,46
India	1310,88	1326,8	1,21
U.S.	321,75	324,12	0,74
Indonesia	257,53	260,58	1,18
Brazil	207,83	209,57	0,84
Pakistan	188,83	192,83	2,12
Nigeria	182,07	186,99	2,70
Bangladesh	160,97	162,91	1,21
Russia	143,45	143,44	-0,01
Mexico	127	128,63	1,28

Table 5.3: Change in population (2015-2016)

figures) before they read the whole text, so these items have to be self-contained.

Give clear and informative titles. Table titles have to describe concisely the purpose or contents of the table and draw the reader's attention to what you want them to notice. In addition, make sure that column heads are clearly and correctly labelled.

Ensure consistency between values or details in a table (e.g., abbreviations, group names, units of measurement such as thousands and millions) and those in the text. Tables that present repetitive information will impair communication rather than improve it. Examine the titles of all your tables and check if they talk about the same or similar things. If they do, rethink the presentation and combine or delete some tables.

When presenting large amounts of information, divide the data into clear and appropriate categories and present it in columns with clear titles. If there is a lot of data that would make the tables too cluttered or long, consider making the tables a part of an appendix or add-on material. Also, ensure that there is sufficient spacing between columns and rows and that the layout does not make the table look too disorganised or crowded.

Finally, remember that, sometimes a picture may be worth a thousand words. While tables have to be used where you need to show a lot of precise numerical values, figures (graphics) can frequently be used in professional texts to show trends, patterns, and relationships between and across sets of data, especially when the general pattern is more important than the exact data values. Graphs, plots, maps and pie charts are all different ways of conveying a better understanding of what might otherwise remain hidden in a long text or

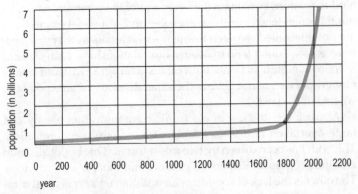

Figure 5.1: world population growth

complex set of tables: how much more attention-grabbing Figure 5.1 is, for instance, than the same data would be just listed in a table!

Social media

'Human relationships are rich and they're messy and they're demanding. And we clean them up with technology. And when we do, one of the things that can happen is that we sacrifice conversation for mere connection. We short-change ourselves. And over time, we seem to forget this, or we seem to stop caring' – Sherry Turkle

Scan around a restaurant and you will struggle to find a person who doesn't have their head down using their cell phone to text, tweet, or update their Facebook status – all while sharing a meal with others at their table. The effect of social media is visible everywhere, so what does this mean for interpersonal communication? Social media certainly affect how we engage with others across all settings and ages. There has been a change in the way we communicate; rather than face-to-face interaction, we tend to prefer email, and we text rather than talk on the phone.

There are three key issues involved in communication using social media. First, when we communicate through social media, we tend to trust the person on the other end of the communication, so our messages tend to be more open. Second, our social connections are not intensified as much through social media as they are face-to-face, so we don't tend to deepen our relationships. Last, we tend to follow and interact only with others who agree with our points of view, so we are not getting the same diversity of viewpoints as we had in the past.

At work too, the use of electronic communication has by and large overtaken face-to-face and voice-to-voice communication. This shift has been driven by two major forces. One is globalisation and the geographic dispersion of more and more of our activities. The other is the lack of comfort with traditional interpersonal communication among a growing segment of our workforce; those who grew up in the internet age, Gen Y and Gen Z. Studies show that these generations – which will comprise more than 50% of the workforce by 2020 – prefer to use instant messaging or other social media than stop by an office and talk with someone. These trends are inevitably affecting the ability to effectively work together, build trust, and create employee engagement and loyalty.

Further, because most business communication is now done via emails, texts, instant messaging, intranets, blogs, websites and other technology-enabled media – all without body language – the potential for misinterpretation is growing. Rushed and stressed, we often do not take the time to consider the nuances of what we are writing. Conflicts detonate over the tone of an email, or that all-important cc-list. When an older person writes a text in all capital letters, does it mean that he is shouting? Are short responses, without the usual politeness formulae, a sign that the person doesn't want to engage? On the other hand, does a smiley really mean they're bought in and aligned? Nowadays, conclusions are drawn on surprisingly little information.

Social media will likely continue to become more and more integrated into the normal human experience, like most of the technologies that came before. As social media becomes more normalised, we will stop seeing it as something new, and start seeing it as what it really is, just another form of communication.

The pitfalls of technology

The effect of technology on communication has been extensive and largely positive. Organisations use websites, email, text messages, chatting and other forms of technological communication channel to transfer information to managers, employees and the public at large. But while technology has enhanced the way organisations conduct business, some disadvantages exist.

One significant disadvantage of technology in business communication is the perception of communication being impersonal. Employees may perceive electronic communication as impersonal if they only receive messages from managers or other employees through email. Email can also create confusion, requiring employees to seek more feedback than normal as compared to more personal communication methods.

Second, technology such as text messages and email allows us to communicate in short, carefully edited sentences that lack proximity and completely remove the contextual information provided by tone of voice and body language. As a result, those who connect with others primarily through technology can find it difficult to engage in a normal conversation. They may have issues understanding non-verbal cues due to lack of practice with face-to-face interaction that cannot be paused, edited or filtered.

Also, many users of technology tend to pay little attention to basic rules of grammar and format when composing their texts. This careless correspondence style reflects a lack of professionalism and may communicate to the recipient a view of the organisation behind the message as equally unprofessional. Much has been written on the vocabulary and peculiarities of online and text messaging jargon. This jargon, usually derived from English, can be extremely confusing for those who are not native English speakers, making it harder to detect the meaning of a sentence; people who regularly text or chat online may end up using it, out of habit, even in situa-

"No. Add some words to make
that sound like maybe,
and email it to everyone."

tions where it is inappropriate or out of place, such as in business messages or professional texts. The ease and informality of the medium should not be confused with the quality of writing necessary to use it properly.

Next, because communicating through technology creates an obstacle between people that isn't there when speaking face to face, some may find it easier to be rude and aggressive. Sherry Turkle suggests that this happens because technology keeps us from having to see the reaction of the person on the receiving end of the message, making it harder to empathise with them.

One more hidden trap of technology is the permanent risk of information overload (also known as 'infobesity' or 'infoxication'). According to Lucy Jo Palladino, a psychologist and author of *Find Your Focus Zone*, information overload happens when a person is exposed to more information than the brain can process at one time. Obviously, technology has had a major effect on our minds in this respect.

Finally, technology allows us to always be reachable if we want to be, no matter where we are or what we are doing. Although this can be helpful, it may also lead to a vicious cycle of stress and anxiety in which people feel pressured to immediately check and answer any incoming messages, emails or phone calls regardless of whether it is appropriate, for fear of being seen as incompetent or inattentive. In turn, this can potentially cause the breakdown of the very same relationships the person is trying to maintain.

Besides the potential negative effects on the quality of our com-

Table 5.4: Which of these sound like you? (Using social media)

UNSATISFACTORY	IMPROVEMENT NEEDED	MEETS EXPECTATIONS	EXCEEDS EXPECTATIONS	EXCEPTIONAL
Creates content that is poorly written, unstructured, grammatically incorrect, or contains too many spelling errors.	Creates content that is disorganised or badly structured.	Uses social media only when appropriate.	Creates content that is consistently clear and persuasive.	Creates content that is always complete, concise, clear, concrete, correct, considerate and courteous.
Spams his/her audience with irrelevant content.	Uses too long sentences, too verbose, or overly complex.	Keeps content short and concise.	Explains issues and ideas clearly and succinctly.	Creates content that consistently addresses all the needs of specific individuals and groups.
Adopts a sloppy communication style on social media.	Uses slang, jargon, acronyms, or unexplained concepts or ideas.	Focuses on the needs of the audience.	Strikes a good balance between detail and the need for clarity.	Creates visually engaging content, illustrated with tables and graphs enhancing the messages to be conveyed.
Does not respect other people's privacy, personal life, or work-life balance.	Makes inappropriate use of colour coding, text formatting, capitalisations, …	Creates visually appealing content with appropriate use of graphical elements.	Applies organisation's branding and style guides in all his/her communication, including on social media.	Conveys the organisation's image and reputation on social media.
Expects other people to be online or responsive all the time.		Respects and implements the organisation's social media policies and netiquette.		

munications, these last two weaknesses of technology may also affect our resilience and our time management competencies – but these are the subjects of two other chapters of this book.

Some Best Practices

Context matters

Without providing some context, your audience may not understand what you are talking about. On the other hand, you may not understand your audience either.

I very much liked the example given by Dan Pink in his thought-provoking book *A Whole New Mind – Why Right-Brainers Will Rule the Future* (2006):

> 'Suppose that one night you and your spouse are preparing dinner. Suppose too, that midway through the preparations, your spouse discovers that you forgot to buy the dinner's most important ingredient. Suppose then that your spouse grabs the car keys, curls a lip, glares at you, and hisses, "I'm going to the store." Nearly everyone with an intact brain would understand two things about the words your spouse just uttered. First, your spouse is heading to Safeway. Second, your spouse is pissed.'

This has to do with how our brain works. To oversimplify a bit, the left half handles *what* is said; the right half focuses on *how* it's said. However tempting it is to talk of right and left hemispheres in isolation, they are actually two half-brains, designed to work together as a smooth, single integrated whole in one entire, complete brain. The manner in which you deliver your message, from the words you say to how you say them, relies on the situational context – what is appropriate in that situation and that particular environment. For example, the broad smiles and good humour that you might show at a friend's wedding are unlikely to be appropriate at a funeral.

The key to understanding your context is to develop a habit of *situational awareness*. Situational awareness refers to your perception of your environment and situation around you on a moment-by-moment basis. In being situationally aware, you can anticipate changes to your environment. In this way, you're always thinking just one step ahead in any given situation or environment, and you are able to adapt accordingly. Cultivating this skill (and it does take time and a keen awareness of your surroundings) is especially helpful when your context may shift or change in subtle or major ways, or in an instant (see the advice on this topic on https://www.boundless.com/communications).

Because context matters, all communication has to be adapted to the audience. The same message needs to be wrapped differently depending on the audience: a lunchtime conference, a presentation to stakeholders or a note to the management on the same topic will have different content and key messages. Because audiences expect different kinds of communications in different situations and settings, you have to understand how to tailor messages for maximum results. Remember that your perception only exists within the context of your own life. Without proper definition your vision can get lost in fragmented versions of other people's view of you.

We often think others know something when in reality they may not. Don't always assume your fellow workers or your clients know what you know because they probably don't. You must never assume that people understand your point of view and understand your vision. Don't cut corners on educating someone about what you do and why you do it. When you are communicating with someone, never forget the critical pieces that will allow people to understand you. Don't assume others know what you know. It would be a big mistake.

Keep it simple

'If you can't explain it to a six year old, you don't understand it yourself' – Albert Einstein

KISS is an acronym for 'Keep it simple, stupid', a design principle adopted by the US Navy in the early 1960s. The KISS principle states that most systems work best if they are kept simple rather than made complicated; therefore simplicity is a key goal in design and unnecessary complexity is to be avoided. Variations on the phrase include 'keep it short and simple' and 'keep it simple and straightforward'.

Applied to human communication, the KISS principle actually attempts to control the context of the conversation, by reducing it to its simplest form, hopefully making it a common denominator between the sender and their audience.

The idea of simplicity is implemented by applying a clear and straightforward structure to the message, if possible linear and using a chronological order. Clearly, long sentences, over-sophisticated vocabulary and jargon are to be avoided, and complex ideas and concepts have to be explained in their simplest possible form, preferably by using metaphors, analogies or real-life examples.

'Broadly speaking, the short words are the best, and the old words best of all', Winston Churchill once said. Churchill's words inspired millions because he wrote his speeches in a language that could be easily understood. Most of us prefer short words, which we also use in our daily conversations.

When you articulate a message in a simple way you make life easier for your audience. They don't have to make an effort to understand what you are saying and the chance that your message will be heard becomes much higher.

Keeping it simple doesn't mean that you are stupid; quite the opposite. The best proof of someone's intelligence – and mastery of a subject – is their ability to simplify the complex. People who are confident in their knowledge won't hesitate to share it with others in terms that are easily understood. In contrast, those who attempt to talk over people's heads through the use of overly complex terms and descriptions are typically those who lack a true understanding of the subject themselves and are trying to hide that fact.

Too often, we over-complicate things in an attempt to display our intelligence, when all that happens is that we end up pushing people away and ultimately losing credibility. We come across as elitists, rather than team players. Truly intelligent people are not afraid to share their knowledge because they don't view other people gaining knowledge as a threat to their own. Rather, they take pleasure in sharing and in teaching others. As a result they become builders of people, and they contribute tremendously to an organisation's overall success.

Keep it short

'Being brief is an essential 21st-century skill,' says Joseph Mc-Cormack, author of *Brief: Make a Bigger Impact by Saying Less*. People are buried with information, and the average attention span is only around eight seconds. You can't hold anyone's attention if you're not brief.

Acronyms

Acronyms are everywhere, and for a good reason: they speed up conversations by eliminating the need to repeat multiword phrases everyone knows already, and they make documents shorter and visually more attractive. Acronyms are a sort of metaphor.

On the other hand, littering a document with acronyms serves only to turn it into alphabet soup and guarantee that readers will remember nothing substantive, only how hard it was to read.

Over-use of acronyms in written communication is bad, lazy writing, but at least with a document, readers set their own pace and can pause to check what the acronyms refer to. Actually speaking in acronyms is a major turnoff. Anyone who works in a specific environment can easily slip into using practically nothing but acronyms. Maybe this is fine when you are with immediate colleagues who share your jargon, but for other people who are not familiar with the acronyms it can be confusing or even seem like they are being excluded.

When you are writing a document, answering questions or doing anything that has to do with communicating, assume that your audience doesn't know what any particular acronym means. Use words and phrases anyone can understand. A good practice when you make use of acronyms is to explain every acronym at least once (except the most obvious ones) at the start of your document or otherwise have a list of acronyms as annex to the body of your text.

By the way, do you know what a TLA is? No? It's a 'three letter acronym'.

Repetition

Human communication mechanisms are anything but perfect. Besides the distortions at the level of the transmitter and the transmission channel, we only receive part of the message because we are simply not listening all the time. It is often a good idea therefore to build some redundancy into your message by repeating the same information.

We rate statements that have been repeated as more valid or true than things we have heard only once – this is known as 'repetition bias'. And when we think something is truer, we also tend to be more persuaded by it. Simply said, we are more influenced when we hear statements of opinion and persuasive messages more than once (publicity agencies make extensive usage of this knowledge).

Psychological studies clearly suggest that moderate repetition has a positive effect on someone's reception of, and agreement with a persuasive argument. John Cacioppo and Richard Petty were two pioneers in this field in the late 1970s and early 1980s. They concluded that low to moderate levels of repetition within a message tend to create greater agreement with the message, along with greater recall. However, their work also suggested that too much repetition has an adverse impact and can lead to stronger disagreement with the argument being made.

The use of moderate repetition can be effective if the argument is constructed in such a way that the repetition is spread out over time. The use of repetition over the long course of an argument, written or spoken, creates a greater familiarity with the message and leads to gradual agreement if the intensity of repetition is gradual itself. Too much repetition in a short span of time or space can defeat the purpose of gradual acceptance by creating a stronger aversion to the argument.

In speeches, or other spoken arguments that are highly emotional in nature, frequent repetition of key emotionally charged phrases or words could be very effective. Martin Luther King Jr.'s 'I Have a Dream' speech is often cited as one of the prime examples of the success of such repetition. However, it may be effective in messages of this nature only because of the already emotional nature of the issue. Applying this technique in the wrong context, in contrast, may have the opposite effect of turning off the audience.

Although repetition can be rewarding as a persuasion strategy, subtlety can be as important as the frequency and intensity of the message. Rather than repeating the same words and phrasing throughout the course of an argument, finding more than one way to make the same argument repeatedly can be a more effective approach. The reader or listener is likely to respond more positively to the same argument stated in several ways rather than having the same message shoved down their throat over and over.

This is what psychologists call the 'illusion of truth effect' and it arises at least partly because familiarity breeds liking. As we are exposed to a message again and again, it becomes more familiar. Because of the way our minds work, what is familiar is also true. Familiar messages require less effort to process, and that feeling of ease unconsciously suggests to us that they are true.

Ethos, pathos and logos

No, these are not the three musketeers (their names were Athos, Porthos and Aramis). These are Aristotle's 'ingredients for persuasion' in his treatise on rhetoric. For Aristotle, the goal of argumentative speaking or writing is to persuade your audience that your ideas are valid – or more valid than someone else's. He divided the means of persuasion into three categories: *ethos, pathos* and *logos*.

Ethos

According to Aristotle, our perception of a speaker or writer's character influences how acceptable or convincing we find what that person has to say. This projected character is called the speaker or writer's ethos. We are more likely to be persuaded by a person who, we think, has personal warmth, consideration of others, a good mind and erudition. People whose education, experience, and previous performances qualify them to speak on a certain issue earn the special ethos of authority. But whether or not we know anything about the speaker or writer, the actual text we hear or read, the way it is written or spoken and what it says, also conveys an impression of the author's character. This impression created by the text itself is known as the intrinsic ethos.

Institutions, public personalities and official publications also project an ethos or credibility. We may assume, for example, that The Economist is a more credible source than our daily newspaper or that BBC News is more reliable than our national broadcast organisation. And we usually assume that a person selected for a public position of responsibility is more credible than someone without official endorsement.

Pathos

'Effective communication is 20% what you know and 80% how you feel about what you know.' – Jim Rohn, American motivational speaker

The influential appeal of pathos is a call to the audience's sense of identity, their self-interest, and their emotions. Appeals to our sense of identity and self-interest exploit common biases; we naturally bend in the direction of what is advantageous to us, what serves our interests or the interests of any group we believe ourselves a part of. Even when advantage is not an issue, writers who belong to groups we identify with, or create groups we can belong to, often seem more persuasive. We also naturally find more convincing the speaker or writer who flatters us (especially indirectly) instead of insulting us. Thus skilful speakers or writers create a positive image in their words of the audience they are addressing, an image their actual readers can identify with.

Logos

Finally, we come to the arguments themselves – the clear reasons the arguer provides to support a position, or logos. There are many ways to describe the support provided in an argument, but a simple way to begin is to consider all the principles the author seems to supply. These can be scattered throughout the argument and expressed indirectly, so identifying premises is a judgement call in itself.

Next ask which of the premises are presented as objects of agreement that the arguer considers as given, elements of the argument taken for granted. Objects of agreement are basically either facts or values. Of course, the facts may not be facts at all and readers may not agree with the values assumed. Some of the premises will be supported further, but basically every argument has got to come down to certain objects of agreement that it presents as shared between arguer and audience.

You can also classify premises into categories:

- Arguments based on definition; in other words, making claims about the nature of things, about what terms mean, what features things have.
- Analogies or comparisons, citing parallel cases.
- Appeals to cause and consequences. This is especially common when policy issues are debated.
- Reliance on testimony or authority by citing the received opinions of experts, or creating some kind of authoritative reference group, citing public opinion on what most people think as support for a particular position.

Metaphors

According to Oxford Dictionaries a metaphor is a 'figure of speech in which a word or phrase is applied to an object or action to which it is not literally applicable.' For example, when we speak of 'gene maps' and 'gene mapping', we use a cartographic metaphor.

Metaphors make for effective communication because analogy – a process of finding the properties of a thing by comparing it to another thing – is fundamental to thought. 'Human thought processes are largely metaphorical,' George Lakoff and Mark Johnson explained in *Metaphors we live by* (1980). 'The human conceptual system is metaphorically structured and defined. Metaphor is as much a part of our functioning as our sense of touch, and as precious.'

We use metaphors all the time. As Lakoff and Johnson point out, we compare:

- Arguments to war. (Attack your position, claims are indefensible, criticisms were right on target, shoot down arguments.)

- Time to money. (Spending time, wasting time, saving time, investing time, costing time.)
- Computers to offices. (Desktops, files, folders, documents, notepads.)

Another fascinating book about metaphors is *I is Another – the Secret Life of Metaphor and How it Shapes the Way We See the World* by James Geary.

When you give information in the form of a metaphor, you effectively pre-process it for your audience. They don't have to invest the mental effort of finding an analogy in their own inventory. When you use a metaphor, then, you are coming about as close as you can to placing a thought directly into the mind of your audience. Speaking of effective communication!

Metaphors are therefore powerful methods of persuasion, because they allow you to convey not just the information, but how you want your audience to think about that information. Scientific American reported a study (http://www.scientificamerican.com/article/figurative-speech-sways-decisions/) in which a group of subjects read a passage that said, 'Crime is a beast'. Another group read a passage that said, 'Crime is a virus'. In subsequent surveys, those who had read the beast passage were more likely to prescribe punishment as a means to control crime, while those who read the virus passage were more likely to prescribe treatment. This way a good metaphor goes beyond effective communication to something approaching thought control. So pick your metaphors carefully and use them responsibly.

The 'bottom line' is: if you are communicating complicated, technical, or scientific information, use metaphors. And this is, of course, another metaphor.

Storytelling

'Audiences forget facts, but they remember stories' – Ian Griffin

Many people have discovered the power of storytelling – they have seen how compelling a well-built story can be. Recent scientific work explains just how stories change our attitudes, beliefs, and behaviours.

Storytelling evokes a strong neurological response. Research by Professor Paul J. Zak indicates that our brains produce the stress hormone cortisol during the tense moments in a story, which allows us to focus, while the cute factor releases oxytocin, the feel-good chemical that promotes connection and empathy. Other neurological research tells us that a happy ending to a story triggers the limbic system, our brain's reward centre, to release dopamine, which makes us feel more hopeful and optimistic. As social creatures, we depend on others for our survival and happiness. Professor Zak discovered that a neurochemical called oxytocin is a key 'it's safe to approach others' signal in the brain. Oxytocin is produced when we are trusted or shown a kindness, and it motivates cooperation with others. It does this by enhancing the sense of empathy, our ability to experience others' emotions. Empathy is important for social creatures because it allows us to understand how others are likely to react to a situation, including those with whom we work.

These findings on the neurobiology of storytelling are of course also relevant to workplace settings. For example, character-driven stories with emotional content result in a better understanding of the key points a speaker wishes to make and enable better recall of these points many weeks later. When you want to motivate, persuade, or be remembered, start with a story of human struggle and eventual triumph. It will capture people's hearts – by first engaging their brains. Why do people on the street care about the project you are proposing? How does it change the world or improve lives? How will people feel when it is complete? These are the components that make information convincing and unforgettable.

In his book *Things That Make Us Smart* (1994), Don Norman accurately summarises the power of storytelling:

'Stories have the felicitous capacity of capturing exactly those elements that formal decision methods leave out. Logic tries to generalize, to strip the decision making from the specific context, to remove it from subjective emotions. Stories capture the context, capture the emotions … Stories are important cognitive events, for they encapsulate, into one compact package, information, knowledge, context, and emotions.'

But be careful. Long rambling anecdotes can quickly lose your audience. Short and memorable is the key.

Humour

'If you're going to tell people the truth, you'd better make them laugh. Otherwise, they'll kill you' – variously attributed

The important thing to remember is that humour is helpful at work as in life. Office humour makes our work more enjoyable, and humour outside the office – at home or with friends – will benefit our resilience, as it allows us to see things from a different perspective. As Dale Carnegie, author of *How to Win Friends and Influence People* (first published in 1936 and a big seller ever since) said: 'People rarely succeed unless they have fun in what they are doing.'

One reason why we suppress humour at work is the fear of what others might think. While it is of course important to consider your image and reputation, many people become preoccupied with what their colleagues, managers, and direct reports think of them. To laugh at something is a revelation of our personality. It tells others what we think is funny, and that scares people. If you are in a meeting involving your line manager and someone makes a joke, the tendency is to glance at your superior to see if they think it's funny – if they laugh, then surely it's OK for you to laugh also. The problem is that your manager is doing the same thing: checking how other people in the room are reacting; after all, managers are normal people too, and they have the same insecurities as the rest of us.

Our daily communications at work consist of much more than the information we give and receive. Emotional tone (pathos) is just as important. Think back to conversations you have had with people you met in the past. Chances are you remember your emotional reaction to that person and the general feeling of the conversation much better than you remember what was actually said. Shared amusement and laughter help ensure that both participants in the conversation will remember the good feeling they had long after the content is forgotten.

This is especially important in situations where the initial mood of the conversation is hostile or confrontational. Research has shown that humour helps reduce hostile feelings among co-workers. The better mood that shared laughter creates puts you in a better position to resolve conflict and get on with your job. The fact is that humour is incompatible with anger and other negative emotions, and that makes it such a great tool for conflict management. Since conflict and stress are so common in the workplace these days, the savvy manager will cultivate appropriately timed humour as a means of keeping tensions, frustration and upset from increasing.

Key points to remember

- *Being able to communicate clearly, both orally and in writing is a key competency for all types of job.*

- *One of the key aspects of good communication is awareness. Awareness, not only of your own strengths and weaknesses, but first and foremost awareness of the environment and the audience: What is the context of the communication? Who is my audience? What is the level of the audience? What are the needs of the audience? Do I have the audience's attention? Do I really get my message across?*

- *The most important thing in oral communication is the ability to listen and understand what the other person is saying. Focus your energy on being interested, not interesting.*

- *Especially in oral communication, stress is a major inhibitor of good performance. The trick is to convert this stress into positive energy.*

- *Besides the words that are spoken or written the surrounding emotions are of vital importance.*

And finally... some things to avoid

- *Giving minimalist or no answers to questions.*

- *Speaking too fast, bad articulation, truncating words or sentences.*

- *Dwelling too much on details, not getting to the point.*

- *Being too hesitant and not engaging spontaneously in conversations.*

- *Ignoring the needs of your audience or the context of the communication.*

- *Being overly verbose in speaking and writing.*

- *Creating documents that are disorganised or contain many grammar or spelling errors.*

- *Communicating 'too much', 'too little' or 'too late'.*

6. Working in teams

**"Isn't this what teamwork is all about?
You doing all my work for me?"**

'It takes two flints to make a fire' – Louisa May Alcott, author of 'Little Women'

Some things are easy to accomplish by working on your own, but there will unavoidably be times when you have to work with other people to get a job done.

Working in teams is the ability to effectively interact, cooperate, work together and manage conflicts with other people in order to complete tasks and achieve shared goals. This includes working with just one other individual, or working in small or large groups of people – for example fellow workers, managers, stakeholders, and contractors.

The reality is that there are a number of disadvantages and risks to working alone:

- Working alone you are limited by your own knowledge and skills.
- Working alone makes it harder to get early and frequent feedback.
- Slower progress from working alone reduces morale.
- The troughs of a project are more depressing when working alone.

Working in teams has a number of very real potential advantages:

- Teams can apply a mix of skills.
- Teams can solve complex problems.
- Teams can create new ideas.
- Teams can coordinate activities toward a common bigger goal.
- Teams can provide support and help to team members.
- Teams can give people a sense of belonging.
- Teams can improve communication.
- Teams can help people to learn from each other and develop.
- Teams can create commitment.

Please note that I wrote 'teams *can*' in the previous list of possible advantages; it's not because you are (forced to be) working in a team that these advantages will automatically happen. It takes the right attitude and skills from all the team members, and clever leadership to reap the benefits of teamwork. Working on a team also increases accountability; peer pressure is a powerful force.

Effectively working with others involves understanding and working within the group's culture, rules and values; joint planning and decision-making; negotiating and compromising; expressing one's opinions and ideas and respecting those of others, including people of divergent backgrounds; and being flexible in terms of roles including knowing when to take a leadership role and knowing when to look for a team approach.

Making others feel important requires that you genuinely appreciate the people around you and remind them of their positive qualities. It embodies the idea that you notice their talents and abilities and that in doing so you boost their self-esteem and increase their sense of self-worth. When people feel appreciated, they are more likely to be happier and more productive. This creates an enjoyable environment that is more conductive to relationships where people like working with each other and are more positive. People inherently want to know that they are valued. If you work on making them feel appreciated you will be validating your relationship with them.

In college, you have most certainly been confronted with group assignments. But these were only to an extent similar to the group- and teamwork you will have to do once you hit the work floor.

In your work, you will be expected to:

- Treat others with respect.
- Encourage and appreciate individual contributions.
- Share information and knowledge with others.
- Share your ideas with other workers.
- Be courteous to colleagues.
- Assist others when your own work has been completed.
- Encourage others to express their views.
- Take account of different opinions.
- Be able to listen to what others are saying.
- Accept input from others regarding ideas for improvement.
- Make an effort to understand other people.
- Be sensitive to the feelings of other people.
- Refrain from gossiping with other workers.
- Refrain from interfering with co-workers' productivity.
- Assist others when asked to do so.
- Be assertive.
- Be clear about what you feel and need and how it can be achieved.
- Balance your personal goals and team goals.
- Attend job related social activities.

Anchors for 'working in teams'

- Treating others with respect.
- Cooperating and collaborating with colleagues.
- Including relevant others in decision-making.
- Working with other cultures.
- Utilising other backgrounds, skills and motivations.
- Empathy and sympathy.
- Being assertive.
- Balancing individual and team goals.
- Resolving conflicts among team members.
- Building productive working relationships.

Table 6.1: Which of these sound like you?

UNSATISFACTORY	IMPROVEMENT NEEDED	MEETS EXPECTATIONS	EXCEEDS EXPECTATIONS	EXCEPTIONAL
Does not seek consensus and co-operation with others.	Sometimes displays behavior inconsistent with workplace courtesy and respect.	Treats others with respect.	Is respectful and welcoming.	Promotes, supports, and influences a culture of respect and courtesy among team members.
Ignores or belittles the contribution of others.	Often prefers to work independently.	Encourages and appreciates individual contributions.	Reaches out and engages with other people.	Inspires collaboration by bridging gaps among diverse individuals and units.
Makes decisions in isolation without consulting others.	Sees little value in letting everybody have their say.	Works effectively and co-operatively with others.	Praises the contributions of others.	Actively involves colleagues in decision-making processes.
Is prejudiced and biased against people from other cultures, judges them based on personal standards.	Lacks understanding of priorities and key issues for other stakeholders.	Shares information and knowledge with others.	Seeks new alliances to expand sphere of influence and enhance quality of work.	Creates opportunities for self and others to improve working relationships and work results.
Fails to consider individual differences in background, skills, or motivations.	Shows little curiosity for understanding the reasons why people behave as they do.	Encourages others to express their views.	Is constantly in touch with colleagues from other departments.	Engages with people outside his/her own team to achieve common objectives.
Shows no concern for the emotional state of others.	Holds strong views and is reluctant to see things from other angles.	Takes account of dissenting opinions.	Understands the importance of non-verbal communication patterns.	Effectively utilises the diverse range of backgrounds, skills and motivations of others.
Does not take steps to deal with underlying tensions at work.	Misreads other people's feelings or states of mind.	Has contacts elsewhere in the organisation to call for support if necessary.	Encourages people to voice their opinions and express their views.	Shows a genuine concern for the emotional state of others.
	Steps on other people's toes.	Is sensitive to the feelings of other people.	Is diplomatic when drawing attention to errors in other people's work or understanding of a situation.	
	Is dismissive of ideas that are not his/her own.	Is clear about what he feels, what he needs and how it can be achieved.		

Table 6.1: continued

UNSATISFACTORY	IMPROVEMENT NEEDED	MEETS EXPECTATIONS	EXCEEDS EXPECTATIONS	EXCEPTIONAL
Has low self-esteem.	Bottles up feelings that eventually explode, leaving no room for communication.	Is able to communicate calmly without attacking other people.	Is able to say 'no', rather than agreeing to do something just to please someone else.	Speaks up for colleagues in distress.
Lets himself be dictated to by other people.	Is not sufficiently assertive when defending his/her views.		Is always willing to try something new.	Is able to talk openly about self and able to listen to others.
Is 'invisible' in group discussions.	Resists new challenges.		Balances individual and team goals.	Goes beyond direct responsibilities to achieve team and department goals.
Is unwilling to work outside comfort zone to support team goals.	Seems uninterested in building skills and knowledge.		When possible, looks for and proposes middle ground solutions.	Seeks and achieves 'win-win' resolutions.
Is not prepared or willing to resolve conflict.				Leads colleagues to inspired cooperation and teamwork in support of department and organisational goals.
Shows lack of interest in and respect for fellow workers				

Groups versus teams

'The nice thing about teamwork is that you always have others on your side' – Margaret Carty

Wherever people work together, groups will be formed. People will belong to one or more groups, with each group having a different goal and purpose. These groups may be formal or informal. Formal groups are created to complete defined tasks, while informal groups are created voluntarily and are made up of people with common interests or roles. Informal groups are not usually recognised by the organisation but they can have a significant effect upon the work of others.

In English, the words 'group' and 'team' can sometimes be used interchangeably, but in other situations there are clear differences in meaning between them. For example, we have a football team, not a football group – or we have a special interest group, not a special interest team. While the distinctions may be subtle, they are in fact different, and we need to understand what those differences are.

In the business world there are work groups and work teams. A work group is two or more people who are either dependent or independent in their activities and may or may not work in the same department. A work team has members who work interdependently on a specific, common goal to produce an end result for their organisation.

In work teams, the leader acts as a facilitator; the members actively participate in the discussions and influence the result. It is the team members who decide on the distribution of work assignments. In contrast, in work groups it is the manager who dominates and controls the group; it is very clear who is in charge, and the manager will conduct the meetings and assign work to the group members.

Usually, work teams meet more often than work groups. Work groups may meet periodically, based on the manager's style, mostly to listen to and share information. Teams, in contrast, do much more than communicate when they meet. Team meetings are opportunities for planning work, solving problems, making decisions about work, and looking at progress. In short, meetings are vital to a team's existence.

Dependent-level work groups are the traditional work unit or department-level groups, with a manager who plays a strong role as the superior. Each person in a dependent-level work group has their own job and works under the close guidance of the manager. In fact, most problem solving, work assignments, and other decisions affecting the group come from the manager.

Independent-level work groups are the most common form of work groups on the business scene. Like a dependent-level work group, each person is responsible for their own main area. But unlike the dependent level, the manager tends not to function like a controlling boss. Instead, staff members work on their own assignments with just general direction and minimal supervision. Sales representatives, research scientists, accountants, lawyers, police officers, and teachers are among the professionals who tend to work in this fashion. People in those lines of work come together in one department because they serve a common overall function, but almost everyone in the group works fairly independently.

Members of an *interdependent-level* entity rely on each other to get the work done. Sometimes members have their own roles and at other times they share responsibilities. However, in either case, they coordinate with one another to produce an overall product or set of results. When this interdependence exists, you have a team.

Group dynamics

One of the main sources of stress at work has to do with work relationships. Group dynamics is a system of behaviours and mental processes happening within a group, or between groups. The study of group dynamics can be useful in dealing with conflicts and stress, but also in understanding decision-making behaviour.

In 1965 Bruce Tuckman, in his work on group dynamics, identified four stages of group development, adding a fifth stage in his later writings.

Stage 1: Forming

In the Forming stage, personal relations are seen as *dependence*. Group members depend on safe, patterned behaviour and look to the group leader for guidance and direction. Group members have a desire for acceptance by the group and a need to know that the group is safe. Serious topics and feelings are avoided. During this stage, group members are testing one another and the scope of the task and how to approach it.

Stage 2: Storming

The next stage, Storming, is seen as *competition and conflict* in the personal-relations dimension and organisation in the task-functions dimension. As the group members attempt to organise for the task, conflict unavoidably affects personal relations. People have to change their feelings, ideas, attitudes, and beliefs to suit the group organisation. These reflect conflicts over leadership, structure, power, and authority. Some group members will like the fact that real issues are starting to surface while others will feel uncomfortable.

Stage 3: Norming

In the Norming stage, interpersonal relations are characterised by *cohesion*. Group members are engaged in active recognition of all members' contributions, community building and maintenance, and solving of group issues. It is during this stage of development (assuming the group gets this far) that people begin to experience a sense of group belonging and a feeling of relief as a result of resolving interpersonal conflicts. Group members are now listening to each other better and identify themselves as part of a group. In some groups, the fact so much work was invested in reaching this stage may mean group members become unwilling to change anything.

Stage 4: Performing

Not all groups do reach the Performing stage. If group members are able to evolve to stage four, their ability, range, and depth of personal relations expand to *true interdependence*. In this stage, people can work independently, in subgroups, or as a total unit with equal facility. There is support for experimentation in solving problems and an emphasis on achievement. The overall goal is working well and getting a lot done.

Stage 5: Adjourning

Tuckman's final stage, Adjourning, involves the *termination* of task behaviours and *disengagement* from relationships. In some texts this stage is also referred to as Mourning. Tuckman's original work simply described the way he had observed groups, whether they were conscious of it or not. Later work recognised that the real value is in identifying where a group is in the process, and helping it to move to the Performing stage. In the real world, groups are often forming and changing, and each time that happens, they can move to a different stage. A group might be happily Norming or Performing, but a new member might force them back into Storming. Leaders have to be ready for this, and help the group get back to Performing as quickly as possible.

There are many other models of group development, to name a few: Tubb's Systems model, Fisher's theory of decision emergence in groups, Poole's multiple sequences model, McGrath's Time, Interaction, and Performance (TIP) theory, etc.

Group structure

A group's structure is the internal framework that defines members' relations to one another over time. As discussed above, groups come together for many reasons and in many ways. However, to ensure that people can work together effectively, it is important that everyone recognises and understands the roles and responsibilities of others, and how they can add to getting things done efficiently and well.

Roles can be defined as a tendency to behave, add and interrelate with others in a particular way. Roles may be assigned formally, but more often are defined through the process of role differentiation. Role differentiation is the degree to which different group members have specialised functions.

In many professional or administrative meetings there is the role of *moderator*. The moderator takes on the role of a formal or informal chair, and has to show awareness of the expected result (the mandate) and manage the sequence of events during the meeting by actively guiding the discussions and making sure that everyone gets a chance to contribute. Thus it is a high profile role in steering the group and achieving a successful result. The main thing is to periodically summarise what has been said by others so far, and also to try to advance the discussions by closing as many open points as possible and then proposing the next step or the way forward.

A second role is that of *timekeeper*. A timekeeper monitors the process from a scheduling point of view. He or she keeps an eye on the clock and warns the group when there is a risk of time overrun. The timekeeper is not a standalone role and anyone, at any point, can remind the group of the time left and where you are in the discussion.

In many professional meetings, there is a secretarial function for taking notes, and drafting the minutes.

Status differentials are the relative differences in status among group members. When a group is first formed the members may all be on an equal level, but over time certain members may obtain status and authority within the group; this can create what is known as a pecking order within a group.

What is an optimal team size?

'Too many cooks spoil the broth', as noted before, means that a team turns out to be inefficient if too many people take part in it, as it becomes very hard to coordinate, communicate with all members and maintain the necessary discipline. The reason lies in the mathematics of networks. To understand the magnitude of this effect, let's look at the number of connections in a team, which is $N(N-1)/2$ – see Figure 6.1.

Notice that after the low-digit numbers the equation tends towards $N^2/2$, with N representing the number of team members. The number of connections within the network grows much faster than the number of team members does. And that creates an obvious

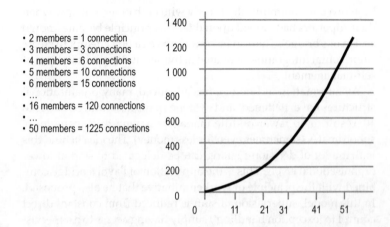

- 2 members = 1 connection
- 3 members = 3 connections
- 4 members = 6 connections
- 5 members = 10 connections
- 6 members = 15 connections
- ...
- 16 members = 120 connections
- ...
- 50 members = 1225 connections

Figure 6.1: Connections in a team

problem: human beings can only handle, or maintain, much smaller numbers of connections. In fact, the optimal size of small teams is the same as the effective range of short-term memory in our brains. Our minds seem to work best in the zone of seven, plus or minus two. On top of that, the connections are not perfect, because of the imperfection of human communication.

This way the ideal size of a team is around three to four people. When more people are needed, the overall efficiency of the team will decrease rapidly.

This simple observation also has far-reaching implications for the so-called span of control of managers and leaders. The commonly accepted definition of 'span of control' is as follows: 'the number of subordinates directly reporting to a leader or a manager.'

In hierarchical organisations of the past it was not uncommon to see average spans of 4 or even less, and the relationship was basically top-down – the manager simply telling the subordinate what to do. In fact, there were even fewer (N) connections, since the subordinates were not even supposed to communicate with each other.

In 1916, Henri Fayol proposed that subordinate workers have to be allowed to communicate directly with each other, but only when their superiors had agreed upon this. This principle became known as 'Fayol's bridge'. This can be considered as a first attempt to create a horizontal integration of related activities under a certain level of self-management.

As information technology has advanced, many organisational structures have 'flattened' and average spans have moved closer to 10, resulting in fewer middle managers having to manage more subordinates (sometimes even for less money). The idea behind this is that a lot of decision-making can be delegated to staff at lower organisational levels. This is the application of Fayol's bridge combined with the principle of worker initiative that he also proposed. In this model, supervision of staff is reduced from constant direct control to 'exception handling'; simply having access to a supervising manager is considered sufficient to satisfy the need for control in standard situations. Peter Drucker referred to this principle as *the span of managerial responsibility* and highlighted the importance of self-directed, cross-functional teams.

This trend has inevitably strengthened the case for the development of essential career skills for all staff at all levels. For a 'flatter' organisation to thrive everybody needs to be aware and responsible – and that takes more than just professional competence in the specific technicalities of one's own tasks. In other words, don't expect to get protective and hands-on management that is aware of what you need to get you up to speed.

How rituals deliver performance

All organisations have rituals – ranging from regular routines like coffee breaks, weekly team meetings and unit meetings, to major, less frequent events like annual meetings and retirement parties. It is important to understand that rituals like these are levers for improving the organisation's performance, because:

- Rituals create a shared identity
- Rituals stimulate the emotions and reduce anxiety
- Rituals reinforce desired behaviours
- Rituals bring team members' external networks into the family

Hence, as an individual, it is important to participate in your organisation's rituals, and not belittle them as a waste of time.

Personality types

The notion of *personality type* will be looked at in detail in Chapter 10 but for now let's assume that there are 16 possible personality types, resulting from four opposing tendencies of preferred behaviour. Even though these 16 type-indicators are not evenly spread across the population one can easily understand that the chances of having to work with people who have a different personality type than yours are huge. For example, in a group of six people, with each person possibly having one out of 16 personality types, the number of possible combinations is 16^6, which is over 16 million!

In practical terms this means that every group of people you ever work with will be different in respect of the mix of personality types around the table. The bad news is that there is not much you can do about this; you have to work with the people who happen to be in the same group as you are. The good news, however, is that you can change your own behaviour in order to successfully deal with the differences, by taking the (assumed) personality traits of the other participants into account.

Working with other cultures

Culture is, basically, a set of shared values that a group of people holds. Every culture has rules that its members take for granted. Few of us are aware of our own biases because cultural imprinting is begun at a very early age.

Of course, no two individuals belonging to the same culture are guaranteed to respond in exactly the same way. However, most caricatures tend to have a substantial slice of truth in them, and generalisations are valid to the extent that they provide indications as to what you will most likely encounter – and how those differences might impact communication.

High-context or low-context cultures

In some cultures, personal bonds and informal agreements are considered far more binding than any formal contract. In others, the meticulous wording of legal documents is viewed as very important.

High-context cultures like the Mediterranean, Latin American, African, Arab, and Asian leave much of the message undetermined – to be implied through context, non-verbal cues, and between-the-lines interpretation of what is actually said. These cultures are looking for meaning and understanding in what is not said – in body language, in silences and pauses, and in relationships and empathy. In contrast, low-context cultures (most of the Germanic and English-speaking countries) expect messages to be unambiguous and detailed. These cultures place emphasis on sending and receiving accurate messages directly, and on being precise with spoken or written words.

Sequential or synchronic cultures

In sequential cultures like English, German, Swedish, and Dutch, people think of time sequentially – as a linear commodity to 'spend,' 'save,' or 'waste'; people give their full attention to one agenda item after another. This can lead to a preoccupation with timelines that plays right into the hands of shrewd negotiators from other cultures; all they need to do is find out about your schedule and wait until right before your deadline to present an offer.

In synchronic cultures (including southern Europe and Asia) the flow of time is viewed as a sort of circle, with the past, present, and future all inter-related. Time is a constant flow to be experienced moment by moment, and as a force that cannot be contained or controlled. This influences how people in those cultures approach deadlines, strategic thinking, investments, developing talent from within, and the idea of 'long-term' planning.

Affective or neutral cultures

Reason and emotion both play a role in communication. Which of these dominates depends upon whether we are affective (readily showing emotions) or emotionally neutral in our approach. Members of neutral cultures (Scandinavians, Dutch, and Japanese for example) do not announce their feelings, but keep them carefully controlled and restrained. In affective cultures – such as Italian and French – people will show their feelings openly by laughing, smiling, grimacing – and sometimes crying, shouting, or walking out of the room.

This does not mean that people in neutral cultures are cold or unfeeling. But in the course of normal business activities, people from neutral cultures are more careful to monitor the amount of emotion they display.

Once again, I need to issue the caveat that these are broad generalisations because people vary greatly, and I challenge you to judge these statements based on your own experience.

In the end there is no single best approach to communicating with one another. The key to cross-cultural success is to develop an understanding of, and a deep respect for, the differences.

Active listening

'Two monologues do not make a dialogue.' – Jeff Daly

A way to become a better listener is to practise *active listening*. This is where you make a conscious effort not only to hear the words that another person is saying but, more importantly, try to understand the complete message that is being sent. In order to do this you must pay attention to the other person very carefully.

There are five important things in active listening. They all help you make sure that you hear the other person, and that the other person knows you are hearing what is said.

Pay attention – Give the speaker your undivided attention, and respond to the message by:

- Looking at the speaker directly, keeping eye contact.
- Putting aside distracting thoughts.
- Not mentally preparing a rebuttal.
- Avoiding distractions like side conversations.
- Observing the speaker's body language.

Show that you are listening – Use your own body language to convey your attention by:

- Nodding every once in a while.
- Smiling and using other facial expressions (avoiding a 'poker face').
- Being aware of your posture and making sure it is open and inviting.
- Encouraging the speaker to continue with small verbal comments like 'yes', and 'hmm'.

Provide feedback – Your personal filters, assumptions, judgements, and beliefs can distort what you hear. As a listener, your role is to understand what is being said. This may require you to reflect what is being said by:

- Paraphrasing: 'What I'm hearing is …' and 'Sounds like you are saying …'
- Asking questions to clarify certain points: 'What do you mean when you say?'
- Summarising the speaker's comments periodically.

Postpone judgement – Interrupting is a waste of time. It frustrates the speaker and limits full understanding of the message:

**"Sorry. I was filtering out
your conversation spam.
What were you saying?"**

- Allow the speaker to finish each point before asking questions.
- Don't interrupt with counter arguments.

Respond appropriately – Active listening is a model for respect and understanding. You are gaining information and perspective. You add nothing by attacking the speaker or otherwise putting him or her down:

- Be open and honest in your response.
- Defend your opinions respectfully.
- Treat the other person in a way that you think he or she would want to be treated.

It is a luxury to be really listened to, to be truly heard. Active listening will support your colleagues both personally and professionally, and it will improve your own productivity.

Empathy and sympathy

Empathy is the experience of understanding another person's condition from their perspective. You place yourself in their shoes and feel what they are feeling. The word 'empathy' was brought into use in 1909 by British psychologist Edward B. Titchener. While the word's spelling borrows from an ancient Greek word, empátheia, which meant 'passion,' Titchener used 'empathy' for the purpose of translating a German word (*einfühlungsvermögen*) and its idea of shared feeling.

Empathy is not to be confused with *sympathy*. When you sympathise with someone, you have compassion for that person, but you don't necessarily share their feelings. Sympathy has broader applications that don't necessarily have to do with one person's feelings for another. You can sympathise with a cause, for instance, or with a point of view that resonates with you. The word 'sympathy' comes from the antique Greek *sunpathos*, meaning 'with/together' and 'suffering.'

The ability to sympathise and empathise is considered vital for a sense of humanity – the ability to understand other humans and their problems. People who lack this ability are often classified as narcissistic, sociopathic, or in extreme cases, psychopathic. However, these terms are only applicable if a person consistently lacks the ability to sympathise or empathise with others.

In general, there are many cases where people may not feel sympathetic or empathetic due to lack of knowledge or because their experiences are different; this does not imply abnormal behaviour. On the other hand, some people are overly empathetic and can eventually be overwhelmed by the negative feelings they take on from their relationships and encounters with other people.

To start using empathy – and sympathy – more effectively when working with others consider the following:

- Examine your own attitude. Are you more concerned with getting your way, winning, or being right? Or, is your priority to find a solution, build relationships, and accept others as they are?
- Try to see things from the other person's point of view. You will probably realise that they are not in fact stupid, evil, unkind, stubborn, or unreasonable; they are most likely just reacting based on the knowledge and understanding they have.
- Recognise the other person's perspective. Acknowledgement does not always equal agreement. You can 'agree to disagree'.
- Practise active listening.

I would also advise you to have a look at the TED talk on empathy given by Daniel Goleman.

Preparing for a meeting

'Knowing is not enough; we must apply. Willing is not enough; we must do' – Goethe

Meetings are a huge part of working life and you will most likely quickly find yourself in a situation where you are involved in preparing a meeting. Meetings are critical for team development and task management. However, meetings can easily fail without adequate preparation and leadership. A large part of what makes a meeting successful occurs in the preparation phase. Although it may vary by committee, department or unit, there are seven key responsibilities expected of chairs or moderators before a meeting happens:

- *Clarify purpose and aims.* The purpose of a meeting has to be stated at the top of the meeting agenda. A weekly or monthly staff meeting may not require meeting aims beyond the agenda items.
- *Create an agenda.* An agenda is a structure that guides and supports the meeting. An agenda helps focus the group's work on achieving desired results. Good agenda items provide focus and structure for a meeting.
- *Schedule the meeting properly.* Scheduling a meeting involves much more than just making a list of attendees. It requires identifying key people who in a perfect world must attend and either finding times that work for them or at the very least notifying them as far in advance as possible of when the meeting will take place. Once an optimal date and time are decided on, a meeting location can be selected. Sometimes, of course, the choice of meeting location dictates the time of the meeting and how long it can go on for. You certainly don't want to find you have to leave a meeting room before your business is finished just because someone else has booked it.
- *Post and send out the agenda.* An agenda has to be sent to participants ahead of time to help them prepare to participate. Don't leave this to the last minute or you will simply irritate people.
- *Circulate supporting information.* You always have to circulate supporting documentation to participants in advance of the meeting. However, deciding how much documentation to send out can present a problem. Some people won't want to look at anything prior to the meeting and some will conscientiously read everything they receive. Focus therefore on the documentation that it is essential people study in advance, and make it clear that that is what you are sending them.
- *Make room arrangements.* Ensure that the meeting room is set up properly. Trivial details (are there enough chairs? Are there drinks, and if so enough cups/glasses?) can certainly influ-

ence people's perceptions of how well a meeting is organised. Most importantly, make sure that all participants are going to be able to see and hear each other properly.

- *Arrange for a secretary*. The secretary of the meeting takes notes on paper, laptop or on flip charts. Meeting notes have to be distributed as soon after the meeting as possible. The longer the delay, the less confidence the members will have that their contribution will result in action. For groups that meet regularly, the secretary is responsible for keeping previous meeting notes and agendas in one place where they can be referenced later such as from a notebook or shared network drive, etc.

Assertiveness

Assertiveness is an attitude and a way of relating to the outside world, backed up by a set of abilities. You need to see yourself as being valuable, and this goes hand in hand with you valuing others equally, respecting their right to an opinion. Many people find it very hard to communicate honestly, directly and openly with other people. It is sometimes said about assertive behaviour that it involves being aggressive. It doesn't! Assertiveness involves clear, calm thinking and respectful negotiation where each person is entitled to their opinion. Assertiveness, properly understood and applied, makes sure that you – and other people – are not hurt, used or abused.

There are only two alternatives to being assertive: being passive or being aggressive. Passive modes of communication are in reality an attempt to punish or undermine the other person: playing games, being sarcastic, or remaining silent all together. Aggression involves bottling up feelings that eventually explode, leaving no room for communication.

Assertiveness includes:

- Being clear about what you feel, what you need and how it can be achieved.
- Being able to communicate calmly without attacking another person.

- Being able to say 'no', rather than agreeing to do something just to please someone else.
- Being happy to defend your position, even if it provokes conflict.
- Being confident about handling conflict if it occurs.
- Understanding how to negotiate if two people want different results.
- Being able to talk openly about yourself and being able to listen to others.
- Having confident, open body language.
- Being able to give and receive positive and negative feedback.
- Having a positive, optimistic outlook.

The nice guy syndrome

'Nice Guys have a very hard time comprehending that in general, people are not drawn to perfection in others. People are drawn to shared interests, shared problems, and an individual's life energy' – Robert Glover

The 'nice guy syndrome' refers to a behavioural pattern of being overly nice to others. A leading book on this topic is *No More Mr Nice Guy* by Dr Robert Glover.

A nice guy's most important goal is to make other people happy. Nice guys are dependent on external validation and avoid conflict at any cost. As a result of this syndrome, nice guys have mediocre careers compared with how skilled they are, no matter how hard they work, and they sabotage almost every aspect of their own lives:

- They appear needy and insecure.
- They end up ignoring their own needs and not taking care of themselves.
- They end up not being there for the people who really matter, because they try to please everybody.
- They are full of repressed rage and they tend to detonate at the most inappropriate times.
- They try to get what they want in indirect, manipulative ways.

If you think you may be too much of a 'nice guy', you will need to consciously change your thinking and change your behaviour. Specific actions may include:

- Expressing yourself more, even when you may upset someone.
- Asking for what you really want and saying 'no' to others.
- Taking more time for yourself and your own needs.
- Ending toxic relationships that go nowhere.

Brainstorming

Brainstorming provides a free and open environment that encourages everyone to participate. Original ideas are welcomed and built upon, and all participants are encouraged to contribute fully, helping them develop a rich collection of creative solutions.

When used during problem solving, brainstorming brings team members' diverse experience and backgrounds into play. It increases the richness of ideas investigated, which means that you can often find better solutions to the problems that you face. It can also help get buy-in from team members for the solution chosen – after all, they are likely to be more enthusiastic about an approach if they were involved in developing it. What's more, because brain-

"Before we start this round of wide-
open brainstorming, I'd just like to
remind you that all ideas that
are not mine must be rejected."

storming is amusing, it helps team members bond, as they solve problems in a positive, rewarding environment.

Brainstorming is popular for two reasons, one good and one bad. The good reason is that a typical brainstorming session brings people together in the creative process, and increases the social nature of the project. If the meeting is run properly, everybody feels as though they are contributing to what they will be working on in the future. More importantly, it gets people thinking and communicating with each other about topics relevant to their work.

The bad reason that brainstorming is popular is that it is an easy way for bad managers to pretend that the team is involved in the direction of the project. A team leader can be convinced that he or she knows how to cultivate and work with ideas that are not their own simply by holding a meeting.

The most important thing about a brainstorming session is what happens after it ends, because some good ideas will surface, no matter how poorly you run a brainstorming meeting. But depending on what happens after the session, those ideas may or may not impact anything.

While brainstorming can be effective, it's important to approach it with an open mind and a non-judgmental attitude. If this does not happen, people are likely to clam up and the number and quality of ideas, and morale, will suffer as a result.

Finally, if you are new in your job be prepared for the possibility that good ideas thrown up in a brainstorm – including your own – may never actually be implemented. It happens!

Six Thinking Hats

Six Thinking Hats is a bestselling book by Edward de Bono that provides a tool for group discussion and individual thinking involving six coloured hats. Team members learn how to separate thinking into six clear functions and roles. Each thinking role is identified with a symbolic 'thinking hat' and team members can adopt in turn the roles and thought patterns associated with each hat.

- The 'White Hat' calls for information known or needed: 'the facts, just the facts.'

- The 'Yellow Hat' symbolises brightness and optimism. Under this hat you explore the positives and probe for value and benefit.
- The 'Black Hat' is judgement – the devil's advocate, or why something may not work.
- The 'Red Hat' signifies feelings, hunches and intuition. When using this hat you can express emotions and feelings and share likes, dislikes, loves, and hates.
- The 'Green Hat' focuses on creativity: the possibilities, alternatives, and new ideas.
- The 'Blue Hat' is used to manage the thinking process. It is the control mechanism that ensures the Six Thinking Hats guidelines are observed.

Networking

Networking is about making connections and building enduring, mutually beneficial relationships. The word 'work' is part of networking, and it is not easy work, because it involves reaching outside the borders of your comfort zone.

There are basically three forms of networking: operational, personal and strategic.

The purpose of *operational networking* is getting work done efficiently, or – in other words – building and maintaining the capacities and functions required of the groups you are part of. Your contacts are mostly internal and orientated towards your current activities. Key contacts are prescribed mostly by your tasks and the organisational structure, so it is relatively clear who is relevant. Operational networks include direct reports and superiors but also fellow workers, other internal players with the power to block or support a project, and key outsiders such as suppliers and clients. Operational networking focuses on depth: building strong relationships.

As you move into a leadership role, your network must readjust itself externally and toward the future. In *personal networking*, improving personal and professional development is key; providing referrals to useful information and contacts. Contacts are mostly external and orientated towards current interests and future possible interests; this means that it is not always clear who is relevant.

According to the famous 'six degrees of separation' principle, your personal contacts are valuable to the extent that they help you reach, in as few connections as possible, the distant person who has the information you need. Personal networking focuses on width: reaching out to contacts that can make referrals.

Finally, for *strategic networking* the purpose is figuring out future priorities and challenges. Contacts are both internal and external and orientated towards the future. Having lateral and vertical relationships with other people outside your immediate control becomes a lifeline for figuring out how your own contributions fit into the big picture. What distinguishes a leader from a manager is the ability to figure out where to go and to enlist the people and groups necessary to get there. As they step up to the leadership transition, some managers accept their growing dependence on others and seek to transform it into mutual influence. Others dismiss such work as 'political' and, as a result, undermine their ability to advance their goals.

Building a network is less a matter of skill than of will. When first efforts do not bring quick rewards, some may simply figure out that networking isn't among their talents. But networking is not a talent; nor does it require an expansive, extraverted personality. It is a skill, one that takes practice.

Key points to remember

- *Focus your energy on being interested, not interesting.*
- *Working with others increases your energy, efficiency and creativity.*
- *Working in teams improves understanding, communication and a sense of shared purpose.*
- *Diversity makes the most of a range of skills and knowledge.*
- *Collaboration is often essential to success.*

And finally... some things to avoid

- *Demonstrating behaviour that negatively impacts the morale and accomplishments of the team.*

- *Ignoring or belittling the contribution of others.*

- *Making decisions in isolation without consulting others.*

- *Being prejudiced and biased against other people.*

- *Being 'invisible' in group discussions.*

- *Showing lack of interest in and respect for fellow workers.*

- *Not being sufficiently assertive when defending your views.*

- *Being dismissive of ideas that are not yours.*

- *Adopting a silo mentality, not co-operating with other departments or groups in the same organisation.*

- *Displaying behaviour inconsistent with workplace courtesy and respect.*

7. Being resilient

"You'll experience a certain amount
of stress in your new job, but don't
worry. We keep a defibrillator here
on my desk."

'The difference between winners and losers is how they handle losing'
– Rosabeth Moss Kanter, Harvard Business School

Being resilient is surviving and adapting in the face of adversity,
trauma, tragedy, threats or significant sources of stress. *Resilience*
– the ability to effectively cope with losing, failing, and not getting
what you want – is an important quality for anyone to cultivate in
order to achieve success and well-being. To live and to work is to
risk failure, and resilience helps people to bounce back from the unavoidable adversities and obstructions that risk involves.

Resilience is ordinary, not extraordinary. Resilience is not a feature that people either have or do not have. It involves behaviours,
thoughts and actions that can be learned and developed in anyone.

Resilience is sometimes confused with *perseverance*, but there is
a difference. In short, perseverance keeps you going when you are

convinced that you are on the right track, but you are just not getting enough traction to get to your destination. Being resilient enables you to build a new track, fix the locomotive and start all over
again when the wheels come off.

Another related idea is *grit*. Grit is a personal characteristic based
on a person's passion for a particular long-term objective, coupled
with a powerful motivation to achieve that objective. Grit supplies
the determination to overcome obstacles and achieve your goals.

Developing resilience is a personal journey. People do not all react
the same to traumatic and stressful events. An approach to building
resilience that works for one person might not work for another.

Resilience

I often use the metaphor of a (coil) spring to illustrate the idea of resilience. Springs are constructional elements designed to retain and accu-
mulate mechanical energy, working on the principle of flexible deformation
of material.

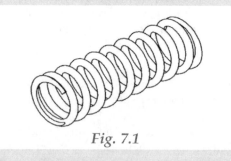

Fig. 7.1

First, imagine that you are compressing the spring and releasing it – gently – afterwards. The spring will come back to its original shape. The energy
that was accumulated during compression will be released completely, and
the spring will not 'remember' anything of the event. That's what a spring
is meant to do, that's what it is designed for.

Now, imagine that, instead of compressing the spring you are extending
it. Just a little bit. When released, the spring will come back to its original
shape, just as it would when having compressed it. However, when you ex-

cont...

tend it too much, the spring will not come back entirely – there will be a permanent deformation. One could say that the spring has 'learned' from the experience, because no matter how often you repeat the experiment (even compressing) the deformation will be permanent, and the spring will never return to its first original state again.

Finally, when you extend the spring too much, it will break. This is also a permanent state that can only be repaired by a serious intervention (soldering, welding or some mechanical fix).

I compare mental resilience with the behaviour of a spring. When subjected to 'normal' levels of stress (compression) we bounce back as if nothing happened. This is what we are meant to do, what we are 'designed' for. This is also what we are paid for at work. However, when subjected to 'abnormal' stress (either too high or in an unusual direction) we only have two options: learn from the experience and bounce back, or break. The mental counterpart of a spring breaking is known as 'burn out', and it will be very hard to repair. The 'permanent deformation' obviously is the learning experience we get from adversity.

I am sure that you have had to be resilient in your academic career. Maybe you flunked an exam – or two – even though you had been working very hard to pass. But, despite the stress and disappointments, you made it. Being resilient at work (and in life) will be very similar, but the challenges may be greater as you will be expected to:

- Be mentally and physically in top condition.
- Continuously work on self-improvement.
- Manage your workload effectively and efficiently.
- Remain calm under pressure.
- Consider failures and setbacks as learning opportunities.
- Be able to control emotions, behaviour and desires.
- Work with the management, not against it.
- Embrace change.
- Be self-motivating.
- Remain optimistic.

Anchors for 'being resilient'

- Relying on social support.
- Living healthily in mind and body.
- Positive thinking.
- Communicating and problem solving.
- Coping with heavy workload and tight deadlines.

Table 7.1: Which of these sound like you?

UNSATISFACTORY	IMPROVEMENT NEEDED	MEETS EXPECTATIONS	EXCEEDS EXPECTATIONS	EXCEPTIONAL
Has little or no social contact with fellow workers, friends or family.	Has an operational network, but no personal or strategic network to rely upon.	Has both an operational and a personal network to rely upon.	Has good operational, personal and strategic network.	Has very good operational and personal network, combined with an excellent strategic network.
Has an unhealthy lifestyle.	Neglects work-life balance.	Eats mostly healthy food, sufficient physical activity, gets enough rest and sleep.	Maintains an optimistic, positive outlook.	Is mentally and physically in top condition.
Concentrates on negative only.	Does not do enough physical activity.		Combines good work-life balance with efficient and effective behaviour at work.	Continuously works on self-improvement.
Is unaware of other people's feelings and emotions.	Is overweight, or has high blood pressure.	Is assertive, not passive or aggressive.		Is a 'giver' not a 'taker'.
Becomes stressed or panics when under pressure.	Gets insufficient sleep or rest.	Keeps cool under pressure, works more intensively and longer hours when pressure is on.	Has strategies for coping with large volumes of work.	Remains calm under pressure.
Regards unsuccessful endeavours as personal failures.	Has low self-esteem.	Takes care of professional and personal development during the calmer periods at work.	Considers failures and setbacks as learning opportunities.	Prepares mentally and physically for busier periods to come.
Loses self-confidence and self-esteem after a failure or setback.	Lacks trust in co-workers.		Turns setbacks and failures to his/her advantage.	Handles failures and interprets setbacks professionally, not personally.
	Is overly perfectionist, indecisive, or impatient with others.			

- Adjusting to peaks and troughs in workload.
- Handling failures and setbacks.
- Working with management.
- Facing changes.
- Self-control.

Table 7.1: continued

UNSATISFACTORY	IMPROVEMENT NEEDED	MEETS EXPECTATIONS	EXCEEDS EXPECTATIONS	EXCEPTIONAL
Is frustrated by the management, has little tendency to work with it constructively.	Responds defensively to criticism.	Accepts that not everything in life works out fine.	Actively seeks feedback from management and builds on it.	Endeavours to become involved in decisions related to his/her work.
Intolerant of ambiguity in work content or organisational situation.	Refuses to learn from failures and setbacks.	Acknowledges own mistakes, and learns from them.	Sees change and reorganisation as an opportunity for improvement.	Sees organisational change as a positive challenge.
Externalises frustrations with management.	Tends to blame the environment for own failures.	Tolerates ambiguity in work content or organisational situation.	Adjusts quickly to unexpected changes.	Is able to control emotions, behaviour and desires in the face of external demands.
Resists organisational change, and sticks to old habits and traditional ways of working.	Does not always take steps to establish with management the conditions for smooth working relations.	Copes with demands by management and understands their role.	Keeps negative emotions under control at all time.	
Feels threatened by change or reorganisation.	Has difficulty adapting to new working environments.	Adapts to new ways of working and broader organisational changes.		
	Is discouraged by organisational change.	Sees organisational change as part of life.		

Change

> *'There are only three certainties in life: death, taxes, and change'* –
> Anonymous

Change is one of the most important sources of stress. Change happens in your daily life (you meet a new friend, go live together or get married, move to another city or even country, get children...) but there will be change in your working environment too – at various levels:

- People: attitudes, expectations, perceptions and behaviours.
- Structure: job, responsibilities, management, and organisational design.
- Technology: work, processes, equipment, methods and software.

One can easily say that at work change is constant, but it varies in degree and direction. Organisational change produces uncertainty, but it is not completely unpredictable, and organisational change creates both threats and opportunities.

Organisational change affects workers differently. While some will welcome it, others will become worried and stressed at the mere mention of change. They will fear that any reorganisation might challenge their standing and worry how they will fit into the new structure. That is why being able to adjust to changing working conditions is one of your essential career skills.

Stress

Stress is the body's response to change. Stress is defined in many ways and the things that cause stress can vary from person to person. Stress affects your performance.

There are four types of stress:

- *Acute stress* is the type of stress you experience on a day-to-day basis – for example, the stress of getting your to-do list finished or the stress of unexpected obstacles.

- When a person rarely gets relief from stress, this is called *episodic acute stress*. This type of stress usually goes on for longer periods of time with little relief.
- *Chronic stress* is characterised as long-term stress, where there is little hope for relief. These are long-term situations where the person has given up trying to find a solution.
- Not all stress is bad; some stress can actually help us to perform better and challenge us. This type of stress is called '*eustress*'.

Dr Peter Nixon, a British cardiologist, developed a diagram called the Human Function Curve (Figure 7.2) that illustrates the balance of good and bad stress.

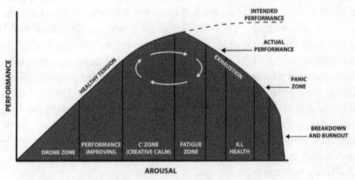

Figure 7.2: Peter Nixon's human function curve

Nixon calls any state where you are awake and reacting to stimuli an arousal state, such as being at work. If you compare the amount of stress to your performance, your performance actually improves when you experience eustress. However, according to this model, there is a point where chronic stress can impede your performance. In Figure 7.2 you can see in the drone zone, for example, that your performance is low. You may be bored and not have enough positive stress to perform at a decent level. In the C zone, in contrast, you may experience eustress, which raises your performance. However, when you reach the fatigue zone, you could be experiencing chronic stress, which interferes with your perform-ance. As you can see, performance is actually improved with a cer-tain amount of stress, but once that stress becomes episodic or chronic, your performance gets worse.

Boreout

According to Peter Werder and Philippe Rothlin in their book *Boreout – Overcoming workplace demotivation* (2008), it is the absence of meaningful tasks, rather than the presence of stress, that is the main problem for many workers. What they call 'boreout' consists of three elements: boredom, lack of challenge, and lack of interest. These authors disagree with the common perception that a demo-tivated worker is lazy; instead, they argue that the worker has lost interest in work tasks. Those suffering from boreout are 'dissatisfied with their professional situation' because they are frustrated at being prevented – by institutional mechanisms or obstacles rather than their own lack of aptitude – from fulfilling their potential. Ful-filling their potential means using their skills, knowledge, and abil-ities to contribute to their organisation's development and/or receiving official recognition for their efforts. Such workers have given up and become resigned to their situation, experiencing bore-out, which is effectively the opposite of burnout (see pages 163-165).

Here are some typical signs of boreout:

- Frequent private surfing on the internet combined with frequent usage of the 'Alt-Tab' shortcut (and if you know what this means you may already have a problem …).
- Burning long hours at work: going as early as possible to the of-fice and leaving as late as possible, without producing much.
- Procrastination: tasks are split up over more periods of time and are constantly interrupted or moved.
- Remaining work is taken home but not worked on.
- Constantly highlighting to fellow workers and supervisors how busy and overloaded you are.
- Feeling unsatisfied by your working situation and constantly feeling unchallenged and bored.

"The secret to being interested in dull
work? You're fired. See? Didn't it just
become much more interesting?"

The dangerous effects of boreout cannot be underestimated: dissatisfaction, apathy and the loss of appetite for life – not to mention the reduction of the organisation's efficiency resulting from bored workers spending hours of company time surfing the net.

Boreout has become widespread among workers around the world, although employers have only recently begun to recognise the problem.

Comfort zone

Your *comfort zone* is any type of behaviour that keeps you at a low anxiety level. Everyday activities that you are used to doing won't make you feel anxious and uneasy, so they are part of your comfort zone.

Brené Brown, a research professor at the University of Houston Graduate College of Social Work, has another definition of comfort zone: 'Where our uncertainty, scarcity and vulnerability are minimized – where we believe we'll have access to enough love, food, talent, time, admiration. Where we feel we have some control.'

Although people often refer to 'getting outside your comfort zone' in terms of trying new things, anything that raises your anxiety levels can be counted as being outside that zone. Anxiety is not something we are prone to go looking for, but a little bit can be surprisingly helpful. We often need just a hint of anxiety to push us to get our work done, or to improve our performance.

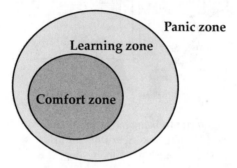

Figure 7.3: Comfort, learning and panic zones

This is illustrated in Figure 7.3, where the comfort zone extends into a learning zone, but eventually leads to a panic zone, where anxiety is too high.

How we deal with uncertainty

A lot of the anxiety that comes from leaving your comfort zone is due to uncomfortable levels of uncertainty. There is a reason that cooking dinner is no big deal when you do it all the time; you know what to expect. Driving a car for the first time, or skydiving, or starting a new job, are all activities that are full of uncertainty, and thus, anxiety. Uncertainty can make us respond more strongly to negative experiences. We are more likely to respond negatively to new things, even though we may come to like them over time.

Familiarity is comfortable and enjoyable, so it is no real surprise that new things get our guard up. From an evolutionary perspective, we see familiar things as more likely to be safe, and so we are more drawn to what we know. Trying new things also takes energy, so we are more likely to lean on old habits than take a new risk.

Breaking out of your comfort zone

So, should you try to break out of your comfort zone? Is it actually good for you to try? The answer is 'yes' – to some degree. 'We need a place of productive discomfort,' says Daniel H. Pink in his must-read book *Drive: The Surprising Truth about What Motivates Us.*

'If you are too comfortable, you are not productive. And if you are too uncomfortable, you are not productive either. We can't be too hot or too cold. The objective is to reach that optimal level so that our skills increase and we become comfortable with that new level of anxiety – then we are in an expanded comfort zone. And in a perfect world, we will get more used to those feelings of "productive discomfort" and won't be so scared about trying new things in the future.'

When mixed with a feeling of success, some anxiety and self-doubt can lead to personal growth. This is why outdoor adventures like rock climbing or skydiving can be so exciting: they induce anxiety and unease but when completed, they give us a huge feeling of accomplishment and increase our base levels of confidence.

A couple of years ago, I had the opportunity to help my daughter to learn how to drive a car. I am sure you can imagine that the first time she took place behind the wheel, not even knowing where to put her feet on the pedals, her 'level of anxiety' was very high; she was in – or very close to – her panic zone. So, I decided not to let her start the engine for that very first time, but just to explain a couple of general principles and showing her where all the controls of the car could be found, and what these were used for. Giving her a bigger challenge would have been pointless, since her level of anxiety was too high.

The next step was to just let her start the engine and move forward for a couple of meters, giving her the feeling of how to play with the pedals to achieve this. Of course, we did this on a quiet parking lot in our neighbourhood, where no other vehicles or obstacles were in the way. Needless to say that the engine stalled many times and the first movements of the car were more like jumping than riding, but after a while (maybe 30 attempts or so) she had the initial 'feeling' of how the car responded to her actions. And that was it. She had accepted the first – small but achievable – challenge, out of her comfort zone, into her learning zone.

Over subsequent lessons, each time with a couple of days in between, I slowly added challenges to her portfolio – driving around in circles (first gear), starting and stopping, emergency braking – until the time had come

to use the clutch. The car, especially the gearbox, suffered a lot, but I considered that this was the price to be paid for her learning experience (it was
my wife's car anyway).

Then came the day that we moved away from the parking lot and went
for a drive on the road. We usually practised during the weekend and in an
industrial area with little or no traffic around. She first had to get a better
feeling of the vehicle, especially when driving at somewhat higher speeds.
At first, the trips we made were very short and always the same; the only
purpose of this was to remove the anxiety that comes with driving in an un-
familiar environment, allowing her to concentrate on the driving.

Many weekends later we went out on real roads. I live in the countryside,
so I could choose roads with very moderate traffic, just to let her gradually
get used to the idea that she is not alone on the road, and that other drivers
may make mistakes as well. In fact, she even had a little accident during
that time. It was dark and rainy and she misjudged her braking distance to
a car that stopped in front of us. There was some small damage to both cars
(she was driving my own car this time) but nobody was hurt. I am sure that
this was a great learning experience for her…

After some months of messing around on country roads we finally went
to a (small) city to prepare her for the driver's exam.

In fact, she failed first time round. Not because of her driving skills, but
because she had misinterpreted a rather complex traffic situation (I was sitting next to her and made the same mistake). Once again, tears were flowing, but once again this was a great learning experience. Anyway, the second
time she got her driver's licence and since then has driven safely thousands
of kilometres in very variable circumstances. I believe she is now inside her
comfort zone.

Fight or flight

The *fight or flight response* – also called the acute stress response – is a physiological reaction that happens in response to a
perceived harmful event, attack, or threat to survival.

When our fight or flight response is activated, sequences of nerve
cell firing happen and chemicals like adrenaline, noradrenaline and
cortisol are released into our blood-stream. These patterns of nerve
cell firing and chemical release cause our body to undergo a series of

very dramatic changes. Our respiratory rate increases. Blood is shunted away from our digestive tract and directed into our muscles and limbs, which require extra energy and fuel for running and fighting. Our pupils dilate. Our awareness intensifies. Our sight sharpens. Our impulses quicken. Our perception of pain diminishes. Our immune system mobilises with increased activation. We become prepared – physically and psychologically – for fight or flight.

When our fight or flight system is activated, we tend to perceive everything in our environment as a possible threat to our survival. By its very nature, the fight or flight system bypasses our rational mind and moves us into 'attack' mode. This state of alert causes us to see everyone and everything as a possible enemy. We may over-react to the smallest comment.

You can see how it is almost impossible to have a positive attitude to work when you are stuck in survival mode. Your rational mind is disengaged. Making clear choices and recognising the results of those choices is not possible. You are focused on short-term survival, not the long-term effects of your choices. When you are overwhelmed with excessive stress, your life becomes a series of short-term emergencies. You lose the ability to relax and enjoy the moment. You live from crisis to crisis, with no relief in sight. Burnout is unavoidable.

Burnout

Burnout is a state of physical, emotional or mental exhaustion combined with doubts about your competence and the value of your work. Burnout can result from different factors, including:

- Lack of control
- Lack of resources
- Unclear job expectations
- Dysfunctional workplace dynamics
- Mismatch in values
- Poor job fit
- Extremes of activity
- Lack of social support
- Work-life imbalance

The difference between stress and burnout is a matter of degree, which means that the earlier you recognise the signs, the better able you will be to avoid burnout. Here are some signals you have to pay attention to:

- *Chronic fatigue.* Lack of energy and feeling tired most days, or feeling a sense of anxiety about what lies ahead on any given day.
- *Insomnia.* Trouble falling asleep or staying asleep, or inability to sleep overall.
- *Impaired concentration and attention.* Lack of focus and for-getfulness, or you can't get your work done and everything begins to pile up.
- *Physical symptoms.* Physical symptoms may include chest pain, heart palpitations, and shortness of breath, gastrointestinal pain, dizziness, fainting, and/or headaches.
- *Increased illness.* Because your body is depleted, your immune system becomes weakened, making you more vulnerable to infections, colds, flu, and other immune-related medical problems.
- *Loss of appetite.* In the early stages, you may not feel hungry and may skip a few meals. In the latter stages, you may lose your appetite altogether and begin to lose a significant amount of weight.
- *Anxiety.* Symptoms of tension, worry, and edginess. As you move closer to burnout, the anxiety may become so serious that it interferes with your ability to work productively and may cause problems in your personal life.
- *Anger.* Interpersonal tension and irritability. This may turn into angry outbursts and serious arguments at home and in the workplace.
- *Loss of enjoyment.* Not wanting to go to work or being eager to leave, or trying to avoid challenges and figure out ways to escape work all together.
- *Pessimism.* A general sense that nothing is going right or nothing matters, issues of trust with co-workers and family members and a feeling that you can't count on anyone.
- *Isolation.* In the early stages, this may seem like mild resistance to socialising; in the latter stages, you may become angry when

someone speaks to you, or you may come into work early or leave late to avoid interactions with fellow workers.

- *Detachment*. Removing yourself emotionally and physically from your job and other responsibilities; you may call in sick often, stop returning calls and emails, or regularly come in late.
- *Depression*. In the early stages, you may feel mildly sad, occasionally hopeless, and you may experience feelings of guilt and worthlessness as a result. At its worst, you may feel trapped, severely depressed, and think the world would be better off without you. (If your depression has reached this point, you have to seek professional help immediately.)

You can read more about this topic in *The Truth about Burnout: How Organisations Cause Personal Stress and What to do about it*, by Christina Maslach and Michael P. Leiter, or – on a lighter note – in *Fried: Why you Burn Out and how to Revive*, by Joan Borysenko.

Surprisingly enough, top performers are most likely to experience burnout, because they are given the toughest assignments with the biggest challenges. They are the most likely to struggle with overwork, and least likely to ask for help or set limits. Burnout is not a simple result of hard work or long hours. The cynicism, depression and lethargy of burnout can happen when you're not in control of how you carry out your job, when you're working toward goals that don't resonate with you, and when you lack social support. If you don't tailor your responsibilities to match your true talent, or at least take a break once in a while, you could face a mountain of mental and physical health problems. Beware!

Resilience factors

For sure, the origins of our stress are often outside of ourselves, and the way our body and mind react are largely physiological and thus beyond our immediate control. However, a combination of factors can contribute to our resilience. Many studies show that the most important factor is having caring and supportive relationships within and outside the family. Relationships that create love and trust, provide role models and offer encouragement and kind words help reinforce a person's resilience.

Besides social support, several additional factors are associated with resilience, including:

- A healthy life style.
- A positive view of yourself and confidence in your strengths.
- The ability to make realistic plans and carry them out.
- Skills in communication and problem solving.
- The ability to manage strong feelings and impulses.

All of these are factors that people can develop themselves. Some, or many of the ways to build resilience in the following pages may be appropriate to think about in developing your personal approach.

Social support

Many studies show that social support is extremely important for maintaining physical and mental health. Both the harmful results of poor social support, and the protecting effects of good social support have been extensively documented. Social support has been described as 'support accessible to an individual through social bonds with other individuals, groups, and the larger community – a network of family, friends, neighbours, and community members.' One might add that the possibility of being able to call on the help of a mentor or a coach could also be counted as social support. Coaches like Ian McDermott (https://www.linkedin.com/in/ianemcdermott) recommend the 'buddy system', especially for managers, in this respect.

As to exactly what social support means, maybe the psychiatrist Sidney Cobb gave one of the best definitions. He proposed that social support was a subjective sensation in which the individual feels: 'That he is cared for and loved. That he is esteemed and valued; that he belongs to a network of communication and mutual obligation.'

Theoretical models of social support specify the following two important dimensions:

- A *structural dimension,* which includes network size and frequency of social interactions.
- A *functional dimension* with emotional (such as receiving love and empathy) and instrumental (practical help such as gifts of money or assistance with child care) components.

Most research has found that the *quality* of relationships (the functional dimension) is a better predictor of good health than the *quantity* of relationships (the structural dimension), although both are important.

For expats, or people working outside the place where they live (commuters), this may pose a particular problem. They have had to leave their homes, their relatives, fellow workers and social networks behind, and may find it very hard to build a new network of social support from the ground up. I have seen brilliant people – highly skilled and motivated professionals – who could not successfully deal with this. I remember from my time working for the EU one Spanish fellow worker who had left his girlfriend back home during the nine months of his probation period. He was so homesick and socially isolated that he decided to quit prematurely, giving up the prospect of life-long employment and an interesting job. I think this was probably the best decision he could make, because, if he had stayed, he was bound to run into serious trouble, deeply unhappy at work, and ultimately a burnout.

International companies with many expats are well aware of this. That is why they are actively involved in the many leisure, sports and cultural clubs open to staff and their families, including athletics, dance, theatre, art and language exchange. I would also advise you to break out of your daily work routine, and join local organisations and (service) clubs. This will help to build a strong network of social support.

The benefits of reading for pleasure

'Reading is to the mind what exercise is to the body' – Richard Steele (1672-1729)

A recent study done at the University of Liverpool explored the emotional, social and mental benefits to adults of regular reading for pleasure.

Regular readers for pleasure reported fewer feelings of stress and depression than non-readers, and stronger feelings of relaxation from reading than from watching television or engaging with social media. Reading creates a parallel world in which personal worries can move away, while also helping people to realise that the problems they experience are not theirs alone. A fifth of people who responded said reading helped them to feel less lonely.

Those who read for pleasure also have higher levels of self-confidence and a greater ability to cope with tough situations. Readers have expanded models and repertoires of experience, which allow them to look with new perspectives and understanding on their own lives. Readers find it easier to make decisions, to plan and prioritise, and this may be because they are more able to recognise that trouble and setbacks are unavoidable facets of human life.

People who read regularly feel closer to their friends and their community than lapsed or non-readers. Reading not only produces greater understanding and empathy with others; it also gives a currency for sharing experience more meaningfully than is possible in ordinary social conversation. Readers also have a stronger and more engaged awareness of social issues and of cultural diversity than non-readers.

The conclusions of the study were that readers feel happier about themselves and their lives. Reading for just 30 minutes a week produces greater happiness, enhances social connectedness and sense of community spirit, and helps protect against, and even prepare for life's struggles.

Mens sana in corpore sano

The expression *mens sana in corpore sano* – 'a sound mind in a sound body' – is widely used to express the idea that physical health is an important part of mental well being. Caring for your physical needs by eating healthy food, exercising, finding time to relax, and getting enough sleep can help you successfully deal with stress:

- *Eating healthily* can help boost your brain's serotonin levels, which will combat higher cortisol associated with stress.
- *Exercise* and other physical activity produce endorphins – chemicals in the brain that act as natural painkillers.
- *Stay well-hydrated* – keeping the body hydrated helps the heart pump blood more easily through the blood vessels to the muscles and your brain.

Stress and smoking

When I was still a smoker – I used to smoke cigars – I was convinced that smoking relieves stress. Studies have found, however, that in reality, smoking has the opposite effect; it causes long-term stress levels to rise, not fall.

In one study done at the London School of Medicine and Dentistry, researchers looked at 469 people who tried to quit smoking after being hospitalised for heart disease. At the start, the subjects had almost the same levels of stress and generally believed that smoking helped them to cope.

A year later, 41 per cent had managed to stay abstinent. After controlling for several factors, the scientists found that the abstainers had 'a significantly larger decrease in perceived stress,' roughly a 20 per cent drop, compared with the continuing smokers, who showed little change.

The scientists' hypothesis was that the continuing smokers were dealing with uncomfortable cravings between cigarettes many times a day, while the abstainers, after facing some initial withdrawal, had greater freedom from nicotine cravings and thus had eliminated a frequent and significant source of stress.

The bottom line: the calming effect of a cigarette is a myth, at least in the long term.

- *Sleep* is a necessary human function – it allows our brains to recharge and our bodies to rest, which in turn reduces stress. Your brain needs downtime to stay sharp. If you don't get enough sleep, you'll tax your memory and start forgetting things. Stay rested so you can keep your mind alert.
- *Limit alcohol intake.* Alcohol is a depressant, which means that it slows down the brain and the central nervous system's processes.
- *Limit caffeine intake.* The effects of drinking coffee are long-lasting and exaggerate the stress response, both in terms of the body's physiological response as reflected in raised blood pressure and stress hormone levels, and also in terms of increasing a person's feeling of being stressed.

The brain is roughly 2% of our body weight, but uses about 20% of the oxygen. The ability to get more oxygen to the brain allows more of the brain to be accessed, and a healthy body can make this happen.

Positive thinking

'Optimism is a moral duty' – Immanuel Kant

A study released in 2013 found that positive-thinking people have a better biological response to stress than pessimists. Researchers at Concordia University's Department of Psychology found that 'the stress hormone' cortisol tends to be more stable in people with a positive outlook.

Joelle Jobin found that pessimists tend to have a higher stress baseline than optimists. Pessimists generally had trouble regulating their sympathetic nervous system when they go through stressful experiences. The inability to look on the bright side causes cortisol to stay constantly elevated.

Like most hormones in our bodies, 'the stress hormone' cortisol is complex with many functions. Although cortisol is linked to many health problems it is also our 'get up and do things hormone,' according to Jobin. Just like we have 'eustress' (good stress) and 'distress' (bad stress), we need cortisol to stimulate our sympathetic nervous system and kick-start our bodies into action.

Each of us has the free will to be an optimist or a pessimist. The daily choices of mind-set and behaviour that we make create biological changes throughout our bodies that have long lasting ramifications.

In his *Rational Emotive Behaviour Therapy* (REBT) US psychologist Albert Ellis argued that:

- Unconditional self-acceptance, other-acceptance and life-acceptance are of prime importance in achieving mental wellness.
- People and the world are fallible and people are better off accepting themselves and others, life's hassles and unfairness, as they are.
- People have to consider themselves valuable just as a result of being alive and kicking, because all humans do both good and bad deeds and have both good and bad attributes and traits.

Clearly, all this can certainly not be an excuse to just 'cop out', i.e. take the easy way out of a sticky situation; you are responsible for your own behaviour and development after all.

Lastly, for reading matter, I would strongly recommend the excellent guides to mindfulness and emotional intelligence by Gill Hasson.

Planning

'To achieve great things, two things are needed: a plan and not quite enough time' – Leonard Bernstein, US composer and conductor

We all come across periods of very high workload and tight deadlines, but some people simply don't know how to handle this. They get really upset, and start running around like headless chickens. Not good enough progress is made and, obviously, the deadlines are not met. This creates even greater stress.

Before I start with our individual behaviour during these periods of high stress, let me talk about what the bestselling author on change and motivation, John Kotter, says about urgency. In his book *A Sense of Urgency* Kotter identifies the single biggest factor to successful change: creating a true sense of urgency. Urgency he says, is 'a compulsive determination to move, and win, now.'

Resilient behaviour in these situations is to keep your cool, step back a bit, and make a plan. The key to managing your stress under these circumstances is to kill the negative emotions and stay in control.

Planning does NOT mean working longer hours, dropping holidays, or taking work home during the weekends. Now I am not saying that – from time to time – you cannot do this, but it has to fit into your plan; if burning long hours at work is your only strategy to cope with workload stress you are bound to run into a burnout.

Planning means staying in control, and not being controlled by your negative emotions. Planning means cutting the big problem into smaller chunks, allocating time and resources, deciding on the priorities, outsourcing, delegating or asking for help, and possibly even renegotiating the expectations in terms of outcome or deadlines. Breaks and time to relax have to also be part of your plan.

Learn to say 'No'. It may be pressures from family and/or work that lead to too much stress, and sometimes it may be expectations that you have of yourself that might not be completely realistic. If you don't set priorities for your own life, someone else will.

Don't allow a heavy workload to frustrate you. When the pressures are coming from something over which you have no control, rather than fight against it, accept it and move on, like a true professional.

Dealing with variations in workload

Variations in workload happen in almost every job; periods of heavy workload are followed by relatively calmer periods. This can be due to the inherently periodic nature of the organisation's activities (e.g. meeting agendas, budget cycle, etc.) or simply because of holiday periods.

We have already seen how good planning can help you successfully deal with the periods of heavy workload, but effective management of your agenda can be very useful during the calmer periods as well. Here are some things you can schedule for the calmer periods at work:

- *Taking care of your pile of unfinished work*. Activities that were delayed during the 'busy' period because they were not urgent – and not so important – can usefully be performed during a calmer period. Typically, dealing with unanswered emails is one of these activities.
- *Cleaning up*. Reorganising your desktop, filing documents, inventory, etc.
- *Anticipating future work*. Preparing forms, lists of questions, checklists, contact lists, etc.
- *Planning*. It is often possible to plan ahead, even when not all the necessary details are available yet.
- *Professional and personal development*. Training, workshops, seminars and conferences.
- *Networking*. Calmer periods are great opportunities to take care of your social support networks.
- *Recharging your batteries*. Clear your brain by taking holidays, physical activity, spending more time on the things you enjoy, etc.

Communicating and problem solving

Mental noise is the constant chatter of the mind that never stops. It is the inner conversation that goes on constantly in the mind. This mental noise is like a background noise that never stops, from the moment of waking up to the moment of falling asleep. It is a sort of inner voice that constantly analyses everything about what you are doing, what is going on around you, and the people you meet.

The mind also repeats the same thoughts over and over again, like in a loop, like a record that got stuck. If these are positive thoughts, that's fine. However, too often, they are negative thoughts that strengthen stress, worry, anger or frustration.

Clearly, thinking is an important activity required for solving problems, analysing, comparing, studying, planning, etc. – but too often, the mind wanders where it will, occupying your attention with trivial matters and unimportant, useless thinking that wastes your time and energy.

The mind is a tool therefore that needs to be kept under control. The mental noise theory states that clear communication happens only when we overcome a certain degree of mental distraction. It further suggests that when people are stressed, they have greater struggle hearing, understanding and remembering information.

Here are some important things to keep in mind when communicating under stress at work:

- *Listen first.* The higher the level of stress, the more important it is to show that you are listening. People are more willing to listen to what you have to say when they believe you are listening to them in turn. In the words of Stephen Covey: 'Seek first to understand, then to be understood'.
- *Clarity, brevity and repetition.* Remember, the greater the stress, the greater the need for clarity, brevity, and repetition. To help people understand your message, provide information in small portions that are easily absorbed. Use familiar words and simple sentences, and repeat important points, to be sure that you are understood.

- *Make it personal.* Use face-to-face communication, not email or text messaging, to help get your message across during times of high stress. When interacting in person, pay particular attention to body language, as this is directly linked to people's emotions.

Another human feature that often blocks communication is our inclination to focus on the negative. This is called negative dominance theory or negativity bias. Because of this bias, people generally attach more weight to negative statements – and remember them longer – and this tendency of concentrating on what is perceived to be negative becomes even stronger when we are stressed out. So it is important to increase the ratio of positive to negative statements in times of high stress.

The more stressful our environment, the more we need to connect and communicate. In times of crisis and anxiety people need to feel listened to, and feel that they belong to the group. In these circumstances, more than ever, our communication must show compassion, conviction, truthfulness and integrity. Our presentations, conversations and documents must be brief, clear and repeat key messages. Remember that the features of good communication don't change under stress; they just become more important.

Self-control

'You have power over your mind – not outside events. Realise this, and you will find strength' – Marcus Aurelius, Roman military leader, philosopher and emperor 161 to 180

Self-control separates us from our primitive ancestors and from the animals, thanks to our large prefrontal cortices. Rather than responding to immediate impulses, we can plan, we can evaluate alternative actions, and we can refrain from doing things we may eventually regret.

For most people, stress or boredom makes them instinctively reach for something to relieve it, and this often takes the instant-gratification form of sugar, alcohol, nicotine or distractions like social media.

Train yourself to be aware when you are entering your danger zone (i.e. feeling stressed out, tired, bored, etc.). Becoming more aware of your mood and the likelihood of lapsing will help you to act with purpose instead of habit. But it is not enough to simply try to break a bad habit; the process is much more effective when actively replacing it with a good habit. If you're addicted to nicotine, try chewing gum to address the oral fixation, but avoid substituting food for the cigarette. Remember, this isn't just a habit you're trying to kick; it's a lifestyle adjustment. Cultivate a new way of being.

Anger management involves spotting the triggers for anger as early as possible and expressing these feelings and frustrations in a cool, calm and composed way. Anger management is about *unlearning* ineffective coping mechanisms and re-learning more effective ways to deal with the problems and frustrations connected with anger. There are many anger management techniques that you can learn and practise by yourself. However if you experience a lot of regular anger then seeking help, in the form of a counsellor, can be more effective.

Dealing with change

At work, change is unavoidable, and dealing with change needs some mental adjustments:

- Approach change as a process; processes take time.
- Embrace change; choose to give positive meaning to changes.
- Move with changes – they are going to happen anyway.

If you are aware of an upcoming change, such as a move or a new job, you can help to reduce stress about the event in multiple ways:

- *Create an action plan.* By setting SMART goals (see Chapter 11) and creating a series of steps to get from one intermediate objective to another, you will feel more in control of the situation, which helps to minimise your stress.
- *One change at a time.* If you have a big change coming up, it's important that you create consistency in the rest of your life as much as possible. For example, if you're going to be changing jobs soon it may be best not to attempt to change personal habits (stop smoking for example) at the same time.
- *Rely on your social support network.*

Sometimes, change happens without warning. Here too, there are some steps you can take to help you cope and adapt:

- *Relax*. Try to take time to relax every day, even if it's only for a few minutes. You can also use relaxation techniques like meditation or deep breathing as a tool for coping with stress.
- *Laugh*. Laughter can help decrease the effects of stress.
- *Seek professional support*. If stress management techniques do not work for you, then seek care from a qualified professional such as a life coach, a therapist, or social worker.

Working with your manager

'The single biggest problem in communication is the illusion that it has taken place' – variously attributed

Members of hierarchical organisations mainly communicate with their immediate superior and with their immediate subordinates. Structuring organisations in this way is useful because it can reduce the communication overhead by limiting information flow. However, this is also its major limitation.

Communication builds working relationships that allow people within an organisation to coordinate their efforts for the common good. Communication flowing up the chain of command gives management valuable information about the state of affairs. Feedback, reports, suggestions and work needs all flow from subordinate to manager. Communications that flow down from one level to the next range from operational to strategic matters. Starting at the top, though, management must also provide leadership by communicating broader concerns – guiding principles, such as the organisation's vision, mission and strategic goals.

The problem is that communication is never perfect. This is because all organisations are built with people, and people aren't perfect. Perfect leaders or perfect managers do not exist; even the most highly esteemed, world-class leaders have their personal weaknesses and blind spots. Your superior may be inexperienced in their new job; they may have been promoted to their 'level of incompetence' (the Peter Principle, mentioned on page 50); or – at worst – they may

"I have a few complaints about
how you're doing your job
as my boss."

have a hidden agenda. In any case, your interaction with management will never be without stress and anxiety.

Having worked with many not-so-inspiring managers in my
own career, I learned that they provided me with unique opportunities for developing my own leadership skills, and learning 'what
not to do' when managing people myself. However bad your manager may be, you can always develop ways to handle your relationship with him or her in a better way. Rather than think of your line
manager as your 'boss', think of them as a difficult 'client' – one
you have to figure out how to work with if you want to get ahead,
even if you'd rather not be in that situation.

In any event, it's better for you to work with the management
rather than against it; here are some strategies to help you on your
way:

- *Know their 'why'*. The better you understand what your manager
  does, and more importantly, why they do it, the better positioned
  you are to deliver results, manage expectations, and avoid lose-
  lose situations. When you know what drives your manager, you
  can structure your views and communicate in ways that line up
  with their core values, worries and main concerns.
- *Adapt your communication style*. If you have ever done a
  personality assessment like the MBTI (see Chapter 10), try to find

out what your manager's preferences are, and how these may be different from yours. It can help you adapt your communication style and save a lot of tension.

- *Work around their weaknesses.* Exposing your manager's incompetence will only reinforce your misery and may even damage your own reputation. By doing what you can to help your manager succeed, you lay a solid foundation for more success for yourself.
- *Keep your mind focused on top performance.* Never let your manager's bad behaviour be an excuse for your own. As Gandhi wrote: 'Be the change you want to see in the world.' In this case, act like the leader you wish your manager was.
- *Have the courage to speak up.* Instead of saying nothing, suffering in silence, or complaining privately to fellow workers, speak up; you at least owe your manager the opportunity to respond.

And don't forget: nothing lasts forever! On average, we only work for the same manager for a couple of years; natural staff mobility will take care of that.

Personality type and stress

Everybody has a different reaction to stress. One of the main differentiators is our personality. Table 7.2 at the end of this chapter lists some possible tactics you can apply, depending on your MBTI preferences (which you can read more about in Chapter 10).

The Upside of Stress by Kelly McGonigal is a book that brings together research on the relationship between resilience and mindset. It works together science, stories, and exercises with the idea of showing you:

- How to cultivate a mindset to embrace stress.
- How stress can provide focus and energy.
- How stress can help you connect and strengthen relationships.
- Why your brain is built to learn from stress, and how to increase its ability to learn from challenging experiences.

McGonigal's TED talk on the same subject has had more than 7 million views.

Key points to remember

- *Being resilient is ordinary, not extraordinary.*
- *Stress is the body's response to change.*
- *Stress is defined in many different ways and stress and the types of things that cause stress can vary from person to person.*
- *Your social support network is by far the most important tool to become resilient.*
- *You can control stress and stay in control by carefully anticipating and planning work and life.*
- *Stress can be turned into positive energy and stressful situations are – in fact – learning opportunities.*

And finally... some things to avoid

- *Having little or no social contact with fellow workers, friends or family.*
- *Having an unhealthy lifestyle.*
- *Maintaining a negative, pessimistic outlook.*
- *Not listening to what other people have to say.*
- *Becoming stressed or panicking when under pressure.*
- *Displaying negative emotions to others inappropriately.*
- *Losing self-confidence and self-esteem after a failure or setback.*
- *Responding defensively to criticism.*
- *Not taking steps to establish the conditions for smooth working relations.*
- *Reacting negatively to change.*

Table 7.2: Stressors and tactics by personality type

Your Preferences	Your Stressors	Possible Tactics
Extraversion	• Working alone • Having to communicate mainly in writing • Lengthy work periods without interruptions • Having to reflect before taking action • Having to focus in depth on one thing • Getting feedback in writing only	• Networking with others outside your team • Asking others to voice their ideas • Paying attention to written communication • Allowing others to think about your ideas before they provide feedback
Introversion	• Working with others • Having to communicate mainly by talking • Interacting with others frequently • Having to act quickly, without reflection • Too many concurrent tasks and demands • Getting frequent and verbal feedback	• Arriving at work early, taking advantage of the quiet time • Intentionally seeking private/reflective time, taking a walk over lunchtime or the long way home • Planning private breaks to collect your thoughts • In meetings, voicing even partially thought-through perspectives
Intuition	• Having to attend to realities • Having to do things the proven way • Having to attend to details • Checking the accuracy of facts • Needing to focus on past experience • Being required to be practical	• Practise presenting information in a step-by-step manner • Providing specific examples of vital information • Honouring organisational values surrounding experience and tradition • Reading the fine print and getting the facts straight

Your Preferences	Your Stressors	Possible Tactics
Sensing	• Attending to own and others' insights • Having to do old things in a new way • Having to give an overview without details • Looking for the meaning of facts • Focusing on possibilities • Too many complexities	• Getting involved in projects that require long-range or future thinking • Practise brainstorming • Preparing yourself to look for patterns • Going beyond specifics, trying to discover meaning and themes
Thinking	• Using personal experience to assess situations • Adjusting to individual differences and needs • Noticing and appreciating what is positive • Focusing on processes and people • Using empathy and personal values to make decisions • Having others react to questioning as divisive	• Working on projects in which alternative causes and solutions are evaluated in personal terms • Reminding yourself that factoring in people is logical even if people aren't • Softening critical remarks, finding the positive too • Asking for others' opinions and concerns; looking for points of agreement before discussing issues
Feeling	• Analysing situations objectively • Setting criteria and standards • Critiquing and focusing on flaws • Being expected to use logic alone to make decisions • Asking questions that feel divisive	• Practise laying out an argument by saying 'if…then', or by considering the causes and effects • Understanding that critical feedback is often given in the spirit of improving your professionalism • Paying attention to stakeholders' concern regarding project/work • Using brief and concise language to express your wants and needs

Table 7.2 – cont.

Your Preferences	Your Stressors	Possible Tactics
Judging	• Waiting for structures to emerge from process • Too much flexibility around time frames and deadlines • Having to marshal energy at the last minute • Staying open to re-evaluation of tasks • Dealing with surprises	• Seeking out projects that have definite planning and milestones • Trying to wait on a decision for a few days, continuing to gather more information and paying attention to ideas that may come up • Understand that work is progressing despite differences in work styles • Making your own milestones and deadlines
Perceiving	• Having to organise their and others' plans • Working with time frames and deadlines • Others' distrust of last minute energy • Having to finish and move on • Developing contingency plans • Being required to plan ahead	• Recognising that deadlines set by the organisation may not be negotiable • Using a past decision you believe others rushed to demonstrate the advantages of slowing down to gather more information • Becoming active in projects where the process is just as important as the outcome • Keeping surprises to a minimum and reducing your options

8. Managing and leading

"From now on, my bad
decisions will be called
leadership experiments."

'Before you are a leader, success is all about growing yourself. When you become a leader, success is all about growing others' – Jack Welch, long-time boss of General Electric

Strong leaders are highly sought-after worldwide, and many universities pride themselves on nurturing the next generation of leaders. For this reason, some universities and business schools offer leadership scholarships. Leadership scholarships reward students who show skills in motivating others in and out of the classroom. If you have taken on a leadership role, whether it was for the university's sport team, your student society, outside organisation, or volunteer group, you may be qualified to earn free money for college.

Even if you didn't take on a leadership role in university or college, at work you will be expected to, and maybe sooner than you think.

But what is 'managing and leading' anyway?

Managing consists of supervising a group of people or a set of entities to achieve a (limited) goal. *Leading* refers to influencing, motivating, and enabling others to contribute toward organisational success. Leaders are those that others look to for direction, inspiration, advice, and to keep others going when the going gets tough.

Influence and inspiration distinguish leaders from managers, not power and control. I will expand on this distinction further on in this chapter, but for now just keep in mind that if you find yourself in this position you will be expected to:

- Explain your vision and ideas clearly and succinctly.
- Strike a good balance between detail and the need for clarity.
- Set specific goals and priorities for completing assignments.
- Design realistic work methods, procedures and timetables.
- Plan and assign work effectively and fairly.
- Set realistic but challenging goals.
- Provide resources, guidance, and training for subordinates to do their jobs.
- Do your work in an enthusiastic and effective manner.
- Work in a way that inspires confidence and trust.
- Adapt communication to your audience.
- Distinguish between 'need to know' and 'nice to know.'
- Speak with conviction and authority.
- Listen to, synthesise, and integrate others' ideas.
- Display openness and transparency in sharing information.
- Be prepared to deliver tough messages when necessary.
- Recommend corrective action or discipline when appropriate.
- Counsel workers privately behind closed doors.
- Inspire and help others to develop skills and competencies.
- Show a high degree of self-awareness.
- Ask others for feedback on your own performance.
- Give others feedback on their performance.
- Communicate performance expectations clearly.
- Be 'real' in everything you do or say.
- Lead and motivate others by example.
- Inspire others to perform at their best.
- Show drive and determination to succeed.

- Delegate work to develop skills and knowledge.
- Make yourself visible and accessible to fellow workers.

Anchors for 'managing and leading'

- Explaining ideas clearly, simplifying the complex.
- Adapting communication to the level of the audience.
- Communicating clearly and knowledgeably.
- Sharing information with others.
- Seeking input from others.
- Understanding and supporting organisational goals.
- Helping others perform at their best.
- Being self-aware and open to feedback.
- Leading by example.
- Delegating effectively.

Managing or leading?

'*I have a dream*' – Martin Luther King Jr.

Leaders lead people. Managers manage tasks. There is a difference.

Managers have *subordinates*; they have a position of authority vested in them by the organisation. Management is transactional; it operates within the framework of a fixed set of rules. The manager tells the subordinate what to do, and the subordinate does this because they have been promised a reward (a salary, a promotion...) for doing so. Managers are paid to get things done (they are subordinates too), often within tight constraints of time, resources and results. Managers are relatively risk-averse and they will seek to avoid conflict wherever possible. Management is 'Motivation 2.0' in Daniel Pink's terminology (see page 250).

Leaders have *followers*. Many leaders do also have subordinates, but only because they are also managers. However, when they want to lead they have to give up their formal authority because following (or being led) is a voluntary activity. This does not mean that leaders do not pay attention to tasks – in fact they are often very

Table 8.1: Which of these sound like you?

UNSATISFACTORY	IMPROVEMENT NEEDED	MEETS EXPECTATIONS	EXCEEDS EXPECTATIONS	EXCEPTIONAL
Appears distracted or uninterested.	Is hesitant and transmits uncertainty with body language or tone of voice.	Engages spontaneously with his/her audience.	Explains vision and ideas clearly and succinctly.	Explains even complex issues and ideas clearly and succinctly; simplifies the complex.
Does not listen to what others say.	Interrupts others to express own point of view.	Tailors information to audience and individual needs.	Effectively adjusts the level of detail and tone to the audience.	Speaks with conviction and authority.
Does not share information in a timely manner, creating problems for fellow workers and customers.	Has difficulty getting to the point.	Appears knowledgeable and enthusiastic.	Appears credible and reliable.	Listens to, synthesises, and integrates others' ideas.
Shies away from delivering tough messages.	Tends to 'hold on' to information; has difficulty distinguishing between critical and noncritical information.	Actively listens to and synthesises perspectives of others.	Shares accurate, timely information with the right people in the right format.	Displays openness and transparency in sharing information with others.
Avoids contact with co-workers and partners.	Keeps communication to a minimum; is reluctant to share thoughts and ideas.	Gives others the information they need in a timely manner.	Encourages others to share ideas and integrates others' thoughts and opinions.	Is prepared to deliver tough messages when necessary.
Maintains focus on immediate, routine tasks.	Does not openly share expertise or information with others.	Assists others in developing skills and knowledge.	Understands and supports the need to align work with organisational initiatives and goals.	Encourages and leads changes that enhance organisational and workforce effectiveness.
Hinders sharing of knowledge and/or expertise, focused largely on own development.	Rarely asks for help or feedback.	Helps people to resolve problems and overcome obstacles.	Coaches and/or mentors others.	
Fails to create development opportunities for others	Keeps too low a profile to make a leadership impact.	Is self-aware and open to feedback from others.	Creates targeted development opportunities for others.	Spots and nurtures potential future talent.
Demotivates others.		Displays integrity.	Sets a good example in terms of enthusiasm and commitment.	

Table 8.1: continued

UNSATISFACTORY	IMPROVEMENT NEEDED	MEETS EXPECTATIONS	EXCEEDS EXPECTATIONS	EXCEPTIONAL
Betrays lack of conviction in chances of success.	Does not react when developments require assertive action.	Is enthusiastic about his/her work and transmits enthusiasm to others.	Encourages and engages staff to make optimal use of skills and knowledge.	Shows a high degree of self-awareness; asks others for feedback on performance; is a continuous learner.
Does not delegate; does most of the work by himself.	Is inconsistent in supporting staff to achieve defined goals.	Plans ahead and organises work.	Makes himself visible and accessible to fellow workers.	Is authentic in everything he does or says.
Assigns work inappropriately.	Doesn't effectively match work assignments to staff talent and proficiencies.	Thoughtfully delegates work to develop staff and achieve goals.	Effectively links work assignments to achieve individual and unit performance goals.	Leads and motivates by example.
Does not keep development and performance goals in mind.	Does little to monitor team progress or provide follow-up.	Monitors team progress and provides follow-up.		Inspires staff to perform at their best.
Has unrealistic expectations and perception of staff skills and knowledge.				Shows drive and determination to succeed.
				Effectively delegates work to develop skills and knowledge.

achievement-focused. What they do realise, however, is the importance of inspiring others to work towards their vision, or the vision of the organisation (the 'Mission Statement'). Leaders are also relatively risk-seeking. They consider it natural to encounter problems and hurdles that must be overcome along the way. They are thus comfortable with risk and will seek routes that others avoid, seeing them as opening up potential opportunities for advantage, and will happily break rules in order to get things done. (Up to a point! Leaders have to set a good example also, and sometimes that means very visibly obeying certain rules – such as presence during core time, seeking or passing on information correctly and at the appropriate time, etc. Some rules can be happily broken – others come at a cost.) Leadership is what Daniel Pink calles 'Motivation 3.0'.

According to John Kotter, bestselling US author and management consultant, management is a set of practices: planning, budgeting, staffing, controlling, problem-solving. Management makes a system function the way it was designed to function while leadership is about creating a vision and motivating people to buy into it.

In his book *Too Many Bosses, Too Few Leaders* (2012) Rajeev Peshawaria presents the underlying dynamics of what it takes to be a great leader. Leadership is a special talent that goes far beyond just being a boss, and he shows that deciding to develop that talent is a critical choice. According to Peshawaria, it is clear that *trust* is one of the keys to organisational or group performance; he therefore calls trust the currency of leadership.

Contrasting the qualities of leaders 'versus' managers of course involves something of a paradox, given that many people have to be both. Managers still can have the responsibility for leading their team into new challenges while making sure systems and procedures operate properly. Also, even the most out-front leaders must make sure that the systems and procedures are in place to deliver on their vision – a general who leads his troops from the front is ill-advised to forget his supply lines. Leadership without management is charismatic chaos; you need both!

	Manager	Leader
Role	Transactional	Transformational
Vision	Short-term	Long-term
Values	Results	Achievements
Approach	Plans around constraints	Sets direction
Concerns	Do things right	Do the right things
Appeals	The Head	The Heart
Decisions	Makes	Facilitates
Control	Formal	Informal
Culture	Endorses	Shapes
Actions	Directs	Inspires
Risks	Minimizes	Embraces
Rules	Makes	Breaks
Direction	Status quo	Challenges
Focus	Managing work	Lead people
Collaborators	Subordinates	Followers

Table 8.2: Managers and leaders compared

Leadership vs. management

John is the manager of a McDonalds franchise and Pierre is the chef of a fine, French cuisine restaurant. John has to make sure that his restaurant is properly operated and complies with all McDonalds' standards, policies and strategies. John cannot choose the style of the decoration, the way food is prepared, the ingredients and even the way he hires and manages staff as everything is written down by McDonalds. McDonalds wants to give the same experience to all its customers, worldwide. John is a manager.

Pierre, on the other hand, has a dream. Pierre wants to create a unique – and excellent – customer experience. He wants to distinguish his restaurant from the crowd. His dream is to gain a Michelin Star – or even two – and he does whatever it takes to get this award, and to keep it for years after that. Besides being an excellent cook and manager Pierre has to inspire his co-workers to follow his dream. Pierre is a leader.

Leadership styles

There are as many ways to lead people as there are leaders.

Leaders usually have a dominant personal style, one they use in a wide variety of situations. However, there is no one 'best' style – leaders must adapt their style to the people being led and to the situation at hand. This is a key point. As a leader, you sometimes have to be autocratic (with some people) while 'laissez-faire' with others. Much depends on the level of independence of the individual concerned: some need a lot more handholding than others. It's a delicate balancing act, and one that we don't always get right. The important thing is that you shouldn't beat yourself up about getting it wrong occasionally, but just learn from the mistake.

Fortunately, a number of useful frameworks that describe the main ways that people lead have been developed. When you understand these frameworks, you can develop your own approach to leadership, and become a more effective leader as a result.

Lewin's leadership styles

Psychologist Kurt Lewin developed his 'leadership styles' framework in the 1930s, and it provided the foundation of many of the approaches that followed afterwards. He argued that there are three major leadership styles:

- *Autocratic* – Also known as authoritarian leadership style. These leaders provide clear expectations for *what* needs to be done, *when* it has to be done, and *how* it has to be done. This style of leadership is strongly focused on both command by the leader and control of the followers. There is also a clear division between the leader and the followers. Autocratic leaders make decisions independently, with little or no input from the rest of the group. This can be appropriate when you need to make decisions quickly, when there's no need for team input, and when team agreement isn't necessary for a successful outcome. However, this style can be demoralising, and it can lead to high levels of absenteeism and staff turnover.

- *Democratic* – Also known as participative leadership style. These leaders make the final decisions, but include team members in the decision-making process. Democratic leaders offer guidance to group members, but they also participate in the group and allow input from other group members. As a result, team members tend to have high job satisfaction and high productivity. This is not always an effective style to use, though, when you need to make a quick decision.
- *Laissez-faire* – Also known as delegative leadership. Leaders give their team members a lot of freedom in how they do their work, and how they set their deadlines. They provide support with resources and advice if needed, but otherwise they don't get involved. This autonomy can lead to high job satisfaction, but it can be detrimental if team members don't manage their time well, or if they don't have the knowledge, skills, or self-motivation to do their work effectively.

The Blake-Mouton managerial grid

A popular framework for thinking about leadership was developed by Robert Blake and Jane Mouton. They defined the following five leadership or management styles.

- *Country Club* – This style of manager is most concerned about the needs and feelings of the members of their team. They operate on the assumption that as long as team members are happy and secure then they will work hard. What tends to result is a work environment that is very relaxed and fun but where productivity suffers due to lack of direction and control.
- *Authority-Compliance* – Managers in this category believe that workers are simply a means to an end. Worker needs are always secondary to the need for efficient workplaces delivering maximum output. This type of manager is very autocratic, has strict work rules, policies, and procedures, and views punishment as the most effective means to motivate staff.
- *Impoverished* – This type of manager is mostly ineffective, failing to lead or manage at all. They have neither a high regard for creating systems for getting the job done, nor for creating a work

environment that is satisfying and motivating. The result is a place of disorganisation, dissatisfaction and disharmony.

- *Middle-of-the-Road* – This style sits somewhere between the 'country club' and the 'authority-compliance' types. It may at first sight appear to be an ideal compromise. However, when you compromise, you can easily end up losing the more positive aspects of the other two styles and keeping only their disadvantages. Managers who adopt the middle-of-the-road style often settle for middle-of-the road results, too, and persuade themselves that this is the most anyone can expect.
- *Team* – According to the Blake-Mouton model, this is the summit of managerial style. These leaders give equal emphasis to the organisation's need for productivity and the needs of the people working for it. Their starting point is that staff needs to understand the organisation's goals and what they need to deliver. When workers are committed to, and have a stake in the organisation's success, their personal needs and the organisation's needs coincide. This creates a team environment based on trust and respect, which leads to high satisfaction and motivation and, as a result, high productivity.

Other leadership theories

There are many other leadership theories around, but this is only an indication of how difficult it is to define a really good leader. To mention just a few:

- The Hersey-Blanchard 'situational leadership'theory
- Six emotional leadership styles by Goleman, Boyatzis and McKee
- Flamholtz and Randle's leadership style matrix

Personality type and leadership

The concepts of personality type and the Myers-Briggs Personality Type Indicator (MBTI) will be discussed more fully in Chapter 10 but it will be useful to say a few words relevant to managing and leading. The MBTI is based on the idea that there are basic human differences in ways of perceiving and processing information. These differences inevitably show up in the working environment and can be the root cause of many interpersonal conflicts.

People who are extravert may find that introverts are hard to read, and may even go so far as to judge them as indifferent, hard-hearted, and even arrogant. Introverts may unfairly judge extraverts as being superficial, unreliable, and dishonest.

A person who values data and focuses on what is actually present (Sensing) will often seem too analytical and detail-oriented to a person who focuses on the big picture and uses intuition.

'Thinking' people can view 'Feeling' people as too emotional, while 'Feeling' people can find that 'Thinkers' are too task-oriented and uncaring.

One of the biggest sources of conflict, however, shows up in differences between 'Judging' and 'Perceiving'. A person whose style is 'Judging' will be an early starter, will organise their work with attention to deadlines, and may find it offensive when others are late or indecisive. On the other hand, perceiving-style people prefer to keep their options open, and wait until the last minute before completing or deciding. The two different personalities can drive each other crazy in a work environment.

Understanding and accepting fundamental differences in human behaviour is essential for managers and leaders alike, and self-awareness is the cornerstone for developing emotional intelligence.

The question 'What personality type makes the best leader?' often comes up. This question does not have a simple answer because all types can be effective as well as ineffective. Studies of thousands of leaders and managers worldwide have shown some profile types to be more predominant, however. This does not imply that these types make better managers, only that they are more predominant in leadership positions. There is a majority of 'Thinking' and 'Judging' preferences among leaders and managers. This is not unexpected, since the structure and values of most organisations favour logical and decisive behaviour. It may even be that 'Thinking' and 'Judging' behaviour has become the accepted description of what it means to lead and people with these preferences are seen as 'leadership material'.

Bear in mind that the most important element in the MBTI – or in any assessment tool – is the improved ability to understand oneself and those one works with.

Leadership in a multicultural environment

In their book *Leadership in a Diverse and Multicultural Environment* (2005) authors Mary Connerly and Paul Pedersen make the case that, no matter how highly skilled, well trained, or intelligent you are, if you make the wrong or culturally inappropriate assumptions, you will not be accurate in your assessment, meaningful in your understanding, or suitable in your interactions as a leader.

It is very hard to know the cultures of others until, and unless, you have an awareness of your own culturally learned assumptions, as these control your life.

A leader has only two choices: to ignore the influence of culture or to attend to it. In either case, however, culture will continue to influence the behaviour of others, with or without the leader's intentional awareness.

Communication

'The art of communication is the language of leadership' — James Humes, US author and presidential speech writer

There's no mystery here. Regardless of whether we are talking about politics, business, the military, or sports, the best leaders are top-class communicators. Their values are clear and concrete, and what they say supports those values. It is simply impossible to become a great leader without being a great communicator.

The best communicators are good listeners and intelligent in their observations. Great communicators are skilled at sensing the moods, dynamics, attitudes, values and concerns of their audience. Not only do they read their audience well, they also possess the ability to adapt their message to the audience without missing a beat. The message is not about the messenger; it is about meeting the needs and the expectations of those you're communicating with.

Real Leaders Don't Do PowerPoint: How to Speak so People Listen (a book by Christopher Witt) highlights a number of very interesting ideas on how to become a more confident, commanding and compelling communicator. The author explains how real leaders speak to make a difference, to promote a vision, to change the way people think and feel and act.

Motivating others

'Control leads to compliance; autonomy leads to engagement' – Daniel H. Pink

Being able to motivate others is the most important trait of both managers and leaders. Managers may be more inclined to use the extrinsic motivators (carrot-and-stick), while leaders will motivate their followers with the three elements of intrinsic motivation – autonomy, mastery, and purpose – in mind.

Autonomy is the extent to which a worker can use their own judgement in making decisions and carrying out their work. Autonomy is strongly related to 'psychological ownership', which is defined as the extent to which a worker feels as though the organisation or the job is 'theirs' – to the point that the organisation and their role in it becomes an important part of a worker's self-identity. Many studies have shown how important the feeling of ownership is for workers. Managers and leaders can increase the autonomy of staff and co-workers and thus their motivation by:

- Involving people in making decisions that influence their work.
- Encouraging people to apply their own judgement.
- Avoiding directive styles of management.
- Making people feel safe to learn from mistakes.

Mastery has everything to do with keeping people in their learning zone, by setting realistic challenges – and allowing them to make mistakes. We all want to get better at doing things. It is why learning a language or an instrument can be so frustrating at first. If you feel like you're not getting anywhere, you lose interest and you may even give up. A sense of progress, not just in our work, but in our capabilities, contributes to our inner drive.

Managers need to calibrate their expectations of what staff *ought* to do by looking realistically at what they *can* do. If the must-do tasks are too hard, people will become worried and feel out of their depth. If the must-do tasks are too easy, they will get bored. The objective has to be to give people tasks, with the necessary space and support, which stretch them in a way that fosters increasing mastery and personal growth. This requires paying more attention to how staff are approaching and feeling about their tasks, in order to avoid them losing heart in trying to cope with tasks that don't match their capabilities.

Finally, *purpose* is also related to psychological ownership through the idea of 'task identity', the extent to which a job allows someone to be involved from the beginning to the end of a project. Managers and leaders can increase 'purpose' by:

- Communicating how workers' activities contribute to the final result so they can see the results of their work and how it fits into the 'bigger picture'.
- Involving workers in more aspects of work by having them participate in the planning, reporting, and evaluation of projects rather than mere execution.
- Providing workers with the opportunity to completely finish any work they start.

Leadership vs. management revisited

I have experienced perhaps one of the more extreme examples of the difference between leadership and management in my own career when working with outsourced staff, also known as 'body shopping'. Body shopping is the practice of sub-contracting where one organisation buys the technical expertise of another organisation's workers. It enables organisations to access skilled individuals or a team of professionals to work remotely or on their premises, in conjunction with its existing teams. Body shopping can help an organisation deal with the pressures of staff shortages on a short or longer-term basis, or to plug critical technology skills gaps within its own staff. For IT staff, body shopping is widely used, especially for developing software.

In my activities as software development manager I had to rely on more than half of my staff being body shoppers; staff that were hired from external companies for the sole purpose of developing software systems. Under Belgian law it is illegal to have a 'hierarchical' relationship with external staff; there can only be a contractual relationship between the customer and the supplier – who is the real 'employer' of these resources. In practice this meant that I did have the responsibility over the results, but not the formal authority; I had to be their leader, but could not be their manager. The 'stick-and-carrot' approach was not applicable in this context, and other – softer – motivation techniques had to be applied.

- Explaining their decisions and how they have come to them.

I strongly urge you to read Daniel Pink's book *Drive: The Surprising Truth About What Motivates Us* (2011). As a manager – or leader – you have to factor this into your own behaviour.

Starting with 'why?'

'Every organisation in the world knows WHAT they do, some organisations know HOW they do it, but very few organisations know WHY they do what they do.'

This is the main idea behind Simon Sinek's book *Start with Why – How Great Leaders Inspire Everyone to take Action*. In studying the leaders who have had the greatest influence in the world, Simon Sinek discovered that they all think, act, and communicate in the exact same way – and it's the complete opposite of what everyone else does. People like Martin Luther King Jr., Steve Jobs, and the Wright Brothers might have little obvious in common, but they all started with the question 'why?'

Sinek claims that there is actually a biological explanation for this; when we are communicating from the inside out we are talking directly to the limbic system. The limbic system supports a variety of functions including emotion, behaviour, motivation, and long-term memory. In fact we are addressing the person through their heart, not their mind. Allow me to suggest that you have a look at Sinek's TED talk where he explains in more detail his simple but powerful model for inspirational leadership.

Coaching and mentoring

'Treat someone as he wants to be and he will become that person' – Goethe

American newspaper columnist George Matthew Adams observed that there are high spots in all of our lives and most of them have come about through support and encouragement from someone else. Whether the encouragement came informally or through a deliberate, formal program, helping us personally or professionally, we can all easily identify people who influenced and shaped our future; those were or are our coaches and mentors.

For managers and leaders it is important to realise that our subordinates and co-workers need our support and encouragement as well. In fact, the degree to which we coach, or mentor, others defines to a large extent how good, or bad, we are as managers or leaders.

It is easy to get confused about the differences between coaching and mentoring. The purpose and expected outcome of each is distinctly different although, at times, some overlap exists.

Mentoring is a pairing of a more skilled or experienced person, usually in the same field of knowledge, with a less experienced person. Ideally mentors have no line management relationship to the mentee. Mentors will often provide direction and advice and open organisational doors for mentees. Mentors have to provide a neutral sounding board, assure total confidentiality, and have no agenda other than assisting their mentees in their development and in reaching their goals. Mentoring involves helping people to develop their career, skills and expertise, drawing upon the experience of the mentor. Mentoring focuses on the 'horizontal' development (learning) of the mentee.

Coaching. While 'master-pupil' relationships have existed throughout human history, coaching as a discipline – and profession – is relatively new. Its first application in a business context was pioneered in the 1980s by Sir John Whitmore and Timothy Gallwey, author of *The Inner Game of Work*, who challenged traditional ideas by claiming that a coach's role was to remove or reduce the internal obstacles to a person's performance, without the need for much technical input from the coach. They defined coaching as: 'Unlocking a person's potential to maximise their performance.'

In their opinion, coaching is about helping people to learn rather than teaching them. Coaches need not have first-hand experience of the coachee's line of work. Leaders and managers can use coaching techniques successfully in the management and development of team members. Coaches will ask 'powerful' questions and not offer or give advice; it is up to the coachee to find the answers. Coaching focuses on the 'vertical' development of the coachee.

Another interesting book is *Coaching for Performance: GROWing human potential and purpose*, by John Whitmore. Over 500,000 copies sold! I had the pleasure of attending a three-day classroom training at Whitmore's institute, Performance Consultants International (PCI). If you ever have the opportunity, I can only recommend it.

There are many models for coaching, depending of the type of coaching, but for performance coaching the widest used model is the GROW model, which is explained in Chapter 11.

Leading by example

Most people in working life have experienced situations where the boss tells everyone to stay late, and then leaves early to pick up the kids from school. There are plenty of supervisors who criticise people for spending time on the internet and have their Facebook open all day long, and merrily do it themselves.

There is hardly anything worse for the troops' morale than leaders who practise the 'Do as I say, not as I do' philosophy. No matter what the situation is, double standards always feel like betrayals. They can be very destructive. Being a poor role model is the easiest way to undermine your own authority.

Don't underestimate the fact that as a leader you are carefully watched by others. This can be for negative reasons, such as envy of your position or, more positively, because people want to follow your example – so make sure that example is a good one!

"Tell everyone who's been following
my example that they're fired."

Team building

Research has shown that the effectiveness of team building differs substantially from one organisation to another. The most effective team building efforts occur when members of the team are highly interdependent, highly knowledgeable, and when organisational leadership actively establishes and supports the team. Effective team building must also include a link to the ultimate objective of the organisation.

These conditions imply that team building only works for real teams, and not for 'groups' of loosely associated people who happen to work for the same boss. I have heard of 'away days' for groups of 300 people and, frankly, I don't believe in their effectiveness. The cost and effort needed to organise such an event will never be compensated by higher productivity of the group as a whole. At such large events people will stick together in small groups of 4 to 6 and spend their entire day like that, without any deeper contact with the other participants.

In addition, the level of interdependence is not high enough, and the 'ultimate objective' is too high-level and unclear to most participants. At best, people will enjoy themselves together with a few of their closest fellow workers during this extra day off, and they will be happy to take advantage of the free food and drink. But their productivity at work will not go up as a result. When this activity is not mandatory, but on a voluntary basis, many people will find an excuse for not participating (too much work to do, have to collect the children from school, not feeling well, etc.) simply because they don't see the point of it.

Leaders and managers have to be aware of these limitations, and organise team-building events only for volunteers, not during office hours, and possibly only partially cover the expenses. Do not use team-building events to boost your own popularity, because people won't buy it.

Feedback

'I praise loudly, I blame softly' – Catherine the Great

Catherine the Great was the most renowned and the longest-ruling female leader of Russia, reigning from 1762 until her death in 1796 at the age of 67. She came to power following the assassination of her husband, Peter III, at the end of the Seven Years' War. During her reign, Russia was revitalised, growing larger and stronger than ever before and becoming recognised as one of the great powers of Europe.

Catherine understood that even absolute despots cannot hold power without the support of others, and if a ruler is able to maintain a position, without leadership skills, people will be led nowhere. You can occupy a throne and accomplish nothing.

Catherine's philosophy of leadership is one of the most vital skills any influencer can develop:

Praise, when given, has to be generous and whole-hearted. When it is public, specific, clear, and generous, loyalty is won. Those who are praised will follow their leader practically anywhere. Others will follow as well, in hopes of earning such praise. However, choose the target for your praise wisely. Some people love the attention – others shy away from it. I've known someone perform less well after public praise because they so hated being praised in public; they did their utmost to prevent it happening again – by lowering their performance. You need to know who will bask in the glow and who'd prefer not to make a big deal of things. In the latter case I talk to them in private and explain that I haven't put the spotlight on them precisely because I know they don't like it. They appreciate that better because they feel I am attuned to their needs and receptive to their feelings, including shyness. That said, I do still mention them at meetings but not in an over the top way – just a word of thanks.

Blaming softly has to be clear, direct, and specific – but private. The aim is to keep the circle of criticism as small as possible and make corrections quickly, gently, and graciously. The leader who blames softly knows that no loyalty is earned through humiliation, and that a person who can save face can develop into a valuable leader as well. We must not destroy people in the process of making them better.

Catherine the Great had a point. If we make a big deal of praise and handle criticism frankly and discreetly, we will develop the kind of leadership that can help us reach for the sky. It is important to remember that the goal of feedback is not to tell people what to do or how to do it. That is mistaking the process for the goal. The actual goal of feedback – even negative feedback – is to improve the behaviour of the other person.

How to give feedback

Praising good performance is easy, but what about those times when someone on your team needs a kick in the butt more than a pat on the back? Here are some ideas to work with:

Make negative feedback uncommon. When a work environment becomes filled with criticism and complaint, people stop caring, because they feel that they will get criticised whatever they do. Also, when managers stockpile problems, waiting for the 'right moment', workers can become overwhelmed. Changes in behaviour are more easily achieved when negative feedback is administered in small doses and in real time, immediately after the fact.

It is better to give negative feedback orally. People who avoid confrontation are often tempted to use email to give negative feedback. Email is more easily misunderstood than oral feedback and it can look like you are 'building a case' against the person you are giving feedback to, by systematically documenting your (negative) feedback in writing. On the other hand, positive feedback is best given in written form because something put in writing usually has longer lasting impact than something dropped into a conversation. I am, I have to emphasise, talking here about one-off feedback unlikely to lead to disciplinary action (i.e. where you are expecting performance to improve).

Ask powerful questions. Most of the time, people know when they are having problems and may even have good ideas about how to improve which need to be drawn out of them. Asking questions such as 'How could you have done better?' and 'What do you think you could do with improving?' involves the other person in building a shared plan. You can give better feedback if you understand how the other person perceives the situation. Asking powerful questions such as, 'Why do you approach this situation in this way?' or better 'What was your thought process?' can lead other people to discover their own solutions and build their own insights.

Listen before you speak. Effective feedback begins with active listening, paying attention, stepping into the other person's shoes, appreciating his or her experience, and helping to move that person into a learning mode.

Be willing to accept feedback yourself. In fact, few things are more valuable to managers than honest feedback from their staff. Feedback from your subordinates is to be treasured rather than discouraged or ignored; after all, nobody is perfect and not even the best manager has nothing to learn.

Management coaches sometimes advise the 'sandwich approach'. In this approach you insert the negative feedback between two pieces of positive feedback. It's a common method, but the sandwich approach may have the effect of undermining both your feedback and your relationships with your direct reports. Effective leaders are transparent about the strategies they use when working with others. The sandwich approach is designed to influence others without telling them what you are doing – in other words to manipulate them. People don't like to be manipulated.

And a final tip: Be careful in the way you give feedback. Some cultures have a very open and accepting approach to feedback, but others don't. You can cause incredible damage if you offer personal feedback to someone who is not used to it, so be delicate, and start gradually.

Appraisal

Appraisal is formalised feedback. From my own experience, I know that appraisal is often looked upon by managers as a tedious, time consuming and highly bureaucratic burden and something those reporting to them are just glad to get over with. However, a manager needs to see this as a real exercise in leadership and the person being appraised also needs to make use of the opportunity in a positive way. Through its formalised nature, both the staff member and the supervisor get the opportunity to have an open and honest conversation, for which otherwise over the course of the year time or courage may be lacking on both sides. In many appraisal systems, self-assessment by the person being appraised is the first and mandatory step in the process. The self-assessment is a golden opportunity to take stock of important events during the past year. The staff member is not being asked to say if he or she is good or bad at their job, but rather to highlight their achievements and their ambitions for the future.

The qualitative appraisal report brings together the information relating to the individual staff member's performance during the past year. The report has to cover the main aspects of the year, including any work that may have been done outside their own organisational entity.

The manager's job is to try to make the appraisal dialogue positive, meaningful, and helpful for staff. The manager has complete freedom to write the appraisal report, but promotion is the responsibility of senior management in a separate exercise.

360-degree feedback

The term 360-degree feedback refers to an appraisal and feedback system in which a worker is evaluated by one or more supervisors, peers, and subordinates.

One of the great advantages of undergoing a 360-degree feedback evaluation is that it increases self-awareness. The feedback allows the individual to discover strengths, weaknesses and blind spots (behaviours and actions that they exhibit but are not aware of). Uncovering blind spots is valuable for continuous improvement and enables the worker to focus on developing skills in overlooked areas.

You are unlikely to encounter formal 360-degree evaluation in most work places, but many managers will informally gather impressions about you from other members of staff and may well feed these back to you during your appraisal. It is important to listen carefully to such feedback and not be dismissive or defensive.

The Pygmalion effect

The power of the *Pygmalion effect* was first described by psychologist Robert Rosenthal. In his famous study of elementary school children, Rosenthal led teachers to believe that certain children in their classrooms had been identified as high potentials. In reality, the students were randomly given the designation of high potentials, but at the end of the school year, these pupils did indeed show higher achievement. This was because the teachers believed in them and unconsciously gave more positive attention, feedback, and learning opportunities to these pupils. This is what is known as the 'Pygmalion effect' – named after George Bernard Shaw's play in which Professor Henry Higgins transforms a common flower seller, Eliza Doolittle, into a lady, because he believed that it was possible (you are probably more familiar with the musical version, 'My Fair Lady').

Tel Aviv University professor, Dov Eden, has confirmed the Pygmalion effect in all kinds of work groups, across all sectors and industries. If supervisors or managers hold positive expectations about the performance of their workers, performance improves. On the other hand, if the leader holds negative expectations, it leads to performance drops (this is known as the 'Golem effect').

Delegation

A leader or a manager cannot – and should not – do everything by themselves; if they try, they will not succeed. Moreover, trying to do everything by yourself is a symptom of poor time management. Learning how to *delegate* is an indispensable skill for a leader or a manager in any organisation. Worst is the 'control freak' type of manager who won't delegate and has staff afraid to take the smallest of decisions independently – and who then leaves the office for days or weeks at a time, leaving everything just blocked until their return.

Delegation involves giving others the authority to act on your behalf, accompanied with (a degree of) accountability for results. Effective delegation distributes the work-load more evenly, helps an organisation to run more smoothly and efficiently and allows more people to become actively involved and motivated.

You can delegate:

- Tasks that are urgent but not important (priority 3 in the Eisenhower matrix that we discussed on pages 77-78).
- When there is a lot of work.
- When someone else has a particular skill or qualification which would suit a specific task.
- When someone expresses an interest in a task.
- When someone might benefit from the responsibility for their own development.

On the other hand don't delegate:

- Things you simply don't like doing.
- Your own important tasks (priorities 1 and 2 in the Eisenhower matrix).
- Things that are usually your specified responsibilities.
- A task to someone who may not possess the skills necessary to do the task successfully.

I would personally not delegate the non-important/non-urgent tasks (i.e. priority 4 in the Eisenhower matrix) because this can convey the message that you don't value the person, which may cause demotivation.

Many people have difficulty delegating. Most often they would prefer to do the task themselves to make sure the 'job gets done right'. While this method can be more convenient, it can also result in the loss of followers. Sharing your authority with others can be the greatest single motivator in retaining followers and strengthening the organisation.

Managers often achieve their positions after being technical specialists themselves. They will have an opinion or view on how to 'fix' situations or problems. They believe that it's faster to tell some-one what to do – or do it themself – rather than give their subordi-nates an opportunity to figure it out. By always providing the answers, managers take away the opportunity for those they man-age to learn and come up with alternative, and potentially better, ways of doing things.

The secret to great delegation is to empower your people to make decisions when you are not around. That way, they won't rely on you to keep the wheels turning. If a manager doesn't let things get through the gate without personally reviewing them, that holds up the entire organisation.

However, you have to bear this important caution in mind. You can delegate work and authority, but not ultimate responsibility. In the case of something going wrong, the blame is all yours if that fail-ure occurs because you delegated a task to someone lacking the nec-essary skills. It is your fault since you delegated to the wrong person.

Unfortunately, the opposite scenario can also apply: a manager, such as the head of a department, can have responsibility but not au-thority. He or she might be held responsible for making something happen, but lacks the actual authority to enforce any directives or in-centives. This is one of the major stressors that middle managers face. This is particularly an issue in the case of underperformance by a member of staff, where managers have very little in the way of tools (other than feedback) to effect a change of behaviour. Some staff take full advantage of this lack of authority (i.e. they happily chomp on every carrot they are given, knowing there is no real stick).

Give and take

'Give, and it will be given to you' – Luke 6:38

According to organisational psychologist Adam Grant there are three types of people in this world: *givers* (those who prioritise help-ing others), *takers* (those who help themselves) and *matchers* (those who seek equal benefit for themselves and others). After investigat-ing years of psychological studies as well as conducting his own re-search, Grant concluded that givers are the most successful. He says:

'Givers bring out the best in others. One big part of that is seeing more potential in people than they see in themselves.
Givers are often looking at the people around them as dia-
monds in the rough, investing in such a way that they're able
to allow these people to achieve greater potential than they
thought possible.'

Givers also become role models and change behaviour norms for
the group, Grant argues, making others more likely to help each
other and share knowledge – which can ultimately contribute to an
environment of greater creativity and innovation. You can read more
in his book *Give and Take – Why Helping Others Drives our Success*.

Leading your former peers

Becoming the manager of your former peers is a particular challenge; you need to establish your authority and credibility, without
acting like the promotion has gone to your head.

Much as for any other upcoming change, you have to prepare
this transition carefully. So, rather than waiting for a promotion to
be announced, think first about what management style you'd like
to apply, then challenge yourself to show those skills while you are
still working side-by-side with your peers. That way, when you are
promoted, there will be no surprises: people will already know

"Congratulations. You've been promoted
to Supervisor! Now, explain why your
people aren't doing enough work."

what to expect, based on their past experience of your planning, decision-making, communication, and collaboration skills.

Here are some tips on what to do when the promotion has become a fact:

- *Address the elephant in the room.* Schedule a meeting to sit down with your new team. This doesn't necessarily have to be in a formal setting; invite them for lunch or a coffee. Even if your promotion hasn't been announced officially yet, you can bet on it that the grapevine has done its job already. Announcing the transition in a friendly atmosphere will remove the uncertainty and break the ice.

- *Establish your authority from day one.* Step decisively into the new role by letting the team know that things have changed, and that you are now their manager. Right after this first meeting, have a conversation with each individual regarding how expectations have changed; don't underestimate the power of a simple, one-on-one conversation.

- *Renegotiate your friendships.* Be honest about how your own responsibilities and priorities have changed, and ask how your friend sees theirs changing as well. Let them know they can count on you to support them in being happy and successful in their role and ask for their loyalty in return, but make it clear that there won't be any special treatment. Accept that you can no longer have close, personal friendships with your former peers. You don't need to become remote and unreachable, but you may want to attend fewer social gatherings.

- *Tread lightly at first.* You probably have loads of ideas about how to lead the team. But don't introduce any major revamps right away. You need to show your new authority without stepping on toes or damaging relationships. You can identify a few smaller decisions you can make fairly quickly, but postpone bigger ones until you've been in the role longer and have time to gather feedback.

- *Make use of your advantages.* You are more likely to find someone you trust to give you feedback than would a complete stranger to the team. After all, you know your former fellow workers very well and know who is trustworthy and who is not. Leverage this knowledge to ask for honest feedback.

- *Look beyond your team.* During this type of transition, it's easy to become overly focused on your former peers. Ask yourself how you can build credibility with new counterparts and how you can build a connection with your own new boss.

How to manage older workers

Imagine you have just been promoted into a management position and are the youngest person in the group. Becoming a manager of people older and more experienced than yourself feels like jumping for the first time into the deep end of a swimming pool; terrifying and exciting at the same time. Here are some tips to survive your first dive into the deep.

- *Be confident in your skills.* If you have been given a leadership position, your bosses must believe in you. So stop worrying about your age, and take self-confidence from the knowledge that you have already made it this far.

- *Don't claim expertise you don't have.* Nobody is an expert in every subject so don't try to pretend that *you* are. Most people appreciate honesty about strengths and weaknesses, so be willing to share yours and encourage others to do the same. Being truthful will also help to build trust. One of the biggest mistakes you can make as a manager (of any age) is to refuse to learn from your team. In fact, your older employees are one of the best resources you can use to adapt to your new position. Sometimes we feel that asking for help creates a weakness in the relationship between a manager and their staff – this is simply not true. It can actually help to build loyalty and trust to show vulnerability now and again.

- *Relate at the human level, not as their boss.* When I started managing employees who were decades older than me, I didn't think I'd be able to relate to their lives. They had spouses, children, and even grandchildren – and I wasn't at that stage of life yet. But even if you're not in the same position in life as your fellow workers, you can still take an interest in their lives. You may not be able to offer advice but you can ask about their families, past work experience, and ambitions in life. Forging a personal connection with your subordinates will help you understand them better – what makes them tick, how they learn and communicate, and what matters most to them. And if an older employee is excellent but has to go home to their family instead of a happy hour, cut them some slack.

- *Be their leader, not their manager.* Generally speaking, the older the employee, the more knowledgeable they are, so there's little point in trying to outperform them on hard skills, or to boss them around. They've survived in your business for a reason and have probably faced some tough experiences you haven't. Instead, get to know the people on your team, so you can take advantage of each individual's areas of expertise. Treat everybody with respect, and give credit where credit is due. Inspire them with your own enthusiasm and commitment. Use your soft skills.

- *Share your vision, but ask for feedback.* Being young doesn't mean that you don't know what you're doing. So share your vision but don't forget to seek their advice and feedback. Most of the time, they have great ideas which they are more than willing to share. They want to be part of the decision-making process, and they are eager to spread their knowledge. Their prolonged experience at the company is usually a sign that they are invested in it, and want to see it succeed.

- *Respect traditions.* A lot of young people come into an organisation looking to make a change. When managing people older than yourself, it is important to understand how and why they are doing things before you start making changes. They may have been with the company a long time – which means they're aware of what works and what doesn't, they've seen almost every possible technical problem, and they know the unique environment better than anyone else. Remember, even when change is necessary, old habits die hard. Give them time to get used to you and your leadership style and until then, just focus on the task at hand.

Integrity

You are what you do, not what you say you'll do' – Carl Gustav Jung, Swiss founder of analytical psychology

Integrity means that we do not behave in ways that go against our essence; that we behave with honesty, reliability, and caring – with ourselves and with others. Doing what you say you will do is a matter of integrity.

I don't trust people who don't keep their word. Decades ago I had a boss who had clearly reached his 'level of incompetence'. He said different things to different people, trying to save face with the person he was actually talking to. To his boss, the general manager, he promised one thing, while he was instructing the external consultants to do something different. The financial manager then got yet another version of his story, and as for his immediate subordinates, well, they didn't know what to think about all of this. I remember this episode as one of the most unhappy of my entire career, because I didn't trust my boss, I felt unsafe.

I lose respect for people whose word doesn't mean anything to them. If you want to feel respected by others, then you need to say 'yes' when you mean 'yes' and 'no' when you mean 'no', and not allow your fear of rejection to get in the way of being a trustworthy person.

We cannot feel worthy when we let others down. People who default on their word do not value themselves enough to act with integrity. Self-worth is the result of treating others with caring and respect.

When people have the sense that a leader is worthy of their trust they will invest time and take risks in ways they never would if their leader had a reputation built upon lack of integrity. Keep in mind that people will forgive many things where trust exists, but will rarely forgive anything where trust is absent.

Authentic leadership

'To thine own self be true' – Polonius, in Shakespeare's 'Hamlet'

In 2003, following a series of corporate scandals in the US, Bill George made the case that we needed new leaders, not just new laws, to get us out of the corporate crisis in his book *Authentic Leadership: Rediscovering the Secrets of Creating Lasting Value.*

According to George, authentic leaders are 'self-actualized' individuals (self-actualization being, as Abraham Maslow puts it, 'The full realization of one's potential, and of one's true self'). They are aware of their strengths, their limitations, and their own emotions. They also show who they really are to their followers. They do not act one way in private and another in public; they don't hide their mistakes or weaknesses out of fear of looking weak. Authentic leaders lead with their hearts, not just their minds. They are not afraid to show their emotions, their vulnerability, and to connect with their workers. This does not mean that authentic leaders are 'soft'. Being open about yourself helps to break down hierarchical barriers. It is only when your staff knows the person behind the façade that you start building the foundations of good leadership: trust and respect.

Besides being open and honest with their followers, authentic leaders always put the mission and the goals of the organisation ahead of their own self-interest. They do the job in pursuit of results for the organisation, not for their own power, money or ego. Authentic leaders focus on the long-term stakeholder value. They realise that to nurture individuals and an organisation requires hard work and patience, but the approach pays large dividends over time.

Followership: the other side of leadership

'I must follow the people. Am I not their leader?' – Benjamin Disraeli, 19th century British prime minister

The other side of leadership is 'followership'. It seems reasonable that if leadership is important to performance, followership must have something to do with it too. But strangely, followership gets only a small fraction of the exposure that leadership does. Followership is a straightforward concept. It is the ability to take direction well, to get in line behind a program, to be part of a team and to deliver on what is expected of you. One could say that it is closely related to 'meeting expectations' as described earlier in this book.

However, being a good follower is sometimes looked down on. This is a pity because the practical reality is that one does not progressively reach more responsible leadership positions without demonstrating an ability to follow and function effectively as part of a group. The fact is that in organisations everybody is both a leader and a follower depending on the circumstances. How well the followers follow is probably just as important to an organisation's success as how well the leaders lead.

Followership will always be in the shadow of leadership. Nonetheless, while it is true that an organisation is only as good as its leaders, it is also only as good as its followers. There are no leaders without followers.

Key points to remember

- *Managers and leaders have to realise that they can be a cause of sub-optimal performance of their staff.*

- *Motivation is an on-going, everyday aspect of managing and leading others.*

- *Trust is the currency of leadership.*

- *Be yourself.*

- *Lead by example.*

- *Shut up and listen.*

- *Replace ego with empathy.*

- *Communicate, communicate, and communicate.*

And finally... some things to avoid

- *Micromanaging.*
- *Assigning work inappropriately.*
- *Making decisions on your own, without consulting your team.*
- *Keeping information to yourself.*
- *Not listening to what others say.*
- *'Holding on' to information.*
- *Failing to create development opportunities for others.*
- *Not keeping development and performance goals of others in mind.*
- *Having unrealistic expectations and perception of staff skills and knowledge.*
- *Not asking for help or feedback.*
- *Demotivating others.*
- *Not delegating; doing everything by yourself.*
- *Not monitoring team progress or provide follow-up.*
- *Being a 'taker', not a 'giver'.*
- *Being unauthentic.*

9. Learning and developing

"Have you finished learning all the new things from yesterday? Because I have all these new things for you to learn today."

'The illiterate of the 21st century will not be those who cannot read and write, but those who cannot learn, unlearn, and relearn' - Alvin Toffler, American futurologist

Learning and developing is one of the most important parts of our lives and our work. Yet, despite having attended many years of education, many of us have no idea how to approach our pursuit of knowledge, and the development of our skills for either personal or professional reasons.

Learning and developing bring about changes in the way we act, think and/or feel about ourselves, about other people, and about the world around us. These changes may be permanent or temporary depending on our own perceptions of the importance and relevance of the knowledge gained.

Learning and developing doesn't end when you finish school or university. For the rest of your professional career, and beyond, you will be expected to:

- Take active steps to improve your knowledge and development.
- Develop new skills on your own initiative.
- Work actively on developing your strengths and overcoming your weaknesses.
- Improve knowledge and skills out of personal interest and natural curiosity.
- Actively seek feedback from others to improve your own performance.
- Pool knowledge and expertise.
- Be aware of the wider context and of your own contribution.
- Actively mentor or coach others.

Anchors for 'learning and developing'

- Explaining ideas clearly, simplifying the complex.
- Developing and applying new knowledge, skills, competencies.
- Taking care of own personal development.
- Asking for advice and assistance.
- Seeing own role within the organisation.
- Seeing the 'bigger picture.'
- Learning other languages.
- Having a learning strategy.
- Active listening.
- Teaching others.

Table 9.1: Which of these sound like you?

UNSATISFACTORY	IMPROVEMENT NEEDED	MEETS EXPECTATIONS	EXCEEDS EXPECTATIONS	EXCEPTIONAL
Allows knowledge levels to remain constant / outdated.	Remains set in their ways.	Speaks and writes clearly, simplifies the complex.	Strikes a good balance between detail and the need for clarity.	Develops new skills on his/her own initiative.
Shows little interest in acquiring new skills or knowledge.	Slow to learn.	Takes new information on board quickly.	Volunteers for new and challenging tasks.	Improves knowledge and skills out of personal interest and natural curiosity.
Sticks to comfort zone and routine.	Sees personal development only in professional terms.	Learns from observation.	Is resourceful when it comes to familiarising himself with the latest developments in his/her field.	Pools knowledge and expertise.
Does little to overcome weaknesses.	Does little to develop his/her strengths.	Adapts to new ways of doing things.	Learns from input and suggestions from fellow workers.	Is aware of the wider – political – context, and his/her own contribution.
Fails to learn from mistakes.	Doesn't learn from experience.	Knows his/her strengths and weaknesses.	Has a clear learning strategy, and applies it successfully.	Actively mentors or coaches others.
Rejects constructive feedback.	Avoids new challenges and learning opportunities.	Identifies personal failings and tries to overcome them.	Actively listens to, and learns from other people's ideas and contributions.	Is a proficient user of more than three languages.
Focuses only on own tasks and role.	Makes limited use of the experience of fellow workers.	Sets personal goals.	Is a proficient user of at least three languages.	
Lacks understanding of organisational objectives.	Fails to learn from mistakes.	Seeks others' feedback		
Only speaks mother tongue.	Unaware of what happens upstream and downstream of own department.	Learns from mistakes.		
Frequently interrupts others.	Is a proficient user of two languages.	Listens to, and learns from other people's ideas and contributions.		
Does not listen to others.	Sees colleagues as rivals.	Considers teaching others as part of his/her job description.		
Keeps own knowledge and understandings for himself.				

What is the difference between learning and developing?

In my classroom training and coaching sessions I explain the difference between learning and developing this way:

- Learning is about hard skills, development is about soft skills.
- Learning is about the gaining of knowledge and know-how, development is about changing your behaviour.
- Learning is a process that takes a certain amount of time (and effort), and you can usually demonstrate the effect by passing a test or an exam. Development is an ongoing process (you start developing when you are born, and stop when you die), and your behaviour can only be observed, or assessed, but not measured with high precision.

Learning and development

In Chapter 7 I used the example of how I taught my daughter to drive a car, in order to explain the idea of 'Comfort Zone'. I explain how I passed on knowledge and knowhow, and how I progressively increased the challenges so that she would learn how to drive a car. Her *learning* experience was successfully concluded by the driver's exam.

From that moment on, however, her *development* started. Mainly by further practice, exposure to various traffic situations, some near misses and a fine, she became more aware of what driving a car is about, and adapted her behaviour.

Both learning and development are important, but they happen at different rates. Learning happens via many channels: school, professional training, self-directed and lifelong learning, practice, or simply through exposure to life. Development is much rarer, especially in adults. It refers to how we learn to see the world through new eyes, how we change our understanding of what we experience, and how we change our views of reality. It describes our increasing awareness, and therefore what becomes part of our understanding and behaviour.

The Leadership Development Profile

The Leadership Development Profile (LDP) was created by Susanne Cook-Greuter and Bill Torbert, and is based on the Leadership Development Framework (LDF) that describes nine sequential changes – or 'action logics' – in how a person understands events, or makes meaning.

Only the seven most commonly encountered action logics in the corporate world are referred to in the LDP. These range from the Opportunist, through the Diplomat, Expert and Achiever, to the stages of Individualist, Strategist and Magician (or Alchemist):

- *Opportunist* – focuses on own immediate needs, desires and opportunities. Seeks short-term tangible advantage and what is good for them personally. They often display cynicism and hostility, resisting feedback and manipulating events to make themselves look good.
- *Diplomat* – seeks approval through socially expected behaviour. Seeks conformity, belonging and friendly, low stress relationships in order to gain approval from others. Diplomats avoid conflict and focus on preserving their status or membership of a group. They will argue to ensure they do not lose face.
- *Expert/Technician* – believes in the 'right way' to do things, seeking to display own skills and expertise in a inflexible way, following procedures and behaving in ways expected of their role. They admire efficiency, consistency, incremental improvement, quality and perfection, but can get stuck in the details and perfectionism.
- *Achiever* – seeks effectiveness through logical application of objectives, plans and controls, in order to deliver results and goals that will secure success within the system. They are proactive and use scientific problem solving techniques to assert their views and set high standards for others. Successful managers will have this logic in their mind.
- *Individualist* – enjoys being appreciated for their own uniqueness, working through diverse relationships, experimenting with own power, developing increased spontaneity and pursuing new ideas. They tend to focus on the interactions between self and system, which means they understand the consequences of

specific actions and are able to question assumptions. As a result they can adjust and adapt what they do to fit the context they find themselves in.

- *Strategist* – sees the world as interrelated processes and relationships, playing many roles in these. Sees the big picture and holds long-term perspective. Values integrity, principles and freedom in creating positive change. Strategists understand that reality is a social construction, which is what makes it complex with many interacting elements and factors. They are tolerant of difference, seeing diversity as a resource for finding win-win solutions.
- *Magician/Alchemist* – committed to transformation of self, organisations and society. Seeks common good. Enjoys interplay of purposes, actions and results. Is mysterious, chameleon-like and powerful. They have the ability to make meaning by combining practical, ontological, systemic and spiritual practices.

In general, every bit of information or topic that can be considered is viewed and acted upon differently by people at different stages. For example, Table 9.2 describes how someone understands and responds to the concept of 'feedback' changing with increasing development.

Opportunist	Reacts to feedback as an attack or threat.
Diplomat	Receives feedback as disapproval, or as reminder of norms.
Expert	Takes it personally; defends own position; dismisses feedback from those who are not seen as experts in the same field (general manager).
Achiever	Accepts feedback especially if it helps them to achieve their goals and to improve.
Individualist	Welcomes feedback as necessary for self-knowledge and to uncover hidden aspects of their own behaviour.
Strategist	Invites feedback for self-actualisation; conflict is seen as inevitable aspect of viable and multiple relationships.
Magician	Views feedback (loops) as a natural part of living systems essential for learning and change and take it with a pinch of salt.

Table 9.2: Responding to feedback

"I'm sorry, I don't understand
what you're talking about
when you criticize me."

If you are interested to see where you stand you can take an assessment at https://leadershipcircle.com/assessment-tools/, though please note that these tools are not for free.

Learning styles

Learning and development is about remembering things, and how to do them. It is believed that on average we actually remember around:

- 10% of what we read
- 20% of what we hear
- 30% of what we see
- 50% of what we see and hear
- 70% of what is discussed with others
- 80% of what is experienced personally
- 95% of what we teach to someone else

These are only averages, because each person prefers different techniques and ways of learning.

Learning styles group common ways that people learn. Everyone has a mix of learning styles. Some people may find that they have a dominant style of learning, with far less use of the other

A learning secret: don't take notes with a laptop

New research by Pam Mueller and Daniel Oppenheimer demonstrates that students who write out their notes on paper actually learn more.

Across three experiments, Mueller and Oppenheimer had students take notes in a classroom setting and then tested students on their memory for factual detail, their conceptual understanding of the material, and their ability to synthesise and generalise the information. Half of the students were instructed to take notes with a laptop, and the other half were instructed to write the notes out by hand. As in other studies, students who used laptops took more notes. In each study, however, those who wrote out their notes by hand had a stronger conceptual understanding and were more successful in applying and integrating the material than those who used took notes with their laptops.

What drives this paradoxical finding? Mueller and Oppenheimer postulate that taking notes by hand requires different types of cognitive processing than taking notes on a laptop, and these different processes have consequences for learning. Writing by hand is slower and more cumbersome than typing, and students cannot possibly write down every word in a lecture. Instead, they listen, digest, and summarise so that they can succinctly capture the essence of the information. Thus, taking notes by hand forces the brain to engage in some heavy 'mental lifting,' and these efforts foster comprehension and retention. By contrast, when typing students can easily produce a written record of the lecture without processing its meaning, as faster typing speeds allow students to transcribe a lecture word for word without devoting much thought to the content.

Technology offers innovative tools that are shaping educational experiences for students, often in positive and dynamic ways. The research by Mueller and Oppenheimer serves as a reminder, however, that even when technology allows us to do more in less time, it does not always foster learning. Learning involves more than the receipt and the regurgitation of information. If we want students to synthesize material, draw inferences, see new connections, evaluate evidence, and apply concepts in novel situations, we need to encourage the deep, effortful cognitive processes that underlie these abilities. When it comes to taking notes, students need fewer gigs, more brainpower.

(http://www.scientificamerican.com/article/a-learning-secret-don-t-take-notes-with-a-laptop/)

styles. Others may find that they use different styles in different circumstances. There is no right mix. Nor are your styles fixed. You can develop ability in less dominant styles, as well as further develop styles that you already use well.

Generally speaking there are seven learning styles:

- *Visual* (spatial) – you prefer using pictures, images, and spatial understanding.
- *Aural* (auditory-musical) – you prefer using sound and music.
- *Verbal* (linguistic) – you prefer using words, both in speech and writing.
- *Physical* (kinaesthetic) – you prefer using your body, hands and sense of touch.
- *Logical* (mathematical) – you prefer using logic, reasoning and systems.
- *Social* (interpersonal) – you prefer to learn in groups or with other people.
- *Solitary* (intrapersonal) – you prefer to work alone and use self-study.

By recognising and understanding your own learning styles, you can use techniques better suited to you. This improves the speed and quality of your learning.

Formal and informal learning

Formal learning is planned learning that derives from activities within a structured learning setting. Formal learning is enrolling on a programme of study, attending lectures, preparing coursework, and engaging in seminar/tutorial discussions.

Informal learning is learning that originates from activities external to a structured learning context, or unstructured learning within a structured learning environment.

Benefits of formal learning:

- Large numbers of workers will learn the same information and/or processes at the same time.

- If properly designed, the course content should be accurate and up to date.
- Workers learning through formal training programs come up to speed faster once they start their jobs.
- Properly designed formal training programs can include a variety of methods to appeal to all learning styles.

Benefits of informal learning:

- Creating informal learning situations can be less costly and more time efficient given technology and the social media currently available.
- Learning informally can be more personal and less intimidating for some people.
- Subject-matter experts may be more willing to share their knowledge with others this way.
- Since learning this way happens more naturally during the workday, workers may be more enthusiastic about learning new skills.

The four stages of competence

The earliest origins of the 'four stages of competence' theory are uncertain and could be very old indeed. Noel Burch, a former worker of the US organisation Gordon Training International, formalised the theory in the 1970s. Burch suggested that individuals are initially unaware of how little they know, or unconscious of their incompetence. As they recognise their incompetence, they consciously acquire a skill, and then consciously use it. Eventually, the skill can be operated without it being consciously thought through: the individual is said to have acquired unconscious competence (Figure 9.1 on the next page).

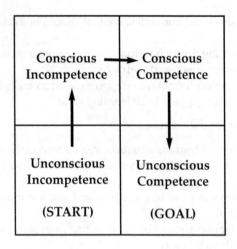

Figure 9.1: The four stages of competence

Unconscious incompetence

- The person is not aware of the existence or relevance of the skill area.
- The person is not aware that they have a particular deficiency in the area concerned.
- The person might deny the relevance or usefulness of the new skill.
- The person must become conscious of their incompetence before development of the new skill or learning can begin.
- The aim of the trainer or teacher is to move the person into the 'conscious competence' stage, by demonstrating the skill or ability and the benefit that it will bring to the person's effectiveness.

Conscious incompetence

- The person becomes aware of the existence and relevance of the skill.

- The person is therefore also aware of their deficiency in this area, ideally by attempting or trying to use the skill.
- The person realises that by improving their skill or ability in this area their effectiveness will improve.
- Ideally the person has a measure of the extent of their deficiency in the relevant skill, and a measure of what level of skill is required for their own competence.
- The person ideally makes a commitment to learn and practise the new skill, and to move to the 'conscious competence' stage.

Conscious competence

- The person achieves 'conscious competence' in a skill when they can perform it reliably.
- The person will need to concentrate and think in order to perform the skill.
- The person can perform the skill without assistance.
- The person will not reliably perform the skill unless thinking about it – the skill is not yet 'second nature' or 'automatic'.
- The person should be able to show the skill to another, but is unlikely to be able to teach it well to another person.
- The person should ideally continue to practise the new skill, and if appropriate commit to becoming 'unconsciously competent' at the new skill.
- Deliberate practice is the single most effective way to move to the next stage.

Unconscious competence

- The skill becomes so practised that it enters the unconscious parts of the brain – it becomes 'second nature'.
- Common examples are driving, sports activities, typing, manual tasks, listening and communicating.
- It becomes possible for certain skills to be performed while doing something else, for example, knitting while reading a book.
- The person might now be able to teach others in the skill concerned, although after some time of being unconsciously com-

petent the person might actually struggle in explaining exactly how they do it – the skill has become largely instinctual.
- This arguably gives rise to the need for long-standing unconscious competence to be checked periodically against new standards.

Our body is constantly creating new neural stem cells, or embryonic brain cells, by a process known as *neurogenesis*. Here is the catch: if you don't learn something so new that you fire those new neurones, they get digested. And it's only in the phases of conscious incompetence and, a bit, of conscious competence, that you are actually learning something new.

The four stages of competence in learning to drive

Let's go back to the example of my daughter learning to drive a car.

As a child she first thought that all she needed to do was sit behind the wheel, and say 'vroom-vroom'. In her imagination she was indeed driving the car. She had no idea that driving skills existed or that she had any shortage in that area. This was the happy stage of unconscious incompetence.

When she first began learning to drive, she soon realised there was a whole lot more to it than she had imagined, and felt a little overwhelmed; there were so many different things to do and think about. This was the stage of her conscious incompetence. In this stage she made lots of mistakes, and doubted if she was even capable of learning. Mistakes are necessary because learning is in essence experience-based; by trial and error. Information can be accrued, but until it is put to use, it's just that: information.

As she practised she gradually moved into the third stage of learning: conscious competence. This felt a lot better, but still she wasn't very smooth or fluid in her driving. She often had to think about what to do next, and that felt a bit awkward. However, with practice she started making fewer and fewer mistakes.

Finally, after a lot of practice, she came to the point where she didn't have to think about every little thing she was doing while driving; she had become unconsciously competent. Because of the ease and elegance in unconscious competence, her driving became much safer.

So the advice to stick to what you are good at is terrible from the perspective of putting your hard-won new baby neurones to work. Better advice would be to start learning something new, and stick with it as long as it feels uncomfortable and you know that you haven't mastered it. As soon as you are good at it, start something new.

The GROW model that is further explained in Chapter 11 relies for an important part on these ideas.

Learning another language

Mastering multiple languages is not only about hard skills; it enables a better understanding of the different cultural backgrounds of your fellow workers and clients and hence develops your interpersonal skills. This is obviously particularly relevant for anyone seeking a career in global companies or international organisations.

The Common European Framework divides language learners into three broad divisions that can be divided into six levels; for each level, it describes what a learner is supposed to be able to do in reading, listening, speaking and writing. These levels are described in Table 9.3 on page 230.

Deliberate practice

'What we hope ever to do with ease, we must learn first to do with diligence' – Samuel Johnson, 18th century

Repetition is maybe the most intuitive principle of learning, traceable to ancient Egyptian and Chinese education. In ancient Greece, Aristotle commented on the role of repetition in learning by saying 'it is frequent repetition that produces a natural tendency' and 'the more frequently two things are experienced together, the more likely it will be that the experience or recall of one will stimulate the recall of the other.'

Repetition is one of the most basic learning techniques. Children use it to learn to speak. Athletes use it to perfect their athletic skills. Repetition is sometimes seen as boring, or looked down upon as an

Basic User	A1	• Can understand and use familiar everyday expressions and very basic phrases aimed at the satisfaction of needs of a concrete type. • Can introduce him/herself and others and can ask and answer questions about personal details such as where he/she lives, people he/she knows and things he/she has. • Can interact in a simple way provided the other person talks slowly and clearly and is prepared to help.
	A2	• Can understand sentences and frequently used expressions related to areas of most immediate relevance (e.g. very basic personal and family information, shopping, local geography, employment). • Can communicate in simple and routine tasks requiring a simple and direct exchange of information on familiar and routine matters. • Can describe in simple terms aspects of his/her background, immediate environment and matters in areas of immediate need.
Independent User	B1	• Can understand the main points of clear standard input on familiar matters regularly encountered in work, school, leisure, etc. • Can deal with most situations likely to arise while travelling in an area where the language is spoken. • Can produce simple connected text on topics that are familiar or of personal interest. • Can describe experiences and events, dreams, hopes and ambitions and briefly give reasons and explanations for opinions and plans.
	B2	• Can understand the main ideas of complex text on both concrete and abstract topics, including technical discussions in his/her field of specialization. • Can interact with a degree of fluency and spontaneity that makes regular interaction with native speakers quite possible without strain for either party. • Can produce clear, detailed text on a wide range of subjects and explain a viewpoint on a topical issue giving the advantages and disadvantages of various options.
Proficient user	C1	• Can understand a wide range of demanding, longer texts, and recognise implicit meaning. • Can express ideas fluently and spontaneously without much obvious searching for expressions. • Can use language flexibly and effectively for social, academic and professional purposes. • Can produce clear, well-structured, detailed text on complex subjects, showing controlled use of organisational patterns, connectors and cohesive devices.
	C2	• Can understand with ease virtually everything heard or read. • Can summarise information from different spoken and written sources, reconstructing arguments and accounts in a coherent presentation. • Can express him/herself spontaneously, very fluently and precisely, differentiating finer shades of meaning even in the most complex situations.

Table 9.3: The Common European Framework

attempt to simply memorise rather than understand. However, repetition is extremely important, because it effectively creates the neural pathways in our brain needed for remembering and understanding new information and skills.

Deliberate practice is not the same as mere repetition, or 'drill and kill'. Simply repeating a task will not by itself improve performance. Deliberate practice involves awareness, attention, rehearsal and repetition, and leads to new knowledge or skills that can later be developed into more complex knowledge and skills. Although other factors such as intelligence and motivation affect performance, practice is necessary, but not sufficient, for acquiring expertise.

The 10,000 hours myth

In 2008, Malcolm Gladwell published his New York Times bestseller, *Outliers*. Based largely on the research of Anders Ericsson (http://projects.ict.usc.edu/itw/gel/EricssonDeliberatePracticePR93.pdf) Gladwell frequently talks about the 10,000-Hour rule, citing it as 'the magic number of greatness.'

A 2013 study by a group of psychologists from five universities, rejects Gladwell's wisdom. 'Different levels of deliberate practice can only explain one third of the variation in performance levels in chess players and musicians', the authors found, 'leaving the majority of the reliable variance unexplained and potentially explainable by other factors.' In other words, practice is great! But practice alone won't make you a world-class expert.

To go back to Anders Ericsson, much of his research has been focused on Deliberate Practice, and the following video explains it well: https://youtu.be/wWuaQ84kGwl

Another, very compelling, video can be found at https://www.youtube.com/watch?v=5MgBikgcWnY. In here Josh Kaufman explains how it is possible to learn anything in just 20 hours. Interesting!

Trial and error

'"Mistakes" is the word you're too embarrassed to use. You ought not to be. You're a product of a trillion of them. Evolution forged the entirety of sentient life on this planet using only one tool: the mistake' – Robert Ford, in the HBO science-fiction series 'Westworld'

Trial and error is a method of learning in which various responses are tentatively tried, and some discarded, until a valid solution is reached.

Edward Thorndike was the chief exponent of the theory of connectionism or trial and error. He conducted Stimulus-Response (S-R) theory experiments with the help of animals. Thorndike was the first to study the subject of learning systematically using standardised procedures and tools. All learning, according to Thorndike, is the construction of bonds or connections between Stimulus and Response.

If circumstances permit, learning from our mistakes is a very powerful way of learning. That is why it is advised to managers and leaders to create a 'safe' environment for those who work under them. A safe environment is an environment where people are not afraid to make mistakes, where they can learn and develop, and are supported rather than punished for whatever goes wrong.

Mind mapping

A mind map is a diagram that connects information around a central topic. At the centre is your main topic, and the branches are related points. Greater levels of detail branch out to subpoints from there, and branches can be linked together. Mind maps link and group together concepts, issues and ideas through natural associations. They prompt you to fill in more and, in the process, find what is missing. Mind mapping helps organise your thoughts, because it imitates the way your brain works.

Mind maps can be used for pretty much any thinking or learning task, from studying a subject such as a new language to planning your career or even building better habits. They are useful for teams to use as well, for brainstorming and interactive presentations.

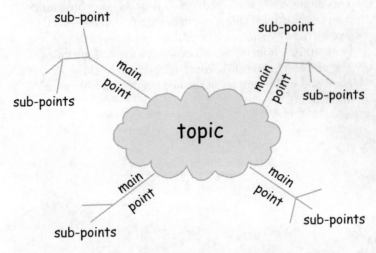

Figure 9.2: Mind mapping

70-20-10 model

The 70-20-10 model is a learning and development model, usually credited to Morgan McCall and his fellow workers, Lombardo and Eichinger, working at the Centre for Creative Leadership

(CCL). In their 1996 book, *The Career Architect Development Planner*, they published the results of a survey asking nearly 200 executives to self-report on how they believed they learned. These results were that lessons learned by successful and effective managers are roughly:

- 70% from tough jobs
- 20% from people (mostly the boss)
- 10% from courses and reading

Lombardo and Eichinger expressed their rationale behind the 70-20-10 model like this:

'Development generally begins with a realization of current or future need and the motivation to do something about it. This might come from feedback, a mistake, watching other people's reactions, failing or not being up to a task – in other words, from experience. The odds are that development will be about 70% from on-the-job experiences – working on tasks and problems; about 20% from feedback and working around good and bad examples of the need; and 10% from courses and reading.'

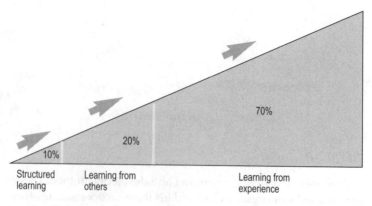

Figure 9.3: The 70-20-10 learning model

Pervasive learning

Daniel Pink's book *A Whole New Mind* first describes how our society has gone from agricultural to industrial to the information age. But then, he describes how we have moved on to a new age where the dominant value for most organisations is created by high-end knowledge workers – concept workers. For concept workers, working and learning merge.

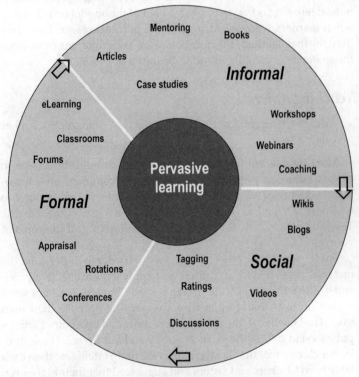

Figure 9.4: Pervasive learning

The idea of *pervasive learning* has been around for some time and makes perfect sense as more and more of us become concept workers. In his book, *Flat Army: Creating a Connected and Engaged Or-*

ganisation Dan Pontefract defines pervasive learning as 'learning at the speed of need through formal, informal and social learning modalities'.

There are some similarities between Pontefract's ideas and the 70-20-10 model, but as others have pointed, out the 70-20-10 model may not be universally applicable to all staff. Instead, Pontefract's 3-33 model often fits better. In the 3-33 model, 33% of learning is formal, 33% is informal, and 33% is social (see Figure 9.4). What is most interesting is that the research behind this model revealed that when learners were asked to give the percentages for how they thought they learned, the numbers were very different from what the researchers actually found to be the case.

Teaching others

'While we teach, we learn' – Seneca, classical Roman philosopher and statesman

Most people are familiar with learning through books, or in classes, but many overlook perhaps the most comprehensive learning experience of all: teaching. The best test of whether or not you really understand a concept is trying to teach it to someone else. Teaching others calls for thorough understanding of the concept yourself.

Students teaching other students work harder to understand the material, recall it more accurately and apply it more effectively. Scientists have called this 'the protégé effect'. Student teachers score higher on tests than pupils who are learning only for their own sake. The benefits of this practice were indicated by a pair of articles published in 2007 in the journals *Science* and *Intelligence*. These studies concluded that first-born children are more intelligent than their later-born brothers and sisters and suggested that their higher IQs result from the time they spend instructing their younger siblings.

Teaching also forces you to communicate your thoughts clearly and precisely. As our society becomes ever more interconnected and interdependent, cooperation becomes more and more important. This cooperation requires communication. However, being heard is not enough; you must also be understood. Your ideas will never be more effective than your ability to make others comprehend them. Teaching helps you develop the extremely important skill of describing your ideas well enough for others to use them.

Teaching others is not limited to a simple transfer of information between individuals, be it in a formal or an informal setting. Teaching others is also coaching and mentoring them for the purpose of learning and developing (Figure 9.5).

My own activities, as a coach and author of books on personal development, are part of my own learning and developing strategy.

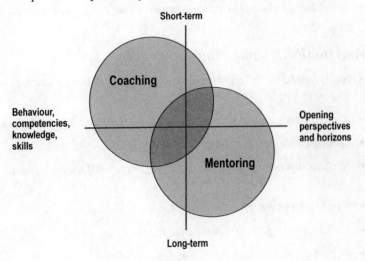

Figure 9.5: Coaching and mentoring

Key points to remember

- *When possible learners should take part in the planning of their learning activities.*

- *Interaction with a mentor or coach is vital.*

- *Learning activities and/or delivery need to be varied.*

- *Self-evaluation and deliberate practice is important.*

- *Build on existing knowledge, link to previous experience.*
- *Appeal to and engage emotions while learning.*
- *Learning increases the capacity to learn even more.*
- *Engage all senses when learning.*
- *Learning should tap into the brain's natural curiosity.*
- *Enhance your motivation by seeing the bigger picture.*
- *Teaching is the most comprehensive learning experience.*

And finally... some things to avoid

- *Showing little interest in developing new skills or acquiring new knowledge.*
- *Staying in your comfort zone and settling for routine.*
- *Doing little to overcome your weaknesses.*
- *Not taking opportunities to ask for personal feedback from others.*
- *Failing to learn from mistakes.*
- *Not accepting constructive feedback.*
- *Focusing exclusively on own tasks and role.*
- *Not listening to what others say.*
- *Keeping information to yourself.*
- *Seeing colleagues as rivals.*

10. Know yourself to understand others

"Everyone says you're really good
at office politics. Or were they
stabbing you in the back with
a compliment like that?"

*'If you know others and know yourself, you will not be imperilled in a
hundred battles; if you do not know others but know yourself, you win one
and lose one; if you do not know others and do not know yourself, you will be
imperilled in every single battle'* – Sun Tzu, Chinese author of 'The Art
of War', 6th century BCE

In 1651, the English philosopher Thomas Hobbes used the term
nosce te ipsum, as the Latin translation of an ancient Greek saying in-
scribed on the temple of Apollo at Delphi, which he translated as
'know thyself' in his famous work, *The Leviathan*. He was going
against popular thinking at the time that you can learn more by studying others than you can from reading books. He states that one learns
more by studying oneself: especially the feelings that influence our
thoughts and motivate our actions. We all have basic skills to lead,
coach, or communicate; but most of us have some mental blocks when

it comes to applying those skills well and consistently. Knowing yourself, and in that way understanding others, will help you overcome your own blocks and unlock your full potential.

Theories of human nature

People behave according to certain rules of human nature, the common qualities of all human beings. Therefore, to understand our own behaviour and the behaviour of others it is important to have some knowledge about human nature.

Maslow's hierarchy of needs

Human needs are an important part of human nature. Ethics, ideas and behaviour differ from country to country and from culture to culture, but all humans have almost the same needs. US psychology professor Abraham Maslow used the terms 'physiological', 'safety', 'belongingness' and 'love', 'esteem', 'self-actualization', and 'self-transcendence' to describe the pattern that human motivations generally move through (see Figure 10.1). Maslow's theory suggests that the most basic level of needs must be met before the individual will strongly desire the secondary or higher level needs. The basic four layers of the pyramid contain what Maslow called 'deficiency needs': respect, friendship and love, security, and physical needs. If these 'deficiency needs' are not met the individual will feel nervous and stressed. At the top of Maslow's pyramid is self-actualization. Self-actualizers finally feel themselves – safe and not anxious, accepted, loved, loving, and alive, certainly living a satisfying life.

Recent research seems to confirm the existence of universal human needs, although the hierarchy proposed by Maslow is questioned. In fact, there is little evidence for the ranking of needs that Maslow described, or for the existence of a fixed hierarchy at all. According to Geert Hofstede, the needs and drives of people raised in individualistic societies tend to be more self-centred than those in collectivist societies. In individualistic societies people focus on improvement of the self, with self-actualization being the highest point of self-improvement. In collectivist societies, the needs of acceptance and community will outweigh the needs for freedom and individuality.

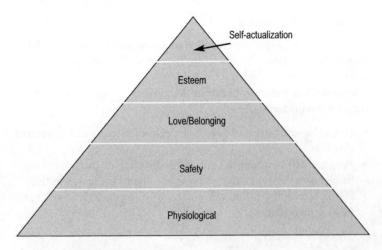

Figure 10.1: Maslow's hierarchy of needs

Herzberg's hygiene and motivational factors

Frederick Herzberg developed a list of factors, which are based on Maslow's hierarchy of needs but more closely related to work:

Hygiene factors or dissatisfiers:

- Working Conditions
- Corporate Policies
- Salary and Benefits
- Supervision
- Status
- Security
- Fellow Workers
- Work-life Balance

Motivators or satisfiers:

- Recognition
- Achievement
- Advancement
- Growth
- Responsibility
- Job Challenge

According to Herzberg, so-called 'hygiene factors' must be present (without them there is dissatisfaction) before motivators stimulate a worker. He used the term job enrichment to describe the process of redesigning work to build motivators.

Theory X and Theory Y

Douglas McGregor developed another view of humanity with his Theory X and Theory Y. These are two opposing perceptions about human behaviour at work.

Theory X is the view that traditional management has taken towards the workforce:

- People have an inherent dislike of work and will avoid it whenever possible.
- People must be coerced, controlled, directed, or threatened with punishment to get them to achieve the organisational objectives.
- People prefer to be directed, do not want responsibility, and have little or no ambition.

Theory Y is different because:

- Work is as natural as play and rest.
- People will exercise self-direction if they are committed to the objectives.
- Commitment to objectives is a function of the rewards associated with their achievement.
- Creativity, ingenuity, and imagination are widely distributed among the population and people are capable of using these abilities to solve an organisational problem.
- People have potential.

Please notice that Maslow, Herzberg, and McGregor's theories all tie together. In fact, Herzberg's theory is the application of Maslow to the workplace and McGregor's Theory X is based on workers trapped at lower levels, while Theory Y is related to workers at higher levels.

Personality

'Chassez le naturel, il revient au gallop' – French proverb (the English equivalent would be 'a leopard cannot change its spots')

The Oxford dictionaries define 'personality' as 'The combination of characteristics or qualities that form an individual's distinctive character' while the American Psychological Association (APA) says: 'Personality refers to individual differences in characteristic patterns of thinking, feeling and behaving.'

There are many theories on personality, and most are in some way based on – or related to – the work of Carl Jung. There are both type and trait theories; trait personality questionnaires are useful in selection and recruitment as they can be more easily mapped to job requirements, whilst the type models are useful in personal and team development, as the type categories are helpful in understanding oneself and others.

Probably the best-known type theory is the *Myers-Briggs Personality Type Indicator* (MBTI) created by Isabel Briggs Myers and her mother, Katharine Cook Briggs.

	Subjective	Objective
Deductive	iNtuition vs Sensing	Perception vs Judging
Inductive	Feeling vs Thinking	Introversion vs Extraversion

Table 10.1: MBTI preferences

Without going into too much detail, it is enough to say that the MBTI is based on the idea that each personality type is composed of four pairs of preferences – or dichotomies – as shown in Table 10.1. Please note that the terms used for each dichotomy have specific technical meanings relating to the MBTI. For example, extraversion means 'outward-turning' and introversion means 'inward-turning'. These specific definitions vary somewhat from the popular usage of the words. Also, the MBTI instrument measures aptitude; it simply indi-

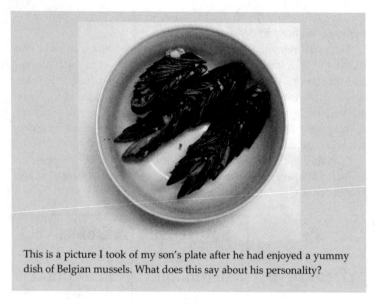

This is a picture I took of my son's plate after he had enjoyed a yummy dish of Belgian mussels. What does this say about his personality?

Figure 10.2: Mussels from Brussels

cates for one preference over another; someone reporting a high score for extraversion over introversion cannot be correctly described as more extraverted: they simply have a clearer preference.

In the MBTI, people are classified according to 16 'type indicators', such as ISTJ (Introversion, Sensing, Thinking, Judging – see Table 10.2). Based on these type indicators a number of common characteristics can be described like:

> 'ISTJ – Quiet, serious, earn success by thoroughness and dependability. Practical, matter-of-fact, realistic and responsible. Decide logically what should be done and work towards it steadily, regardless of distractions. Take pleasure in making everything orderly and organised – their work, their home, their life. Value tradition ands and loyalty.' (From 'Introduction to TYPE' – sixth edition)

ISTJ	ISFJ	INFJ	INTJ
"Doing What Should be Done"	"A High Sense of Duty"	"An Inspiration to Others"	"Everything Has Room For Improvement"
ISTP	**ISFP**	**INFP**	**INTP**
"Ready to Try Anything Once"	"Sees Much But Shares Little"	"Noble Service to Aid Society"	"A Love of Problem Solving"
ESTP	**ESFP**	**ENFP**	**ENTP**
"The Ultimate Realists"	"You Only Go Around Once in Life"	"Giving Life an Extra Squeeze"	"One Exciting Challenge After Another"
ESTJ	**ESFJ**	**ENFJ**	**ENTJ**
"Life's Administrators"	"Hosts and Hostesses of the World"	"Smooth Talking Persuaders"	"Natural Leaders"

Table 10.2: MBTI personality types

It is sometimes argued that the MBTI test is unreliable because 50% of people who take the test a second time get a different result. What this really means is that most people who take the test will score near the middle on at least one dichotomy. So second time around the dichotomy could tip one way or the other over the threshold. The real problem with MBTI is not the stability issue however, but that many people take the test too literally, especially when they go around classifying people and assuming that they now understand the person because they have found a category. This error is the same as assuming that all people are the same.

Many people who take the MBTI ask whether or not their personality type can change. According to type theory, basic type preferences for perception or judgement are innate and do not change. However, it is also known that people, as a result of interacting with their environment and through life experiences, also develop behaviours, habits, and strategies that are not consistent with their type description.

One can compare our 'preferences' with the innate preference of being left-handed or right-handed. A naturally left-handed person (like myself) can learn to write with their right hand. However, when hammering a nail into a wall, they will automatically use their left hand. The 'preference' hasn't changed, but the behaviour is adjusted to the situation.

So why is this important? For one, you may have natural preferences (or innate tendencies) that are not fully used or have been suppressed by your education or environment. Or, you may have facets of your personality that you would like to modify so that you don't fall into the same unhelpful patterns time and again. The sophistication of MBTI is that it is a dynamic system that acknowledges and encourages an individual to change as a part of healthy type development (even as one's basic type theoretically does not change). There is evidence that either the environment or deliberate intention can in fact bring about these changes. This is very good news!

Another important caveat is that your behaviour is also influenced by the context. For example, one person can behave as an extravert when going out with friends, or at home, and show introvert behaviour in the classroom as they don't feel comfortable with the teacher of the subject. So, you should not consider the 'typing' of your personality (or the personality of another person) to be the absolute truth; it's more like an 'average' taken over a variety of contexts you might find yourself in. This, of course, sheds an entirely different light on who a person really is.

"I'm afraid we found annoying
personality markers in your DNA.
I can't hire you."

Who am I?

I am an engineer, brought up and shaped in the Cold War military environment. I started my career in the Belgian Air Force as a technical officer, responsible for an outfit of technicians dealing with the maintenance of military aircraft. When I took the MBTI for the first time the verdict was that I was an ISTJ (see page 244). Looking back, this really corresponded to who I was, and it was a near-perfect match with the kind of person I was expected to be at that time.

In 1993, shortly after the end of the Cold War, I left the military to join a public sector organisation involved in the socio-medical field. After being an IT project manager I moved into the role of Chief Information Officer. In this role I had responsibility for all aspects relating to the IT environment supporting my employer and had to take a much more holistic view. Then, in 2000, I joined the EU administration, still in a managerial position related to IT. Around 2005 I had the opportunity to become Head of Unit for Budget and Finance and had to take management training for that. During this training I took my second MBTI test and, guess what, I had become an INTJ. INTJ's are described as 'Architects', imaginative and strategic thinkers with a plan for everything. Notice how my previous 'Sensing' preference had turned into a more 'Intuitive' one. In fact, the engineer had turned into a manager. In 2013 I started my own business, as a coach and trainer for people who want to become EU officials. From a manager working for an employer, I had become an entrepreneur. Out of curiosity and in the context of another book I wrote, I took another MBTI test. Surprisingly, it turned out that I am an ESTJ now. ESTJ's are 'Executives', excellent administrators, skilled at managing things or people. In short, I went back to the 'Sensing' mode and switched my 'Introversion' preference to 'Extraversion', at least in my behaviour. Please note that the 'Thinking' and 'Judging' parts of my personality have remained unchanged throughout my entire career.

How to make sense of this?

I believe that the consecutive personality types (ISTJ – INTJ – ESTJ) were – and are – pretty close to who I really was or am at these different stages of my life. I was influenced by my environment and adapted my behaviour according to what (I believed) was expected of me. In the role of an engineer I had to behave in the 'Sensing' way, while as a manager and leader I needed to rely more on my intuition. On the other hand, as an employee, I could follow my natural 'Introversion' tendency, while as an entrepreneur I have to behave in the 'Extraversion' mode. I must admit, it took me some years before I fully realised this necessity…

Personality tests tend to be referred to as 'questionnaires', as there are no objective 'right' or 'wrong' answers. It is more about understanding what is helpful or less helpful to achieve personal goals and aspirations. I do recommend that you take a personality questionnaire yourself. Ideally, you would have this done by a real specialist, accredited for example in the MBTI, but a good start can be to take a free online test (http://www.16personalities.com/personality-types). You will be amazed at how much you will learn about yourself. I have treated the more practical use of personality type in the chapters on 'Working in Teams' and 'Managing and Leading'.

One last thing: there are no 'good' or 'bad' personality types. After all, life would be boring if people were all the same.

Culture

Every person carries within him or herself patterns of thinking, feeling, and ways of acting that were learned throughout that person's lifetime. Much of this was acquired in early childhood, because at that time a person is most susceptible to absorbing influences. As soon as certain patterns of thinking, feeling, and acting are established, people have to unlearn these patterns before being able to learn something different, and unlearning is harder than learning for the first time.

In his bestseller *Cultures and Organisations: Software of the Mind* Geert Hofstede uses the comparison of the way computers are programmed. He calls such patterns of thinking, feeling, and acting *mental programs,* or, as per the book's subtitle, *software of the mind.* Allow me to expand on this metaphor. Our 'mental programming' could be compared with the Operating System (OS) of our mind (you know, Microsoft Windows, Mac OSX, or Linux). Much like the operating system of a computer determines its basic behaviour, culture determines ours. The normal programs that are run on top of the OS are only 'learned' behaviour, and are much more easy to upgrade or replace. Also, normal programs are only charged in memory when we use them, while the operating system is there all the time.

It is therefore not surprising to see that one of the anchors for the 'Working in Teams' competency deals explicitly with your attitude towards cultural differences: are you aware of, and tolerant of people from other cultures, or – on the contrary – do you ignore cultural differences and judge people based on your own (cultural) standards?

Xenophobia is the irrational fear of that which is perceived to be different or strange. Xenophobia can manifest itself in many ways such as fear of losing identity, suspicion of the other's behaviour, aggression, and desire to eliminate the other's presence. There is an interesting series of booklets you may already have come across: *A Xenophobe's Guide to* [XYZ], an internationally successful series that highlights the unique character and behaviour of nations. Candid, mocking and funny – almost guaranteed to cure xenophobia (www.xenophobes.com).

Gender and age

Men Are from Mars, Women Are from Venus is a famous book written by the American author and relationship counsellor John Gray. The book argues that most common relationship problems between men and women are a result of basic mental differences between the genders. However, it is my experience that, at least in the places where I worked, these gender differences don't play a major role in the workplace. I have the impression that men and women of about the same age and in comparable positions behave more or less in the same way. Their cultural background and age matters more than the gender difference.

There will soon to be up to four different sociological 'generations' (not the same as family generations) crashing into each other at work.

In shorthand terms, Baby Boomers, born between 1946 and 1964, are often pictured as competitive and loyal to their employer. Gen Xers, born between 1965 and 1977, are held to be more likely to be sceptical and independent-minded. Gen Ys – also known as Millennials – were born in 1978 or later, and usually like teamwork, feedback and technology. Finally, there is Gen Z. Born after 1995; they grew up in a highly sophisticated media and computer environment and will supposedly be more Internet savvy and expert than their Gen Y predecessors. No other generation in the history of humanity has had the technical ability to connect the majority of people on the planet to each other and in the process to provide the potential opportunity for each person to be fully educated, and socially and economically engaged.

It is clear that these 'generations' are very broad concepts, and that individuals vary widely in every generation. A lot of research has been conducted, and a lot of publications written about the differences between the generations, but I tend to agree with Thomas Koulopoulos and Dan Keldsen when they state: 'Generational thinking is like the Tower of Babel: it only serves to divide us. Why not focus on the behaviours that can unite us?' This is the essence of their book *The Gen Z Effect: The Six Forces Shaping the Future of Business*.

There is also an interesting video on TED called 'Closing the Gap – A millennial proposal for a happy multigenerational workplace' by Patrice Thompson, a recently graduated millennial.

Motivation

Motivation is the 'inner force' that drives people to accomplish personal and organisational goals.

In his book *Drive: the Surprising Truth about What Motivates Us*, Daniel Pink describes three eras of motivation. 'Motivation 1.0' – a basic instinct to survive – came in the earliest days of humanity. As more complex social structures evolved, there arrived 'Motivation 2.0' – a desire to seek rewards and avoid punishment. Now, Pink argues, we are in the age of 'Motivation 3.0' – dominated by the desire to direct our own lives and be creative. Pink further argues that what drives successful people in the 21st century are autonomy, mastery and purpose. These are 'intrinsic' motivators related our personal need for satisfaction in what we do, as opposed to 'extrinsic' motivators such as rewards, praise or punishment. *Autonomy* is a degree of freedom in what we do, *mastery* is growing through continuous learning, and *purpose* is a sense that what we do has a value beyond simply earning a living.

Psychologists Teresa Amabile and Steven Kramer interviewed over 600 managers and found that 95 per cent misunderstood what motivates workers. They thought that all that mattered was making money, getting raises and bonuses. Dan Pink maintains that the exact opposite is true: 'The larger the monetary reward, the poorer the performance. – Money doesn't motivate us, at all, instead emotions do.'

Intrinsic motivation is a stronger predictor of job performance than extrinsic motivation. The more people focus on their salaries, the less they will focus on satisfying their intellectual curiosity, learning new skills, or having fun, and those are the very things that make people perform best. But, the basic Motivation 2.0 desire to seek reward and avoid punishment is always there somewhere, except for a lucky few. Also, a person's motivation can change over time, depending on the circumstances of their life. Most of us will have periods in our working lives when we are highly motivated, and other periods when our motivation – and because of this our performance – is below standard. The trick is to work out how to deal with it.

Complementary to McGregor's 'Theory X and Theory Y' (see page 242), Dan Pink created the notions of 'Type I and Type X' behaviour:

- *Type I behaviour* is a way of thinking and an approach to life built around intrinsic, rather than extrinsic, motivators. It is powered by our innate need to direct our own lives, to learn and create new things, and to better ourselves and improve our world.
- *Type X behaviour* is fuelled more by extrinsic desires than intrinsic ones and concerns itself less with the inherent satisfaction of an activity and more with the external rewards to which the activity leads.

You can find out about your own behaviour on Dan Pink's website: www.danpink.com/drive.html

The advantages of workplace diversity

Workplace diversity refers to the variety of differences between people in an organisation. Diversity encompasses race, gender, ethnicity, culture, age, personality, intellectual style, education, background and more. Diversity not only involves how people perceive themselves, but how they perceive others. Those perceptions affect their interactions. An organisation's success and competitiveness depends upon its ability to embrace diversity and realise the benefits. To name a few:

- Attract and retain talent
- Variety of viewpoints
- Increase in creativity

- Better problem solving
- More effective execution
- Increase in productivity
- Increased adaptability
- Broader service range
- Broader market coverage
- Competitive advantage
- Positive reputation

Key points to remember

- *All human beings are different due to their personality, gender, age, cultural background and education.*

- *Every person is unique, and has more potential than can be seen at the surface.*

- *Diversity is an asset, not a handicap for an organisation.*

- *Learning about ourselves gives us the tools to understand others better, and to work better with other people.*

11. What's next?

As a trainer and coach who has helped prepare hundreds of candidates for jobs in the European Union institutions I can hardly be accused of underrating the value of coaching. Coaching is a line of work that takes skill, experience and understanding of human behaviour. To help young professionals improve their game, coaching also demands a deep understanding of how to bring about lasting change.

Unfortunately, there are millions of young people who cannot afford the services of a coach. A young professional buried deep within the organisation may want to improve their game, but sadly, coaching is usually only given to those who are further up in the 'food chain'. For the young professional, there is only one way to create a new future for themselves. That solution is *self-coaching*.

The GROW model

Coaches use models, and the model I am going to describe here is the GROW model. The GROW model is a simple, yet powerful method for goal setting and problem solving. It was developed in the United Kingdom, mainly by Sir John Whitmore and is used a lot in corporate coaching. The principle behind the GROW process comes from the 'Inner Game' theory developed by the American Timothy Gallwey (www.theinnergame.com). Both methods start from the observation that many individuals struggle to reach their goals because they are not learning from experience, and are not aware of the available knowledge that could help them:

'In every human endeavour there are two arenas of engagement: the outer and the inner. The outer game is played on an external arena to overcome external obstacles to reach an external goal. The inner game takes place within the mind of the player and is played against such obstacles as fear, self-doubt, lapses in focus, and limiting concepts or assumptions. The inner game is played to overcome the self-imposed obstacles that prevent an individual or team from accessing their full potential.'

The power of the GROW model lies in the fact that it leads to a clear result in four simple steps. Because it is *the person being coached* who expresses the problem – and generates the ideas – the solution sticks better and leads to lasting results.

The GROW model is a four-step sequence of questions; the acronym stands for:

- **G**OAL – What do you want?
- **R**EALITY – What is happening now?
- **O**PTIONS – What could you do?
- **W**AY FORWARD – What will you do?

(Note: some authors refer to 'Obstacles' for the 'O', and to 'Will' for the 'W', but the underlying ideas of the model remain unchanged.)

A useful metaphor for the GROW model is that of planning a journey. You start with the map: where do you want to go (Goal) and where are you now (Reality)? Then you look at the possible routes (Options). Finally, you pick one route and plan the journey, taking into account all the conditions and obstructions (Way forward).

The GROW model provides a framework for having an effective conversation for achieving any goal or dealing with any kind of problem or challenge. GROW is only a model, not the truth! It is of little value without awareness and responsibility. Awareness increases input, interest, learning and recall. Responsibility is created by offering choice, which leads to self-esteem, confidence and self-motivation.

GROW is flexible in terms of sequence of the steps. The process usually starts with Goal questions and then explores the present with Reality questions. After this, you can move freely between the four elements, as needed. The goal may change along the way. New understanding and awareness may require a return to the Reality section, followed by more Options and actions (Way Forward) related to them.

Please note the similarities between the GROW coaching model, the IDEAL problem-solving model, and the PDCA quality cycle that we looked at earlier. This is no coincidence!

Setting your goals

When setting a goal, in the G part of GROW, there are certain factors which will make the goal stronger and more realistic.

You may already be familiar with SMART goals. SMART is a mnemonic for the 5 steps of Specific, Measurable, Attainable, Relevant, and Time-framed goals. It is a simple tool mostly used by businesses and organisations to go beyond the world of fuzzy goal setting into an actionable plan for results, but it can also be used for individual goal setting.

- *Specific* – Goals have to be simply written and define clearly what you are going to do. This is your vision for the future.
- *Measurable* – Goals have to be measurable so that you have concrete evidence that you have completed the goal. Usually, the whole goal statement is a measure on its own, but there are often several short-term or smaller measurements built into the goal.
- *Attainable* – Goals have to be possible: they must stretch you so that that you feel challenged, but be defined well enough so that you can actually achieve them. You can meet almost any goal when you plan your steps wisely and establish a timeframe that allows you to carry out those steps. As you carry out the steps, you can achieve goals that may have seemed impossible when you started. On the other hand, if a goal is impossible to achieve, you may not even try to accomplish it. Attainable goals motivate – but impossible goals demotivate.
- *Relevant* – In the context of your performance development, your goals have to be linked to a competency and a specific anchor, within the list of your current priorities.

- *Time-framed* – Goals have to be linked to a timeframe that creates a practical sense of urgency, or results in tension between the current reality and the vision of the goal. Without such tension, the goal is unlikely to produce a result.

Besides being SMART, your goals can also be PURE (Positive, Understood, Relevant, and Ethical) or CLEAR (Challenging, Legal, Environmentally Sound, Agreed, and Recorded).

It is important to recognise that there are different levels of goals, and that we have to attend to each level in our journey:

- Dream Goal: your vision or dream
- End Goal: the concrete manifestation of your vision
- Performance Goals: tangible, SMART, PURE, CLEAR
- Process Goals: small, intermediate goals on your way to performance goals.

Exploring your options

Once you have identified the areas where there is room for improvement you can start thinking about your options. These may be simple things like reading some books on the topic or getting some formal training in your domain of activity. But sometimes more extreme options, like a career change have to be carefully thought about.

The purpose of step three in the GROW model is to create ideas that can add to the solution of your problems. It is key to bring alive a creative thinking process that is not hampered by censorship or feasibility considerations. It can help to ask the following questions:

- What could I do to address the problem?
- Who might be able to help?
- What if there were no obstacles?
- What are the pros and cons of this option?
- Which are the considerations I will use to choose this option?
- What else could I do?

In this stage quantity is more important than quality, so try to create as many options as you can.

Commitment

The last step of the GROW coaching model is your commitment to the Way Forward. Here, you carefully select the actions that you will undertake from the list of options that was created during the previous step. The selection is made on the basis mainly of feasibility. Once you have selected the actions you make a plan that matches your SMART Goals, and commit.

Move forward in small, achievable steps. Identify 'quick wins' (process goals) that will make you gain confidence once accomplished, before tackling your performance goals. Personal development takes time, a lot of time, and it is too easy to get discouraged when the distant goals are not reached at the first attempt. And remember: YOU are responsible for your own development, not your manager, your fellow workers, your coach, or your mentor. And neither is the HR department.

More things you can do to develop your essential competencies

Take a class. This may not be the right fit for everyone, but if you have time in your schedule and would like some formal assistance while developing your soft skills, taking a professional development course is an option. Many universities offer these courses in their curriculum.

Volunteer. What better way to practise skills like teamwork and meeting expectations than to work for an organisation that doesn't pay you? Volunteering not only helps out your community, it requires you to work on skills you may not use during other parts of your working or academic life. Plus, if you're interested in managing and leading, this is a great way to develop those skills by chairing a committee, planning an event or even leading the entire organisation.

Become a mentor. Leadership, managing time, meeting expectations, solving problems – name any competency, you can practise it while mentoring. Mentoring gives you real world experience helping someone else work through problems (academic or otherwise).

Teach others. Teaching isn't possible for everybody, but if you have the opportunity, take advantage of your time on the other side of the classroom. You have the opportunity to work on every competency while gaining valuable insight into the inner workings of groups.

Key points to remember

- *You can always improve your competencies, no matter how old or experienced you are.*

- *To start developing your competencies you need to be aware and take responsibility.*

- *Proceed in small steps; don't try to do everything in one go.*

- *In the end, you are the only one in charge of your own development.*

Annex 1. How to land your first job

While the recruiting process differs widely by industry, company and even department, the result is the same: 'many are called but few are chosen'. It is therefore essential that you present yourself in the best possible way at every stage of the process.

In most cases a more-or-less formalised sifting process is involved in which a large number of candidates is progressively reduced to one successful candidate or sometimes a pool of successful candidates. These successive steps are discussed below.

How and where to apply

If you are actively looking for a job you will probably be exploring the classified ads in newspapers, specialised magazines, job boards, etc. It is important to be aware that most job openings at most companies go unadvertised; they are posted only on the company's 'Careers' page. The market for new jobs is so competitive that most companies don't see the need to spend money on third-party recruiting firms or posting their jobs on job boards just to get candidates to apply. To uncover those unadvertised openings, all you need is Google but knowing people who already work for the firm you are interested in can definitely help too.

Writing a spontaneous application directly to an organisation can be a quicker and more direct route into a job. Researching the company (to understand how your interests and skills meet their needs) takes time, but the result is that you are more likely to know if you would be a good match. There is always the risk that your letter goes unanswered or that you receive a rejection, but it's also a strategy that puts you more in charge of your job search, and allows you to discover opportunities that might not have previously existed.

It is always a good idea to take care of your social media presence. You don't want to be ruled out because of a sloppy, incomplete or out-dated profile. Your Facebook or other profile could instantly disqualify you in certain cases (e.g. inappropriate language about minorities, evidence of reckless behaviour) so be alert to this issue also. Your private life and thoughts are not private if they are plastered all over social media.

The classic first jobseeker's 'Catch 22' is lack of experience – employers are nearly always looking for experience in one form or another, but how do you get experience without first having a job? In seeking a job, therefore, try to take a realistic view of whether there is something in your CV – an internship maybe, or voluntary work requiring a relevant skill set – that can overcome the no-experience handicap, and make sure you emphasise it. Unfortunately, the job market has got a lot harder than it once was for those who haven't had internships or volunteered or at least taken relevant training courses. Make sure, too, you can 'speak the language' of the sector you are looking for a job in; if you can seem confident and knowledgeable about that industry, this will show through.

Also, try to read between the lines of job specifications – if you have the opportunity, talk to someone who has been through the process plenty of times and ideally also knows the sector or even the specific company and can tell you what matters most. Sometimes the requirements are absolutely binding (for instance, if specific professional or technical qualifications are asked for) but sometimes not everything that is asked for is actually expected – and if you can get to the point of showing your potential, there will always, eventually, be someone to give you a chance even if you lack experience. Don't just bin a job advert because you don't seem to qualify on one or two aspects.

Bear in mind, too, the universe of small and medium-sized enterprises, not to mention micro enterprises and start-ups. While these may lack the impressive glamour of giant corporations, and of course don't have the career structures, they may offer different opportunities of their own, and may have a more open-minded recruitment policy. They may be more likely to give you a chance based on your potential and a fairly informal assessment of whether you might be a good fit with their ambitions. And, for sure, if your dream is to one day be your own boss, you will probably gain more from working in such an environment where every aspect of your skillset could be called into play even as a first-jobber.

Sometimes it also pays to think laterally. If your university course was very technical or vocational you will most likely be looking for a job specifically in that field – if you have studied veterinary science, for example, it is a fair bet you will be looking for a job working with animals. However, most university courses are, in relation to the world of work, very 'generalist' – if you have studied history, or English language, or business studies, the potential targets for employment are much more diffuse. Think laterally and you may surprise yourself with the ideas you come up with. Brainstorm them with other people. Above all, be open-minded. Many people end up happily and successfully in careers they could never have imagined when they graduated and which certainly make no obvious call on the subjects they studied at university.

Here it can pay to think carefully about your soft skills. Assuming you have already read this book, and not just gone straight to this annex, you should have learned plenty and given lots of thought to what your strengths and weaknesses are when it comes to your soft skills. Do you really like working in teams or are you actually only comfortable when working by yourself? Do you like to lead from the front or do you prefer to take a back seat, letting others set the course for you? Are you comfortable handling difficult interpersonal work situations or do you dread conflict and avoid it at all cost? If you have created your competency 'spider's web' with the app that goes with this book, you should have got a clear perspective on where your strengths and weaknesses lie. Of course, you should try to strengthen your soft skills across the board, it goes without saying – but it also makes sense to think about what career paths might mesh best not just with your formal qualifications but with what you have discovered to be your strengths in your soft skills.

One thing you will find is that at every step of the recruitment process, whatever direction you take, your soft skills are likely to be key. Only in the most specialised professional technical areas will hard skills be all that is required. You need to regard looking for a job as a job on its own, and you will need to call on (and practise) all your competencies.

CVs and application letters

If you want to secure an interview and get a job it is extremely important to make a good first impression on a possible employer with a résumé or Curriculum Vitae (CV). In looking at CVs, diplomas, previous experience, etc. are inspected, looking mostly for the relevant 'hard skills' specific to the job. How this is done, the time it takes, and the number of applicants selected to go on to the next step varies, but there are some patterns. Some screeners carefully read every submission that comes in, while others search for certain keywords among applications. Also, there are screeners who consider motivation letters in their evaluations and those who ignore them. In most cases, however, this is done only on paper.

Your CV has to be presented correctly, so that your strengths are underlined and key points are highlighted – most likely your CV will in the first instance only be skimmed, so present the facts clearly and concisely so your key personal selling points are not going to be missed. Do not leave gaps in the chronology or it may look like you have something to hide. And work backwards in the chronology, from what you are doing now: employers are going to be interested in the now and the recent past, not the newspaper delivery round you had when you were 12 years old. A clear CV which draws attention to the positive aspects of your career to date will grab the employer's attention and show your potential suitability for the job.

Whenever you send off an application, make sure to include a motivation letter. This does not necessarily have to be a separate document but could be simply a well-crafted email to which you attach your CV. In your motivation letter, you can also include (for example) a hyperlink to your LinkedIn profile if you have one, for additional information and to show off any endorsement or recommendation that it may include.

In your motivation letter or your social media profile, make sure to highlight all the elements that make you suitable for the job concerned; if you have the detailed job description, you can explicitly connect your academic and professional achievements to the requirements for that job to reinforce the idea that you are in fact a good candidate.

One of the most common mistakes candidates make is that they talk too much about their skills and achievements without actually linking them to the specific job they are applying for. You should connect your skill set with the needs of your future employer, and avoid them having to figure out such a link for themselves – something which most likely won't happen given the limited time spent on looking at any application. If you do this mental shortcut for them, your chances of raising their interest level and inviting you for an interview increase significantly.

In addition, a good visual presentation of both your motivation letter and your CV are essential for success. Bullet points, moderately but strategically used; highlights or links in the email; short and well-defined paragraphs; an overall 100-150-word length – all can add a lot to your application. It is absolutely fundamental to avoid spelling mistakes or grammatical howlers – for most jobs there are plenty of applications, so you are going to fail at the first hurdle by looking careless and unconcerned.

Finally, try to avoid gushing prose saying how passionate you are and phrases that look like they have been taken from standard letters you found on the internet. If what you say about yourself at this stage doesn't really reflect who you are, that will be easily spotted if you reach the interview stage.

Formalised testing

Typically the sifting of CVs involves the elimination of the great majority of candidates; each person, therefore, who makes it to the next stage, is being seriously evaluated for their potential in terms of the contribution they can make to the employer's organisation.

Everything from this point is costing the employer time and therefore money, so you can be sure they are taking it seriously, and you need to take it seriously too as you have a chance of getting the job.

In some cases you may be asked to take a series of formalised tests, in others you may go straight to an interview, most likely with your potential line manager and/or someone else senior in the department, commonly with someone from human resources sitting in on the process. Generally speaking, the recruitment process has more steps the higher you go in your career: this is because the costs and risks to the employer of a bad appointment are so much greater. However that is not always the case. For example, first-post recruits to civil service jobs usually face very serious exams rather like graduating exams. This is because these have been, traditionally at least, 'jobs for life' so, again, the risks to the employer are so much greater. Turnover of staff in the private sector is higher and poor choices of staff usually move on – or get fired.

Some employers, especially very large ones, use a highly sophisticated mechanism called an Assessment Centre to evaluate candidates. Basically, an Assessment Centre (AC) consists of asking candidates to complete a varied set of exercises that are designed to simulate different parts of a role and work environment. A team of assessors who make judgements on the candidates' performance observes candidates by watching their behaviour during the AC in terms of what 'good' and 'poor' performance looks like. You will be observed by a number of assessors (typically four) throughout the event, to minimise the likelihood of any bias on the part of assessors. All the competencies as described in this book will be carefully examined, even though there will probably be differences in the competency framework that is used for the specific post. Also, during an AC the candidate's 'hard skills' will often also be assessed, along with the 'general intelligence' as described in Chapter 1.

The interview

In an interview a lot of the time will likely be spent talking about your hard skills. This will probably be mainly within your comfort zone (unless you are clearly unsuitable for the job, so it would be a mistake for you to want to go further with it anyway). However, there are almost certainly going to be other candidates with fairly comparable hard skills to yours, so it is your soft skills which will most likely prove decisive. You can be sure that the person from human resources, who will probably not pay much attention at all to the discussion of hard skills, will be focusing very closely on how you come across on your soft skills competencies. These are people who see candidates day-in, day-out, so you will find it very hard to disguise the fact if you have problems with your soft skills.

Of course, the relative importance of the various soft skills will vary from job to job – in some roles, such as customer-facing jobs, qualities like resilience and communicating will be to the fore, whereas in roles where you work mainly on projects with a few colleagues within the organisation aspects like working in teams or managing time would loom large. It would be worth spending time, before you get into the interview room, trying to think through which of the competencies discussed in this book are likely to be key to the job you are applying for, so you take any opportunity you have to demonstrate or refer to your capabilities in those areas.

A challenge in interview situations is to try to identify who will be making the decisions – is it, for instance, one person on the panel, or a collective decision? You may think you have worked out the answer to this and address your comments to the key person only to have misjudged the situation, so be inclusive in your responses, and try to engage with everyone involved. Bear in mind also that the person asking the toughest questions may not in fact be the one who is least enthusiastic about you: on the contrary, they could be the one who thinks you are the right choice for the job but wants to press you a bit with probing questions, just to confirm their hunch. It is very important in that sort of situation that you sound mature and professional and don't react in a touchy way that suggests you are over-sensitive to criticism and could be difficult to work with.

While the format of interviews varies, they commonly conclude with the candidate being asked if they have any questions. Make sure you ask one! Preferably this should be a question that builds on the interchanges you have had in the interview itself and shows you are already getting to grips with the demands of the job and the culture of the organisation. Needless to say, you should absolutely avoid asking a question that has already been answered in the information you have been sent about the job. That will simply look like you couldn't be bothered to prepare properly. Furthermore, once you have asked your question and had an answer, leave it at that. Don't start off on another question on another topic. There is probably another interview scheduled and you need to respect the panellists' time.

And, however tough the interview, make sure you leave the room thanking the interviewers and looking and sounding undefeated and professional. You would be surprised how many people miss getting one job but are called back for interview for another job in the same organisation having made a good impression first time round.

For some positions, a medical check-up is performed, although strictly speaking this is not part of the selection procedure (it is a 'go-no-go' test). If you are asked health-related questions you must answer them truthfully or this could create major difficulties later.

There is more on the vital topic of the interview in Annex 2, so make sure you read that as well!

Key issues at each stage

At each stage of the recruitment process, whatever the exact form it takes, the same basic questions and issues are being examined. Your best approach is to try to think with the recruiter's head. In most cases the recruiter will know nothing about you other than what you have said in your CV, covering letters and maybe your social media profile. That is true whether it is the CV-sifting stage or the interview stage.

As the recruiter tries to get a fix on who you are and what you can do, they will always be thinking about the same questions:

- Is the candidate formally eligible for this post?
- Is their job experience relevant to the specific tasks they would need to do in this role?

- Which specific elements of their profile would fully correspond to the tasks?
- Do they have the right skills that were spelled out in the vacancy notice, or those that were not written there but are implied by the job description?
- Do they have good team working, communication and diplomatic skills?
- Will it take a long time for them to get started in the job, and once they get started, will they need to learn a lot before they become autonomous and operational?
- Are they available for an interview in person, or would they need to travel from far away (which may add complexity, time and administrative burden to the hiring, and unless they are a stellar candidate, others may be more accessible)?
- Do they have the right attitude and 'cultural fit' for our organisation?
- Are they extraverts, or more analytical, or both, depending on what I am seeking?
- If they already work, is their current job relevant to the new post?
- Do they have anyone as a reference I could speak to?

If you manage to answer or take away these 'anxieties' in the motivation letter and the CV, you will have a much better chance of being invited to an interview. You can expect the same issues to come back in the interview, with any difficult areas likely to be probed. As mentioned above, many candidates only give a 'static' description of their strengths and experiences, without directly linking these to the specific requirements of the job. The most important principle here is to answer the question: *'how can you be an asset to my team?'*

What if you were not selected?

In Chapter 7, I have defined resilience as your ability to adapt to stress and adversity. People show resilience when they face difficult experiences and rise above them – or 'bounce back'.

It goes without saying that not getting a job can sometimes be depressing and dispiriting. But bear in mind this is not your unique experience – in fact, it is rather rare to find someone who has not gone through such periods. It is a mistake to think that people who are resilient experience no negative emotions or thoughts and display optimism in all situations. That is rarely the case. The truth remains, however, that resilience is demonstrated by people who can overcome disappointments, finding ways of navigating their way around negative experiences and using effective methods of coping with them.

It is in a way toughest to be eliminated at the final interview stage – you were maybe the 'second choice' but unfortunately there can (usually) be only one winner. You should keep the thought that you are one of the few to have made it to the interview stage. Most of the other candidates didn't make it that far. It is an achievement in itself to have got as far as you did. Furthermore, being interviewed is, like with most skills in life, something we can get better at with practice. Don't just wipe out the memory of an interview where you 'failed'. Don't justify yourself with the idea that 'they already had an internal candidate lined up' or make the excuse to yourself that 'I wouldn't have liked working there anyway'. Review the experience and, again, try to put yourself inside the recruiter's head – where did you perhaps go wrong, *from their point of view.* For sure, if the problem was some aspect of your attitude or approach, the way you expose a flaw in one of your soft skills, you can work on that and make sure you get it right next time.

Walt Disney put it this way: 'The difference between winning and losing is most often not quitting.'

Resources

- *Ready Made CVs* by Lynn Williams
- *The Ultimate EU Test Book – Assessment Centre Edition* by András Baneth and Jan De Sutter
- *How to Succeed at an Assessment Centre* by Harry Tolly and Robert Wood
- http://europass.cedefop.europa.eu/

Annex 2. How to prepare for a job interview

"My strengths? I'm especially good at answering the typical job interview questions. My weaknesses? I don't really like working."

Interviewing methods differ greatly depending on the industry to which you're applying, the company and even the position within the company. The interviewers may focus on one style or engage you in a combination of several interview types. The best thing you can do to prepare is to understand each style and its intention from the interviewer's perspective.

Standard interviews

Often, the people doing the interview are not human resources professionals, but they will be seasoned professionals in your field of expertise, and they may be you future supervisors or fellow workers. These people will be interested in both your hard skills (education and experience) and how they feel about you as a person and a future colleague, which is where your soft skills come in.

They will most often come up with a first question asking you to say something about yourself. They may quite possibly not have read your CV at all, or just briefly glanced at it before the interview, so it is very important to answer this question in a well-thought-out, specific and truthful way. The purpose of this first question then is to put them 'in the picture', to give them the necessary background information to better understand your answers during the rest of the interview. I suggest you think of the following metaphor. Imagine that – when you enter the room – you are an empty canvas, and the intention of the interviewers is to paint your portrait on that canvas. What you have to give them during those moments of self-introduction are the contours of your portrait, and it's up to them to complete the painting with all the details – and colours – they notice during the interview.

While presenting yourself also remember to make their lives easy. The interviewers may have seen dozens of candidates before you and they may be doing this as a side-assignment on top of their regular job. One way of making their life easy is to tell your story in a chronological order, without jumping back and forth in time.

In a CV or a written application you can only express a bit of your personality and motivation – and you can also disguise who you really are in well-designed sentences and carefully chosen adjectives. It is much harder to do so in a face-to-face situation where you have to think on your feet.

At the very least it would be essential for you to be 100% on top of every fact and figure, especially things like exact dates of previous experience that you mentioned in your CV. Interviewers get nervous about any inconsistencies that emerge in discussing a CV as they worry about what else might be hidden – so it would be most useful the day before the interview to systematically review your CV in your head so you can give exact chapter and verse on everything.

You could also benefit from reviewing any weaknesses in your CV, and to some degree 'pre-script' effective answers to the questions that might probe those weaknesses. You could do this by tri-

The secrets of a handshake

Your handshake is a vital part of creating the right first impression; it is the only opportunity where the interviewers actually get to have a physical interaction with you (though not all assessors offer to shake hands). The 'ideal' handshake conveys confidence and equality. If you are sitting in a waiting area always stand up as remaining seated looks rude. Wait for the other person to offer their hand; they are on their territory, so they should initiate the handshake. Step towards the person confidently, not too close and not too far away. SMILE! Make direct eye contact and hold it for the whole handshake. A good little trick is to try to observe the other person's eye colour during this time, which will inevitably result in you looking deep into the other person's eye for a second or two. Give a brief squeeze, not too gently, not too strong.

alling with a friend acting as an interviewer and working from the data used for your CV.

Here are a few tips to help make sure you are not scored lower than what you deserve based on your achievements and overall profile. Always make sure, nevertheless, to provide truthful and relevant information, and never invent anything that is not 'rooted in reality'.

- Remember *it is a subjective exercise*. The interview is purely scored by humans and not by computer algorithms.
- *Terminology matters*. At the same time, using relevant terminology or references to your job-related activities can have an important impact on your scores. Moreover, the way you communicate your specific knowledge during the interview will also influence the interviewers' understanding of your professional background.
- *Less is more*. To paraphrase Einstein, 'everything has to be as short as possible, but not shorter'. This means that while you need to provide extensive information about your achievements, job-related experience and qualifications, no interviewer will want to hear a lengthy reply to the various questions in the interview.
- *Don't boast*. No interviewer wants to see an overconfident candidate who is too full of themself. Be specific about your achievements and positive but not over-the-top about your potential contribution.
- *Link your achievements to the interviewers' objectives*. Even when a question relates to 'your' commitment, motivation, achievements or experience, always make sure that you link your personal background and work experience to the needs of the employer.

Behavioural interviews

No interviewer is going to ask you if you have a soft skill; they're going to ask you to *show them* how you have implemented that skill in or out of the workplace. Behavioural interviews – also known as competency based interviews – focus on the past so interviewers can attempt to predict future behaviour.

The questions you will get during a behavioural interview have a 'generic' format:

Tell us about a situation where XYZ happened, what did you do and what were the results of your actions?

You are then supposed to talk about a specific situation in your past – preferably work-related – and explain how you responded (what you did) and what were the results of your actions. I want to stress the importance of being specific. Many people have a tendency to reply with a general 'this happened frequently', or simply 'yes' but that is not what is expected. You are supposed to describe a very precise episode in your life and explain exactly what you did. This is a very large degree of freedom you get here, and you have to use this freedom to find the best possible example.

A waterproof method of answering a behavioural question is known as the *STAR model*. STAR is the acronym for Situation, Task, Actions, and Results:

- *Situation* – What was the challenge or situation in which you found yourself? (what?, where?, when?).
- *Task* – What did you have to achieve? What was expected of you? (Why?)
- *Action* – What did you do? How did you do it? How did you respond to the situation? (How?)
- *Results* – What was the outcome of your actions? What did you achieve? Did you meet your objectives? What did you learn from this experience and have you used this learning since?

There is often confusion in people's minds about the Task part of a STAR answer. Many people believe that they have to say what their boss had told them to do, or which explicit instructions they had received. Not so. In the Task part you have to explain *what was expected of you, given the situation* (think of the Meeting Expectations competency). As such, in many cases you could limit yourself to telling them about your role. In combination with the situation this will be more than enough background information for them to understand the reasons for your actions.

I cannot underline enough the importance of using the STAR model in a behavioural interview. Using the STAR model is easy for you, because it will allow you to tell your 'stories' in a natural way; you won't have to think about *how* to tell the story because the order is very natural. On the other hand, you will make the interviewer's life easy as well. Behavioural interviews are usually conducted by professional interviewers who have been trained in this kind of interviewing. They will know the STAR model, have practised it during their training, and will be very happy to hear you kick off with a situation and a task because they already know what's coming next.

The most important part of your STAR answer is the 'Actions'. Remember that they want to observe your behaviour in the past and draw conclusions about your future behaviour. For that reason I suggest you spend more than half the time of your answer in describing your actions. Say you spend 60% on the 'Actions' part, you would then spend 20% on the 'Results' (because without tangible results your actions were in vain) and the remaining 20% in 'Situation' and 'Task' combined (since these cannot been seen independently and they explain the reasons *why* you did the 'Actions').

All good and well, but how can you prepare in practice for a behavioural interview?

Without any doubt, the interviewers will be interested in your general competencies as described in this book. You could then try to find a relevant example for every anchor as listed at the beginning of each chapter. When you have done so, you will be ready to answer virtually every question they may ask you, because the set of anchors as given in this book is very comprehensive. You can – of course – do this preparation in writing, but please don't learn your 'stories' by heart because you want them to sound natural when you deliver them during the interview. The STAR model will help you with that.

If by any chance the competencies sought after do not entirely match the framework of this book you have to try to find out where are the differences, and prepare your stories accordingly. This could be the case for very specific functions in for example sales and marketing, or public relations, but you can get an idea by carefully reading the vacancy notice.

People often confuse behavioural and situational interviews, which are described next. Questions may seem similar, because an employer is assessing your behaviour in a particular situation, but the purpose is different.

Situational interviews

Situational interview questions are similar to behavioural questions, but instead of asking you to tell about a past experience and explain how you handled yourself in that situation, you're presented with a hypothetical situation. Situational interviews concentrate on future performance rather than past performance (which is the focus of behavioural interviews). The interviewer will give you a problem and ask how you would deal with it. For example:

You are working on a project with a tight deadline but you find that you are unable to complete your part because your fellow workers are unavailable to answer a few key questions. How do you deal with this situation?

Interviewers want to know how you would solve a problem, and in some cases, they want to measure your expertise. Always be honest and specific. Address the problem, and describe your solution and the actions you would take.

Situational interviews can be looked upon as role-play exercises. You are given a scenario and act as if you were the person in the assigned role.

The best way to prepare for such an interview is to practise. Sit down with a friend and ask them to come up with some situational questions. Be sure to adjust the format of the questions and the type of scenario to the specific company and position you are interviewing for. When you have finished answering, take a few minutes to discuss the answers together to make sure that your answer is in line with the 'positive indicators' as outlined in this book.

Sometimes, instead of a situational interview, employers use computer-based tests like situational judgement or in-tray exercises because these are less labour-intensive (for the evaluators) and are believed to be more objective. I personally have my doubts about that.

There are, of course, other forms of job interviews than the ones described above. These can be case interviews, presentations, panel interviews, or any variation/combination of these. It is impossible to describe a preparation strategy for every permutation within the

---

A recruiter's point of view

Sure, I will think about your qualifications, but what I am really looking for goes far beyond that.

I want to work with people I like, and who like me. A candidate who makes a great first impression and sparks a real connection instantly becomes a big fish in a very small short-list pond. You may have solid qualifications, but if I don't think I'll enjoy working with you, I'm probably not going to hire you.

I want you to stand out. A sad truth of interviewing is that later I often don't recall, unless I refer to my notes, a meaningful amount about some of the candidates. The more people I interview for a job, the more likely I am to remember a candidate by impressions rather than by a long list of facts. I will remember you by 'hooks' – whether flattering or unflattering – so use that to your advantage. Your hook could be your clothing, or an outside interest, or an unusual fact about your life or career. Instead of letting me choose, give me one or two remarkable ways to remember you.

I need to know whether I should hire you, but just as importantly I need you to make sure my job is a good fit for you. So I want you to ask questions. You are the only person who knows what makes you tick. I don't. There's no other way to really know whether you want the job unless you ask questions.

I know you want a positive work-life balance, but let us first find out if you're the right person for the job, and whether the tasks, responsibilities, duties, etc. are right for you. Then we can talk about the rest.

I also appreciate a brief follow-up note. A follow-up note is nice. But 'nice' may not separate you from the pack. What I really like is when you follow up based on something we discussed. The more closely you listened during the interview, the easier it is to think of ways to follow up in a natural and unforced way.

Remember, we're starting a relationship – and every relationship is based on honest interactions.

limits of this annex, but there is one common denominator: *practice*. Google the type of interview you want to prepare for, find some 'typical questions' and practise, practise, practise. And remember: tailoring your answers to the needs of the employer is key.

Most common interview mistakes

- Not doing research on the company before the interview
- Not dressing for the occasion
- Answering a mobile phone or texting during the interview
- Avoiding eye contact with the interviewers
- Mismatch between body language and what you say
- Not behaving 'naturally'
- Being overly nervous
- Being overly confident
- Speaking negatively about current or previous employer
- Answering in general terms, not being specific
- Not focusing on your strenghts
- Not keeping in mind what's in it for them
- Asking questions about working conditions or salary
- No follow-up letter or email

Resources

- *The Ultimate EU Test Book – Assessment Centre Edition* by András Baneth and Jan De Sutter
- *Job Interview Success – Be your own Coach* by Jenny Rogers
- *Now you've been shortlisted* by Denise Taylor
- http://www.interview-skills.co.uk/free-information/interview-guide

Annex 3.   Bibliography

Allcott, Graham *How to be a Productivity Ninja* (ISBN: 9781848316836)

Alred, Dave *The Pressure Principle: Handle Stress, Harness Energy, and Perform when it Counts* (ISBN: 9780241240847)

Anderson, Chris *TED Talks: The Official TED Guide to Public Speaking* (ISBN: 9781472244437)

Arendt, Hannah *The Human Condition* (ISBN: 9780226025988)

Baneth, András and Jan De Sutter *The Ultimate EU Test Book: Assessment Centre Edition* (ISBN: 9780992974879)

Barr, L. and N. Barr *Leadership Development: Maturity and Power* (ISBN: 9780890159453)

Blake, R. and J. Mouton *The Managerial Grid III: The Key to Leadership Excellence* (ISBN 9780872014701)

Blein, Bernard *Prendre la parole en public* (ISBN: 9782035843562)

Blyth, Catherine *The Art of Conversation: A guided Tour of a Neglected Pleasure* (ISBN: 9781592404971)

Borysenko, Joan *Fried: Why you Burn Out and how to Revive* (ISBN: 9781401925512)

Brown, Bren *The Gifts of Imperfection* (ISBN: 9781592858491)

Cain, Susan *Quiet: The Power of Introverts in a World that can't stop Talking* (ISBN: 9780141029191)

Carnegie, Dale *How to win Friends and Influence People* (ISBN: 9780671027032)

Carr, Nicholas *The Shallows: What the Internet is doing to our Brains* (ISBN: 9780393339758)

Christian, Brian and Tom Griffiths *Algorithms to Live by* (ISBN: 9780008166090)

Connerly, Mary and Paul Pedersen *Leadership in a Diverse and Multicultural Environment* (ISBN: 9780761988601)

Cottrell, Stella *Skills for Success: Personal Development and Employability* (ISBN: 9781137426529)

Covet, Stephen *The 7 Habits of Highly Effective People* (ISBN: 9780684858395)

Covey, Stephen *First Things First* (ISBN: 9780684802039)

Coyle, Daniel *The Talent Code* (ISBN: 9780099519850)

Csikszentmihalyi, Mihaly *Finding Flow* (ISBN: 9780465024117)

Davenport, Thomas H. and John C. Beck *The Attention Economy: Understanding the New Currency of Business* (ISBN: 9781578518715)

Davenport, Thomas H. *Thinking for a Living* (ISBN: 9781591394235)

De Bono, Edward *Six Thinking Hats* (ISBN: 9780316178310)

De Bono, Edward *The Use of Lateral Thinking* (ISBN: 9780140137880)

De Sutter, Jan *The Ultimate EU Career Development Book* (ISBN: 9780993454936)

Duarte, Nancy *HBR Guide to Persuasive Presentations* (ISBN: 9781422187104)

Duckworth, Angela *Grit: The Power of Passion and Perseverance* (ISBN: 9781785040184)

Flamholtz, Eric and Yvonne Randle *Growing Pains* (ISBN: 9780787986162)

Ford, Martin *Rise of the Robots: Technology and the Threat of Mass Unemployment* (ISBN: 9781780748481)

Friedman, Thomas L. *Hot, Flat, and Crowded* (ISBN: 9780141036663)

Friedman, Thomas L. *The World is Flat* (ISBN: 9783125737990)

Galinsky, Adam and Maurice Schweitzer *Friend and Foe: When to Cooperate, When to Compete, and How to Succeed at Both* (ISBN: 9780307720214)

Gallo, Carmine *The Storyteller's Secret* (ISBN: 978047009160)

Gallwey, Timothy *The Inner Game of Work: Overcoming Mental Obstacles for Maximum Performance* (ISBN: 9781842030158)

George, Bill *Authentic Leadership: Rediscovering the Secrets of Creating Lasting Value* (ISBN: 9780787969134)

Gigerenzer, Gerd *Gut Feeling: Short cuts to better decision making* (ISBN: 9780141015910)

Gigerenzer, Gerd *Risk Savvy: How to make good decisions* (ISBN: 9780143127109)

Glover, Robert *No More Mr Nice Guy* (ISBN: 9780762415335)

Goleman, Daniel *Emotional Intelligence: Why It Can Matter More Than IQ* (ISBN: 9780553383713)

Goleman, Daniel et al *Primal Leadership* (ISBN: 9781422168035)

Goleman, Daniel *Working with Emotional Intelligence* (ISBN: 9780553378580)

Grant, Adam *Give and Take: Why Helping others Drives our Success* (ISBN: 9780143124986)

Gray, Dave, Sunny Brown and James Macanufo *Gamestorming: A Playbook for Innovators, Rulebreakers, and Changemakers* (ISBN: 9780596804176)

Hersey, Paul et al *Management of Organisational Behaviour* (ISBN: 9788120335455)

Hofstede, Geert, Gert Jan Hofstede and Michael Minkov *Cultures and Organisations: Software of the Mind* (ISBN: 9780071664189)

Imai, Masaaki *Kaizen: The Key to Japan's Competitive Success* (ISBN: 9780075543329)

Janis, Irving *Victims of Groupthink: A psychological Study of foreign-policy decisions and fiascoes* (ISBN: 9780395140444)

Jeffers, Susan *Feel the fear and do it anyway* (ISBN: 9780091907075)

Johnson, Spencer *Who moved my Cheese?* (ISBN: 9780091816971)

Kahneman, Daniel *Thinking, fast and slow* (ISBN: 9780141033570)

King, Patrick *Encore!* (ISBN: 9781523872152)

Kline, Nancy *Time to Think: Listening to Ignite the Human Mind* (ISBN: 9780706377453)

Kotter, John P. *A Sense of Urgency* (ISBN: 9781423369356)

Kotter, John P. *Our Iceberg is Melting* (ISBN: 9780230014206)

Koulopoulos, Tom and Dan Keldsen *The Gen Z Effect: The Six Forces Shaping the Future of Business* (ISBN: 9781629560311)

Kurzban, Robert *Why everyone (else) is a hypocrite: Evolution and the modular mind* (ISBN: 9780691154398)

Lakoff, George and Mark Johnson *Metaphors we live by* (ISBN: 9780226468013)

Locke, Edwin et al. *A theory of goal setting and task performance* (ISBN: 9780139131387)

Lombardo, Michael and Robert Eichinger *The Career Architect Development Planner* (ISBN: 9780965571241)

Maslach, Christina and Michael P. Leiter *The Truth about Burnout:*

How Organisations Cause Personal Stress and What to Do About it (ISBN: 9781118692134)

Mason, Antony *Xenophobe's Guide to the Belgians* (ISBN: 9781906042226)

McCormack, Joseph *Brief: Make a Bigger Impact by Saying Less* (ISBN: 9781118704967)

McGonigal, Kelly *The Upside of Stress: Why Stress is good for You, and how to get Good at It* (ISBN: 9781583335611)

McGregor, Douglas *The Human Side of Enterprise* (ISBN 9780070450929)

Messinger, Joseph *Ces gestes qui vous trahissent* (ISBN: 9782290035016)

Michalko, Michael *Thinkertoys: A Handbook of Creative Thinking Techniques* (ISBN: 9781580087735)

Murphy, Herta A. et al *Effective Business Communications* (ISBN: 9780070443983)

Myers, Lorii *Targeting Success* (ISBN: 9780986790003)

Nassim, Nicholas Taleb *Fooled by Randomness: The Hidden Role of Chance in Life and in the Markets* (ISBN: 9780141031484)

Nisbett, Richard E. *Mindware: Tools for Smart Thinking* (ISBN: 9780374112677)

Nisbett, Richard E. *Intelligence and How to Get It* (ISBN: 9780393337693)

Nisbett, Richard E. *The Geography of Thought* (ISBN: 9781857883534)

O'Connell, B., S. Palmer & H. Williams *Solution Focused Coaching in Practice: Essential Coaching Skills and Knowledge* (ASIN: B00ZT0WXVK)

Osborn, Alex F. *Applied Imagination: Principles and Procedures of Creative Problem Solving* (ISBN: 9780930222734)

Palladino, Lucy Jo *Find Your Focus Zone* (ISBN: 9781416532019)

Parkinson, C. Northcote *Parkinson's Law: Or the Pursuit of Progress* (ISBN: 9780141186856)

Paul, Richard and Linda Elder *The Thinker's Guide to the Art of Socratic Questioning* (ASIN: B0065RPUGG)

Peshawaria, Rajeev *Too Many Bosses, Too Few Leaders* (ISBN: 9781451646672)

Peter, Laurence J. and Raymond Hull *The Peter Principle: Why Things Always go Wrong* (ISBN: 9780062092069)

Pink, Daniel H. *A Whole New Mind: Why Right-Brainers will rule the Future* (ISBN: 9781594481710)

Pink, Daniel H. *Drive: The Surprising Truth About What Motivates Us* (ISBN 9781594484803)

Pinkner, Susan *The Village Effect: Why Face-to-Face Contact Matters* (ISBN: 9781848878594)

Pontefract, Dan *Flat Army: Creating a Connected and Engaged Organisation* (ISBN: 9781943425419)

Schwartz, Barry *Why we Work* (ISBN: 9781471141812)

Sibbet, David *Visual meetings: How Graphics, Sticky Notes & idea mapping can transform group productivity* (ISBN: 9780470601785)

Sinek, Simon *Leaders eat Last: Why some teams pull together and others don't* (ISBN: 9781591845324)

Sinek, Simon *Start with Why: How Great Leaders Inspire Everyone to take Action* (ISBN: 781591846444)

Syed, Matthew *Black Box Thinking: Marginal Gains and the Secret of High Performance* (ISBN: 9781473613805)

Syed, Matthew *Bounce: The myth of talent and the power of practice* (ISBN: 9780007350544)

Tapscott, Don and Anthony D. Williams *Wikinomics: How Mass Collaboration Changes Everything* (ISBN: 9781591843672)

Turkle, Sherry *Reclaiming Conversation: The Power of Talk in a Digital Age* (ISBN: 9780143109792)

Werder, Peter and Philippe Rothlin *Boreout: Overcoming workplace demotivation* (ISBN: 9780749453398)

Whitmore, John *Coaching for Performance: GROWing human potential and Purpose* (ISBN: 9781857885354)

Witt, Christopher *Real Leaders Don't Do Powerpoint: How to Speak so People Listen* (ISBN: 9780749942601)

Wright, Milton *The Art of Conversation* (ASIN: B000H1DGTE)

Annex 4.   Other resources

Inspiring TED Talks

TED (www.ted.com) is a non-profit organisation devoted to spreading ideas, usually in the form of short, powerful talks (18 minutes or less). TED began in 1984 as a conference where Technology, Entertainment and Design converged, and today covers almost all topics – from science to business to global issues – in more than 100 languages. Meanwhile, independently run TEDx events help share ideas in communities around the world. Below is a list of my favourite talks.

- The puzzle of motivation – Dan Pink
- How great leaders inspire action – Simon Sinek
- What makes us feel good about our work – Dan Ariely
- Got a wicked problem? First, tell me how you make toast – Tom Wujec
- The case for letting business solve social problems – Michael Porter
- The career advice you probably didn't get – Susan Colantuono
- Why its time to forget the pecking order at work – Margaret Heffernan
- Dare to disagree – Margaret Heffernan
- Why good leaders make you feel safe – Simon Sinek
- How to manage for collective creativity – Linda Hill
- Your body language shapes who you are – Amy Cuddy
- The power of vulnerability – Brene Brown
- 10 ways to have a better conversation – Celeste Headlee
- Inside the mind of a master procrastinator – Tim Urban

- Why you think you're right, even if you're wrong – Julia Galef
- How to speak up for yourself – Adam Galinsky

MOOCs

A Massive Open Online Course (MOOC) is a model for delivering learning content online to any person who wants to take a course, with no limit on attendance. Below is a list of courses on the essential competencies as described in this book which I found on Coursera, a major MOOC provider, but I'm sure you will find other interesting courses with the other MOOC providers at https://www.class-central.com/providers.

- **Solving Problems**
o Career Success – University of California, Irvine
o Think Again I: How to understand arguments – Duke University
o Think Again II: How to reason Deductively – Duke University
o Think Again III: How to reason Inductively – Duke University
o Think Again IV: How to avoid fallacies – Duke University
o Creative Problem Solving – University of Minnesota
o Effective Problem Solving and Decision Making – University of California, Irvine
o Cracking Creativity Code: Discovering Ideas – Technion, Israel Institute of Technology
o Game Theory – Stanford University

- **Meeting Expectations**
o Career Brand Management – State University of New York
o Successful Negotiation: Essential Strategies and Skills – University of Michigan
o Introduction to Personal Branding – University of Virginia
o Strategic Self-Marketing and Personal Branding – State University of New York
o Career Brand Development and Self-Coaching – State University of New York
o Career Options: Exploring a new Career – University System of Georgia

- **Managing Time**
  o Work Smarter, Not Harder – University of California, Irvine

- **Communicating**
  o Career Success – University of California, Irvine
  o Dynamic Public Speaking – University of Washington
  o Effecitve Communication – University of Colorado, Boulder
  o Effective Communication in the globalized Workplace – University of Singapore
  o Introduction to Public Speaking – University of Washington
  o Presentations: Speaking so that People Listen – University of California, Irvine
  o Advanced Writing – University of California, Irvine
  o Writing Professional Emails and Memos – University System of Georgia
  o Successful Presentation – University of Colorado, Boulder
  o Giving Helpful feedback – University of Colorado, Boulder

- **Working in Teams**
  o Culture-Driven Team Building – University of Pensylvania
  o Personality types at Work – University of Florida
  o Types of Conflict – University of California, Irvine
  o Building High-Performance Teams – University of Pensylvania

- **Being Resilient**
  o A life of happiness and fulfilment – Indian School of Business
  o De-mystifying Mindfulness – Universiteit Leiden

- **Managing and Leading**
  o Career Success – University of California, Irvine
  o Coaching Skills for Managers – University of California, Davis
  o Inspirational Leadership – HEC, Paris
  o Influencing People – University of Michigan
  o Inspiring Leadership through Emotional Intelligence – Case Western Reserve University
  o Conflict resolution Skills – University of California, Irvine

o Self-Awareness and the Effective Leader – Rice University
o A Practical Guide to Managing People at Work – University of London, Birkbeck
o Leadership in 21st Century Organizations – Copenhagen Business School
o Leadership and Emotional Intelligence – Indian School of Business

- **Learning and developing**

o Learning how to Learn – University of California, San Diego
o Intellectual Humility: Theory – University of Edinburgh
o Understanding Memory – Wesleyan University

Other interesting web sites

- http://www.bbc.co.uk/science/humanbody/mind/
- https://www.psychologytoday.com/basics
- http://www.brainrules.net/
- http://www.youramazingbrain.org/
- http://bcs.mit.edu/
- https://en.wikipedia.org/wiki/Portal:Psychology
- http://changingminds.org/

Index